THE snapshot survey

QUICK, AFFORDABLE MARKETING RESEARCH FOR EVERY ORGANIZATION

LLOYD CORDER, PHD

KAPLAN PUBLISHING

Vice President and Publisher: Cynthia A. Zigmund
Senior Acquisitions Editor: Michael Cunningham
Development Editor: Karen Murphy
Director of Production: Daniel Frey
Creative Director: Lucy Jenkins
Typesetting: Todd Bowman

Published by Kaplan Publishing,
a division of Kaplan, Inc.

Printed in the United States of America

07 08 10 9 8 7 6 5 4 3

Library of Congress Cataloging-in-Publication Data

Corder, Lloyd.
 Snapshot survey : quick, affordable marketing research for every organization
 /Lloyd Corder.
    p. cm.
 Includes index.
 ISBN 1-4195-0696-X
 1. Marketing research. I. Title.
 HF5415.2.C64 2006
 658.8'3--dc22

2005028673

For information about ordering Kaplan Publishing books at special quantity discounts, please call 1-800-KAP-ITEM or write to Kaplan Publishing, 888 Seventh Avenue, 22nd floor, New York, NY 10106.

PRAISE FOR *SNAPSHOT SURVEY*

The title of the book speaks for itself..A practical, easy decision-making tool.
**DR. ILKER BAYBARS, DEPUTY DEAN AND PROFESSOR OF OPERATIONS MANAGEMENT AND
MANUFACTURING CARNEGIE MELLON UNIVERSITY TEPPER SCHOOL
OF BUSINESS, PITTSBURGH, PA**

*Lloyd has captured many valuable lessons from his personal experiences and
provides a practical approach which can be applied to your business.
The Snapshot Survey is a great investment for any organization.*
-M. CHAD WERTZ, SENIOR ACCOUNT MANAGER, TELCOVE

*The Snapshot Survey is a great, cost-effective tool that helped MSA launch an
ntirely new consumer brand. It not only helped us better understand the market and
consumer attitudes toward safety, it provided us with a credible publicity tool that
generated increased awareness of the MSA Safety Works brand.*
MARK DEASY, DIRECTOR, PUBLIC RELATIONS & STRATEGIC COMMUNICATIONS, MSA

*Dr. Corder's Snapshot Survey demystifies the dark art of marketing research.
A must-read and indispensable tool for decision makers to quickly and
clearly discern the basis of an opportunity or problem.*
WALTER E. "PETE" PIERCE, III, LIEUTENANT COLONEL (RETIRED) UNITED STATES ARMY

DEDICATION

To all the women in my life!

Patti, my soulmate.
Molly, Megan, and Maura, my hip and beautiful young daughters.
Loy, my mom and inspiration.
Charlene, Sabrina, and Elke, my sisters.
Pretzel, my slobbering Chesapeake.

Contents

Acknowledgments xi

Preface xiii

PART ONE
PRINCIPLES AND PROCEDURES

1. THE SNAPSHOT SURVEY *Conducting Attitude Research–with Attitude!* 03

   How Ten Organizations Benefited from Lightning-fast Feedback 07

   What, Exactly, Is a Snapshot Survey? 11

   Taking the Guesswork Out of Making Important Decisions 12

   Ten Tough Questions the Snapshot Survey Can Answer 13

   Why the Snapshot Survey Is Valid—the Gory Details 16

   How the Snapshot Survey Stacks Up to Other Marketing Research Tools 20
   1. Focus Groups 22
   2. Telephone Surveys 23
   3. Mail Surveys 24
   4. Intercept Surveys 25
   5. Face-to-Face Interviews 26
   6. Experiments 27
   7. New Media Research (E-mail and Web-based Surveys) 27

2. BOOT CAMP *How to Run Your Own Snapshot Survey* 31

   Selling Your Snapshot Survey 32

   Five Steps to Running Your Own Snapshot Survey 37
   1. Asking the Right Questions 37
   2. Deciding Who to Talk To 43
   3. Gathering Feedback 45
   4. Analyzing Your Data 47
   5. Summarizing Your Results 52

PART TWO
BASIC APPLICATIONS

3. SIZING UP THE COMPETITION *How to Drill Deep Enough to Discover Your Organization's True Image and Reputation in the Marketplace* 61

Why You Have as Much Competition as You Deserve   62

Scratching the Surface: Basic Techniques for Learning about Your Competitors   64

Going Deeper: How to Discover Strengths and Weaknesses   65

Using Attribute Ratings as Your Yardstick   70

How to Evaluate Your Attributes   72

Using Personification Questions to Get a Good Sense of Your Competitors   74

To See the Bigger Picture, Ask Other Audiences What They Think   78
    External   79
    Internal   80
    Opinion Leaders   81

Why Size Doesn't Matter If You're Talking with the Right People   82
    Coordinating Company and Product Brand Names with Customer Feedback   82
    Creating a More Entrepreneurial Image   83
    Building a Marketing Infrastructure Program   83

Striking Pay Dirt: What to Do When You Find the Mother Lode   85

4. CUSTOMER SATISFACTION, CUSTOMER LEADS *How to Get Referrals, Create Loyalty, and Develop Lifelong Partnerships*   87

Using Your Customer Satisfaction Survey to Pay the Bills   88
    Determine Awareness   90
    Offer More Product Information   91
    Solicit Referrals   92

Squeezing More Juice Out of Your Satisfaction Questions   95

They May Be Satisfied, But Is It Important to Them?   98

Lifetime Customer Value: Why Customers Are More Precious Than You Think   102

What I Have Learned from Customers Like Yours   106

5. BUILDING A MARKETING PLAN THAT WORKS *Ensuring Your Messages and Tactics Resonate with Your Target Audience*   111

Ten Building Blocks of a Typical Marketing Plan   118

Selecting a Marketing Mix That Makes Sense   121
    Consumer (B2C)   123
    Business-to-Business (B2B)   123
    Consulting and Professional Service   124

How to Ask about Price without Giving Away the Store   126

Maximizing Your Electronic Marketing   129
   Ten Ways to Improve Your Web Site's Navigation   129
   25 Tips for E-mail Newsletters   134

Finalizing Your Blueprint   137

6. WHAT SHOULD WE CALL IT? *Picking the Right Name for Your Organization, Products, and Services*   141

The Power of Naming   144

Choosing a Name You Can Live With   146
   Steps for Selecting Names and Taglines   146
   Six Ways to Generate Names   150

Regional Marketing: Naming and Logo Testing for Pittsburgh   154
   Building a Baseball-only Ballpark for the Pittsburgh Pirates   155
   How the Pittsburgh Pirates Used Feedback from Young Fans to Build a Winning Logo and
      Uniforms   155
   Naming PNC Park   157
   Naming Three Rivers Park   158
   Fighting Pittsburgh's "Brain Drain"   158

PART THREE

ADVANCED APPLICATIONS

7. GETTING NEWS COVERAGE *How to Identify Trends, Insights, and Survey Results That the Media Want to Publish*   163

Creating News with the Snapshot Survey   164

Where You Can Publish Your Findings   170

Why Publicity Surveys Must Be Scientific   171
   Consumer Polls   172
   B2B Surveys   172
   Proprietary Research   173

Dramatic, Thought-provoking Insights Start with the Right Questions   174

Packaging Your Results in a Media Kit   178
   Prepare a Media List   178
   Develop a Media Kit   179

Tips for Working with the Trade Media   181

Pitching Your Story: How to Entice an Editor to Make You Famous   183

8. ADDING POWER TO YOUR PROPOSALS *How to Win More Business by Focusing Your Sales Presentations on Your Prospects and Their Desires*   185

How to Win More Sales Proposals   186
   Walking a Mile in Your Buyer's Shoes   187
   Shoot-out Results Using the Snapshot Survey   190

Scientific Selling: Using the Snapshot Survey to Sell Bigger Projects   198
  Why Physicians Are Great Salespeople   198
  Transforming Your Sales Process   199
  Quantifying Pain   202
  The Needs Assessment   203

Getting On Track to Win More Customers and Bigger Projects   207

9. INTERNAL MARKETING *Using the Snapshot Survey to Gather Employee Feedback*   209
  Ten Reasons Why You Should Ask Your Employees for Feedback   210
  Success Stories: How Six Organizations Used Employee Feedback   212
    1. Using More of Your Employees' Talents   213
    2. Developing a Stronger Marketing Culture   217
    3. Evaluating a Marketing Tactic   224
    4. Marketing Specific Ideas and Programs to Employees   224
    5. Redesigning Employee Compensation Packages   226
    6. Communicating and Simplifying Employee Benefits   229
  A Dozen Tips for Gathering Employee Feedback You Can Use   232

10. MEASURING MARKETING ROI *How to* Prove *and* Improve *Your Marketing Effectiveness*   235
  How Did You Find Out about Us?   236
  Three Steps for Determining Your Marketing ROI   237
    1. Determine Who Bought What   237
    2. Tally the Results   237
    3. Determine the Cost to Make Each Sale   238
  Seven Levels of Marketing ROI Measurement   240
    1. Marketing Activity   242
    2. Placements   243
    3. Awareness   245
    4. Attitude   247
    5. Contacts   250
    6. Sales   254
    7. Lifetime Customer Value   257
  Five Crucial Steps to Assessing the Value of Your Marketing Effort   258
    1. Set Measurable Marketing Goals   258
    2. Agree on What's Being Counted   259
    3. Use More Than One Measurement Tool   261
    4. Use Existing Measures before Creating New Ones   263
    5. Effectively Communicate and Present Your ROI Findings   263
  The Bottom Line   264

About the Author 265

An army of colleagues, clients, students, and friends made this book possible.

One of the great fortunes of my professional life is to have a vast network of colleagues who have supported my work by recommending the snapshot survey to their clients and organizations. Their passion and committment allowed me to first develop the concepts in this book and then to perfect them over the years.

I've also been blessed with a terrific client roster that includes some of the biggest and best local, regional, national, and international firms. The snapshot survey concept was developed for them—and I am humbled by how they have championed it.

Conducting a snapshot survey and teaching someone else to do it are two entirely different skills. I want to personally thank the hundreds of MBA and master's students who have tried this concept while studying at the Tepper School of Business at Carnegie Mellon University. I also am thankful for the chance to share these ideas with several thousand undergraduates from the University of Pittsburgh, Chatham College, and the Pennsylvania State University over the years.

Finally, I would like to acknowledge several special individuals who believed in what I was trying to do and turned this book into a reality. I am grateful to all the folks at Dearborn Trade, including Michael Cunningham, Karen Murphy, Leslie Banks, and Jack Kiburz. Sam Deep, John Bell, John Graf, Jarrod Miller, Judy Kelly, and Dave Mastovich found the right encouragement when it mattered the most. Bob Sonnet has been my right-hand man; his terrific mind has helped me sharpen my focus—and keep us in business while I spent time writing this text. Thanks also to my brother, J. B. Corder, who helped me sell the snapshop survey nationally. Finally, and most important, I want to thank the best scientist I know, my dad, Clinton Corder. For the past decade he has asked me this simple question again and again: "How's your book coming along?" I can now confidently reply: "Dad, it's ready to go."

God has wisely given us two ears and one mouth
so that we might hear twice as much as we speak.

Epicticus, ancient Greek philosopher

In its simplist form, marketing research is about listening—getting feedback about your product, service, or idea from customers, prospects, peers, employees, and other target audiences. It is supposed to make you smarter and more confident.

The problem is that marketing research isn't living up to its potential. In many organizations, research is considered an expensive, time-consuming, and often frustrating experience that provides little practical value. Instead of using research as a tool for running their businesses more efficiently, they elect to use it very sparingly or not at all. When faced with making important decisions, these businesspeople rely on their instincts and hunches. Sometimes those guesses are on the money; other times they are dead wrong and costly.

So why should you read this book? The snapshot survey is the opposite of what people think about when they hear the term *marketing research*. I'll show you how to ask highly focused questions of a limited sample of your target audience to get what I call "directional" feedback. It's the kind of insight you need in most of the marketing situations you face. Instead of being exactly sure, this type of research tells you whether you're headed down the right path. Because it's focused, it usually takes a lot less time, money, and energy to gather this type of feedback than to do full-blown, lethargic surveys.

Don't worry if you've never conducted your own research project. I'll show you how to quickly perform your own survey from start (putting a proposal together) to finish (analyzing and summarizing your results). I've also included dozens of examples of successful surveys that organizations from all kinds of industries have used to address their unique challenges.

I'll also let you in on the secrets I've learned over the past two decades of conducting more than 1,000 of these surveys, frequently addressing organizations' most pressing challenges.

- Do you know how you stack up to your competitors and what you can do separate yourself from the pack? If not, the ideas in Chapter 3 will help you.
- If you'd like to get more out of your customer satisfaction surveys—and turn them into legitimate lead-generation tools for finding more business—read Chapter 4.
- Do you need a marketing plan for a new product or service or a more effective way to promote your organization? I provide a blueprint on how to use the snapshot survey to do this in Chapter 5.
- Are you having trouble figuring out the best names for your products or services? If so, you can use the snapshot survey to gather opinions from customers, prospects, and other groups. Read more about this in Chapter 6.
- If you'd like to generate more positive media coverage (free advertising), you can use the snapshot survey to identify trends, insights, and survey results the media want to publish. Learn the nitty-gritty techniques on this type of research in Chapter 7.
- Are you tired of losing business to competitors during big presentations or shoot-outs? Why not use the snapshot survey to gather feedback from your prospect's customers and include those findings in your presentation. Chapter 8 shows you different ways you can try this technique.
- Do you want to learn more about what your employees are thinking—and what it's going to take to get them to more enthusiastically support your plans? Chapter 9 shows you how to use the snapshot survey inside your organization.
- If you'd like to find out what, exactly, you're getting for the money you're spending on marketing, you'll want to read Chapter 10, which is devoted to the different ways you can measure marketing return on investment (ROI).

As you'll see throughout this book, the snapshot survey is a concept that has been tested on some of the most successful organizations around—with some of the toughest and most demanding clients. It's worked beautifully for them. And it will work for you, too. All you have to do is get started.

Part One

PRINCIPLES AND PROCEDURES

1

THE SNAPSHOT SURVEY
Conducting Attitude Research–with Attitude!

There is no great trick to doing research. The problem is to get people to use it–particularly when the research reveals that you have been making mistakes. We all have a tendency to use research as a drunkard uses a lamppost– for support, not for illumination.

David Ogilvy, Advertising Executive

If you listen *carefully enough,* your customers will tell you how to make a fortune. They'll leave you a trail of subtle clues that will lead to ideas for new products and services that you never would have dreamt up. They'll give you inspiration and energy— and reward you for helping them pursue their dreams.

Some years ago, two of my customers left such a trail of clues that led me to the snapshot survey. The first clue happened the day I started working for Ketchum, a leading public relations and advertising firm. Jim Ficco, the president of one side of the business, Ketchum Advertising, told me that it was becoming increasingly difficult to convince customers to buy large research studies—the valuable intelligence about markets, customers, prospects, and other people that serves as the backbone of great marketing strategies and smart advertising. Customers were tired of paying $25,000, $50,000, or even $100,000 for a study that took weeks to complete and even more energy to digest, understand, and apply. They didn't want to keep buying research that was too theoretical and rigid and that eventually sat on the shelf collecting dust.

Don't get me wrong. Jim truly believed in research. He had sold a great deal of it during his career, starting as an account executive and working his way up the agency ladder. He constantly recommended research, because he believed that when customers based their advertising decisions on feedback from the people they were trying to persuade, the advertising agency could develop stronger, more effective communications. Without research, advertising was little more than high-stakes gambling.

Jim also understood that marketing is not a battle of products or services. It's a battle of perceptions. It's a fight for what gets into and stays in our minds. Marketing and selling are all about shaping the opinions and attitudes we hold, so that when it comes time to make a buying decision, prospects decide to buy from us and become customers again and again. Marketing research is one of those tools that helps us determine what attitudes and perceptions our customers hold about us, our company, and how we're doing business. Once we know that, we can figure out the right things to say and do—at the right time with the right frequency.

As I was trying to figure out where my desk was, Jim blurted out this challenge: "If you can find an inexpensive, fast way to do marketing research, we can sell a ton of it."

I paused for a moment and stammered, "Well, then. Okay. I'll think about it." I had no earthly idea of what he was talking about, much less how I might find a way to conduct effective, inexpensive, or even quick research. How was I going to figure out a way to start doing the opposite of what I had been doing my whole life?

It wasn't until sometime later that I realized Jim's challenge was my first clue about discovering the snapshot survey.

I picked up my second clue a few months later. I also happened to be working for Ketchum's public relations division at the time I was selling and running those massive marketing surveys that took weeks to complete. One of my clients, a health care provider, asked us to help straighten out an image problem that resulted because the health system's administrators and physicians were fighting with each other in the media.

As with most health care systems, the hospital administrators and physicians group are actually separate organizations. In this case, both shared a common name, which created additional confusion.

For nearly a year, the hospital administrators and physicians traded jabs and took shots at each other in the media through a slew of negative stories.

During this same time, members of the health care system noticed a significant decline in the number of patients who were coming to the hospital for treatment. These numbers were lower than historical averages and represented a major decrease.

The hospital administrators believed that the public fighting with the physicians group was what was driving patients away and, therefore, if they rebuilt their image through a public relations and advertising campaign, they could win back the patients they had lost.

Before creating a plan for rebuilding the hospital's image, we suggested they get some feedback from the community, employees, and other groups. A big, slow-moving research study was put together that included these components:

- Senior executive interviews with all the top brass to find out what they thought were the issues and what could be done to get the hospital back on track
- A community perception telephone survey of more than 1,000 residents to learn what people living throughout their service region thought of the hospital and its services
- Interviews with more than 100 employees through 10 focus groups, one at each of their facilities (more about this technique at the end of this chapter)
- A telephone survey with more than 50 reporters and editors from the local newspaper, radio, and television stations
- A telephone survey of more than 200 people who contributed financially to the hospital

In total, we talked to nearly 1,400 people before making any recommendations on how to fix the hospital's image and attract the patients it had lost.

Not too far into the community perception survey project, my client asked me a simple question: "Can you give me a brief summary of the results after the first day or two of calling? I'd just like to see how the interviews are going and what people are saying." Of course, I agreed.

Within a couple days, we had finished more than 150 phone interviews. So I tallied the answers to every question and faxed a copy of what I found. Several weeks later during a preliminary report of the entire study, my client made a terrifying comment during the meeting: "You know, Lloyd, the numbers from your final sample of more than 1,000 residents really aren't that different from the numbers you gave me after the first couple of nights of interviewing," he said. "The percentages have changed by a point or two one way or the other, but none of the conclusions have."

I was mortified. I thought to myself that if there were no real differences between a big survey and a small survey, how in the world would I get customers to buy bigger surveys? My first thought was that I should never give clients an update on how their research was going before the total interviews were completed—no exceptions.

As we continued with the meeting, we talked about how the results revealed some very important insights: Namely, the health care system actually had a terrific image and all the disagreements expressed in the media were not driving patients away. Something else was. And that something else was managed care, a new type of insurance that limited where people could go to receive treatment. If they didn't go to hospitals that were within their "plan," they had to pay for those services with their own money and their visits wouldn't be covered by their insurance. Because a number of local companies were switching to managed-care plans to reduce their health care costs, employees were being forced to go to competing hospitals. This hospital didn't need a new image. It needed some of the managed-care contracts.

A few days after the meeting, the client's comment continued to bother me. We had already learned the hospital had a great image after the first couple days of interviewing. All we gained from the next 850 interviews was more confidence in our initial findings. But was the extra time, energy, and cost really worth the confidence? After all, none of the conclusions had changed. We already knew the bottom line.

About this time I remembered Jim Ficco's challenge of finding a way to conduct a fast, highly focused, cost-effective survey. I thought to myself, what if I looked at the question as what it really was: a second clue that would lead me to the snapshot survey. Maybe a legitimate way does exist to run surveys that are fast and affordable and that provide great insights to customers.

I asked myself, what would happen if I designed surveys that could be completed in a couple of days, not in weeks or months? What would happen if we used smaller sample sizes, 25, 50, or even 100 people to obtain insights quickly? After all, if the percentages were changing by only a couple of points one way or the other—but none of the conclusions were—wouldn't that type of research be good enough for a lot of marketing, sales, and management situations? If the surveys were smaller and more affordable, could we find tons more buyers for this product? I wasn't sure of the answers to any of these questions, so I decided to see if I could get anyone to buy the concept and in what situations they might find smaller surveys most valuable.

> **F** *l a s h #* **1**
> _____
>
> The snapshot survey is the opposite of what most people think of when they hear the term *survey research*. By asking a limited sample of your target audience a set of highly focused questions, the snapshot survey gives you valuable insights in just a few days—not in weeks or months.

HOW TEN ORGANIZATIONS BENEFITED FROM LIGHTNING-FAST FEEDBACK

My customers and prospects didn't wait long to start trying the snapshot survey. In fact, I sold more than 100 surveys within the first couple of years, because they obtained immediate and valuable information. Here are ten examples of how they did it:

1. *Marketing/promotional decision.* A leading regional family-style restaurant chain that competes with Denny's, Bob Evans, and Perkins, wanted to offer a take-home drinking glass promotion featuring Pittsburgh Steelers football players. For a nominal fee, consumers could purchase a series of four drinking glasses. The chain was planning to imprint 100,000 glasses and didn't want to be left with a large inventory that it couldn't sell. Internally, a strong debate was being waged about whether to include current-day stars or Hall of Fame players. Only 115 telephone interviews were conducted with consumers to find out which players they wanted to see on the glasses and how likely they would be to make a purchase. The results overwhelmingly showed the Hall of Fame Steelers were favored. So that's what the chain had imprinted. The promotion was very successful and sold out in just a few days, exceeding everyone's expectations.

2. *Customer satisfaction and brand-reputation assessment.* A small manufacturer who makes programmable stampers to mark pipes, steel, and other metal products wanted to find out what customers and prospects thought of the company, its products, and its service performance. The manufacturer had been noticing that some customers and prospects were not aware of its new products and services. The company wanted to figure out how to focus its marketing and communications efforts. A total

of 50 telephone interviews were completed, half with current customers and half with prospective customers. The interviews were blind and did not reveal the sponsor of the survey. Questions focused on who respondents thought were the leaders within the industry and what they thought of each of the manufacturers who produced similar equipment. The company found out it was the "Cadillac" of the industry, primarily because it had machines it built 20 or 30 years ago that were still working well. The problem was it didn't want to be a Cadillac; it wanted to be a Mercedes, and thus used the snapshot survey results to create a plan to rebrand its image.

3. *Creating a strategy to launch a new product.* A large manufacturer of gas-detection equipment primarily used in HVAC settings wanted to enter the automotive air-conditioning repair market, but didn't know the best approach or what to charge for its product. Historically, air-conditioning repair technicians used dye testing to find leaks, because the electronic equipment is unreliable. The manufacturer was convinced that its sensors were superior and could perform better than those of its competitors. The manufacturer was initially planning to offer this electronic device through automotive parts stores and distributorships and package the product with add-ons, such as a flashlight, a rubber boot to hold the tool, and a hard plastic carrying case. In two days, 25 air-conditioning repair technicians were interviewed. The results showed that mechanics prefer (1) to buy from tool trucks that come to their locations (not automotive distributorships) and (2) have strong opinions concerning the packaging of the instruments. The findings were used not only to package the product but to create a marketing plan and launch the product.

4. *Gathering feedback from a senior executive advisory panel.* To convince business leaders to relocate in Pennsylvania, former governor Tom Ridge, who later became the head of the Department of Homeland Security, created an economic advisory panel of about 30 business leaders from major companies across the state, calling the group and program *TeamPA*. The idea was that if the state made itself more business-friendly and promoted these changes, it would help bring companies, jobs, and more prosperity to Pennsylvania. The executives served as the sounding board for many of the program's ideas, strategies, and marketing materials, but getting them together frequently in a central location was a significant challenge. So, the

snapshot survey was used many times to gather their feedback, which helped transform the image of the Commonwealth and convince more businesses and workers to relocate to the state.

5. *Persuading millionaires to purchase financial investments.* One of the nation's largest banks used a snapshot survey to interview 100 high-net-worth individuals about what they look for and want from private banking services. What are their hot buttons? What are they not getting from their current bankers that they would like to be getting? Answers to questions like these helped the bank create marketing strategies for reaching these wealthy individuals, as well as find ways to describe how the bank's services are substantially better than those of its competitors. Incidentally, you cannot purchase a list of millionaires, but you can buy a list of people who have bought expensive products or services such as yachts, European sports cars, megahomes, and other big-ticket items. By merging multiple databases, you can find individuals who have made several significant purchases and, naturally, needed to be millionaires to do so.

6. *Creating marketing messages.* The snapshot survey can help you create marketing messages. When pitching to a large trucking manufacturer, a major jet manufacturer, and many other companies to try to win their advertising business, five to ten interviews were enough to get an initial idea of what the target audience cared about most. For example, buyers who purchase truck fleets were asked about how their trucks stacked up against other brands such as International and Freight Liner. Jet purchasers were asked how their planes compared to other players. The results provided clues about the kinds of messages that made an impact on these audiences.

7. *Gathering distributor, dealer, and sales representative perspectives.* Many businesses sell their products and services through distributors, dealers, independent sales reps, agents, and others. One leading property and casualty insurance company used the snapshot survey to talk regularly with its agents about marketing, territory, promotions, and other issues. The snapshot survey helped include their perspectives and ensured that a cross section of agents were the ones giving the feedback—not only those who were disgruntled or who had an ax to grind.

8. *Listening to employees.* The snapshot survey can help you listen more closely to your employees, especially if you have 10 or more. A national nonprofit organization used a snapshot sur-

vey to ask 40 of its employees in one of its regional offices how they thought things were going. Included were questions about assorted issues, for instance, the amount of communication, direction of the company, management effectiveness, and training needs. The results were used to help identify where improvements could be made to help everyone do their jobs more effectively and to understand the overall direction of the organization.

9. *Developing a new product/service.* The snapshot survey can help you assess whether your ideas for a new product or service will fly with the people you want to buy those products or services. A university used the snapshot survey to test the viability of offering three new majors—one each in the sciences, performing arts, and professional services. Interviews with potential students, industry professionals, and possible employers were completed to learn what they thought of each major and what potential the major might have. As it turned out in this case, one of the three new majors looked very strong, one looked like a bomb, and the other one was a risk, but doable. Simply deciding to move ahead with all three without testing them would have brought on a lot of angst and frustration—not to mention financial difficulty when not enough students could be recruited or couldn't be placed once they received their degrees.

10. *Refining a product or service offering.* When customers have a lot of options to choose from, what is it going to take to get them to pick your product or service over someone else's? A leading engineering association used the snapshot survey to plan specific programs within some of its major conferences. By asking members what they'd like to see covered and where they wanted the conference to be focused, the association was able to better design those conferences and attract the right people. Without it, members and industry professionals would have been more tempted to go to competing shows or to not attend at all.

In each of these examples—and hundreds of others just like them—a limited number of interviews were used to gather valuable perspectives in a couple of days. The snapshot survey is revolutionizing marketing research and helping many organizations (even big ones) obtain the feedback they need without investing too much time, money, or energy. This tool dramatically improves the total value of marketing research.

WHAT, EXACTLY, IS A SNAPSHOT SURVEY?

Because I was fortunate to have so many opportunities to share the snapshot survey concept with customers and use this tool to help them better understand their challenges, I tried to listen very carefully to how they talked about it. What words did they use to describe it? What examples did they use to explain it to their colleagues? I figured the more I used their words, the easier it would be to continue promoting the product.

One thing I quickly learned was that I originally used the wrong name for the product. I had started out calling it the "SoundByte Survey." Because "sound bites" are a public relations term for short, memorable statements that can be quoted in the media, I thought a concept that was a play on these words and also included "information" (byte as in computer information) would work (at least it did in my own mind). I even had a product logo and other materials designed around it.

Before long, I noticed that my customers would describe the SoundByte Survey as a "snapshot" survey. Instead of filming a full-length motion picture, you're just "taking a photograph or a snapshot" they would say. I finally gave in and decided to call the product by its natural name, because it was a lot easier to explain and customers were able to see easily and quickly its value. I never regretted the decision.

I also found myself answering five basic questions about the snapshot survey. These are the same questions you should be asking yourself to see if the snapshot survey is the right tool for your situation:

1. *What is the snapshot survey?* The snapshot survey is 10 to 15 custom-designed questions that include 2 or 3 open-ended questions. I tell customers that the snapshot survey is a poll that asks a limited sample of a target audience highly focused questions. There's no beating around the bush. Because the survey is short and the interviews are tightly defined, most surveys can be completed in two or three days and summarized in a short report, a welcomed alternative to typical research time frames that can take weeks or months. The tool is *not* what most people think of when they hear the words *survey research.*

2. *Why should I use the snapshot survey?* The snapshot survey helps you outmaneuver and outstrategize competitors, because it quickly gives you the insight you need. It places leverage on your recommendations, because you're basing them more on your

personal opinion and reputation (nothing seems to persuade decision makers more than the "voice" of their customers). You can base marketing and communications decisions on fact rather than on guessing. The snapshot survey is a process for learning perceptions and opinions.

3. *Who should use the snapshot survey?* The types of people who use a snapshot survey and benefit from it are senior management, marketing, sales, human resources and public relations directors, product managers, hospital and nonprofit administrators, and many others. The snapshot survey makes marketing research accessible to virtually everyone, not only to the upper echelon.

4. *When should I use the snapshot survey?* You should use the snapshot survey in the following situations:
   - When market trends are changing and you want to figure out where they're shifting
   - To verify if marketing and communications strategies or tactics worked and what it will take to improve them
   - To create publicity and make your news stories or trade articles more interesting
   - To validate hunches and suspicions
   - To create a strategy for developing new products or markets

5. *Where can I use the snapshot survey?* The snapshot survey can be used at any local, regional, national, and international location, as well as within the consumer marketplace, industry-specific segments, or in conjunction with events such as trade shows, forums, business briefings, and more.

TAKING THE GUESSWORK OUT OF MAKING IMPORTANT DECISIONS

It never ceases to amaze me how many companies are willing to make important decisions on little to no market data. They rely on hunches and guesswork and seem content to sit in a conference room and debate with each other about where they are going and how they are going to get there. They then go out and spend a lot of money to market their products or service. That's the whole idea behind marketing research. By asking the people you're trying to influence what they know and think, you can build a marketing program that has a good shot at working.

F *l a s h* **# 2**

Because marketing is a battle of perceptions, you need to know what your customers and prospects think. If you can't afford the time or money to understand these perceptions through a full-scale study, the snapshot survey beats your only other alternative—guessing.

At the same time, it has been my experience that most marketing situations do not require highly precise marketplace feedback. Generally, you don't need to know within a tenth of a percentage point how many people like or don't like a new product concept. You simply need to know if you are heading in the right direction. You need something I call *directional feedback*. This is what the snapshot survey provides. It's like coming to a stop sign. The snapshot survey tells you whether you should go left, right, or straight ahead. It does not tell you to go two degrees to the north.

Figure 1.1 outlines the basic options you have for making an important marketing, sales, operational, management, or other decision. On the left side is "guessing," or basically deciding what to do with no real input from anyone other than yourself. This is great if you're certain you know exactly what's going on.

On the right-hand side is "science," or the type of research that is rigorous and repeatable. Forget about trying to reach this end for most marketing and selling situations. It's complete overkill, unless you're testing products such as medications, equipment, or similar items. In the middle is where you'll find a range of marketing research options, including the snapshot survey. The further toward the right you go, the more valuable your research, because it gives you insights from people such as customers, prospects, and others who typically aren't as easily accessible as the colleagues you see and work with every day.

TEN TOUGH QUESTIONS THE SNAPSHOT SURVEY CAN ANSWER

While the snapshot survey is an interesting tool by itself, it is even more interesting when it is applied to common operations, marketing, and management challenges you are likely to find yourself grappling with from time to time. While conducting more than 1,000 surveys over

FIGURE 1.1

The options for making important business decisions

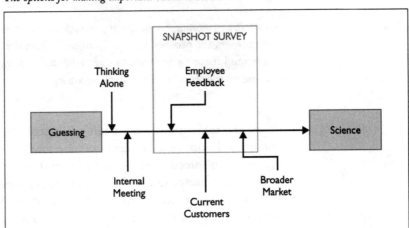

the past two decades, I've discovered 10 common themes that many organizations face. (In Parts Two and Three of this book, I'll show you how many different organizations have successfully used the snapshot survey to help them make smarter decisions about the issues they were facing.)

1. *How well are we taking care of our employees?* The snapshot survey is a terrific tool for gathering employee feedback about issues ranging from how satisfied they are about their benefits packages to better understanding their morale levels.

2. *How satisfied are our customers, distributors, or end users?* A quick and easy way to measure customer satisfaction or determine their level of loyalty is to use the snapshot survey. By asking questions about how aware customers are of your current products and services, whether they want more information about any of them, and whether they would be willing to provide a referral, the traditional customer satisfaction surveys can be transformed into sales-lead generation tools—that do not violate the ethical standards of marketing research. Depending on the type of company using the survey, the leads generated can easily pay for the cost of conducting the research.

3. *How well do we stack up against our competitors?* The snapshot survey can help you evaluate how and where you're stronger than competitors, and if not, what you need to do to close the gaps.

4. *What kind of corporate citizen do people think we are?* For businesses who operate within communities, presenting a positive image is key. The snapshot survey can help find out what that image is and how well your programs, messages, and other activities are working.

5. *What should we say in our marketing materials and how should we say it?* The snapshot survey can help prioritize which key messages resonate with the people you are trying to reach and which ones are likely to be ignored.

6. *How can we generate more visibility and news coverage?* The snapshot survey can be used as more than a strategy tool—it can be a marketing tool. By asking questions of a target audience a trade or consumer publication cares about, the results can be fashioned into news stories and positive publicity about the organization. When conducted and promoted properly, they offer fresh publicity opportunities traditional media relations can't deliver.

7. *Will our new product or service be successful?* Before developing a product or placing it into full production, the snapshot survey can be used to test the viability of a concept, product, or service.

8. *What should we call our company, products, or services?* The snapshot survey is a terrific tool for conducting naming research. By testing reactions to alternative names—before one is adopted—the snapshot survey helps gauge the potential positive or negative connotations associated with your words, acronyms, or logos.

9. *How can we win the business?* The snapshot survey has been used successfully dozens of times in agency shoot-outs and other new business pitches. By conducting a brief survey, the presentation can be transformed from "Look how great we are" to "Here's what we initially found out about your situation and what we think you ought to do about it." It embodies the concept of consultative selling.

F *l a s h* **# 3**

Ninety-five percent of the marketing and business decisions you need to make don't require that you know absolutely everything about everything. Instead, you simply need to know if you're headed in the right direction. This is how the snapshot survey works. It gives you directional feedback so you can make smarter decisions in less time.

10. *How well is our marketing working?* The snapshot survey can help you track and measure marketing return on investment (ROI). In short order, you can find out which of your marketing tools are working and what you need to do to improve the results you're getting.

WHY THE SNAPSHOT SURVEY IS VALID— THE GORY DETAILS

How can such a limited number of interviews collected in a snapshot survey produce such interesting and accurate results? Through rigorous testing, I discovered that as long as the sample selected for a snapshot survey is *random,* the results should mirror a larger survey.

The operative word here is *random.* The options you have when conducting research are to try to talk to everyone, which is completely impractical in most situations, or to talk to only some of them (a sampling). How you take your sample matters greatly. There are two approaches:

1. *Nonrandom samples (also called nonprobability).* These samples are based on convenience, personal judgment, or some other factor that *does not give* each and every person in the target audience an equal chance of being selected. If you interview everyone who comes into your store for a day, how do you really know that sample is representative of the entire population? The fact is that you don't know. You can still get valuable insights from these customers, but you can't be sure that these customers have the same feelings as do all your customers. Much of marketing research falls in this category, regardless of whether you're doing a full-scale or a snapshot survey.

2. *Random samples (also called probability).* These samples give everyone an *equal* chance of being selected. There are many ways you can get a random sample, such as simple (create telephone lists from a computer that randomly generates the last four digits of phone numbers within known area code3s and exchanges), systematic (select every nth person), or stratified (divide the population into groups and randomly select people from each group).

Figure 1.2 shows the results from a single question included in a random sample from a national consumer telephone survey that asked, "Which material has the most modern or high-tech image?" There are

FIGURE 1.2

Smaller samples (100 consumer interviews) reveal the same conclusions as much larger (1,000+) samples

WHICH MATERIAL HAS THE MOST MODERN OR HIGH-TECH IMAGE?				
	All Consumers (1,018)	Sample 1 (100)	Sample 2 (100)	Sample 3 (100)
Material A	13%	17%	13%	13%
Material B	18%	13%	22%	17%
Material C	**59%**	**58%**	**60%**	**61%**
Don't Know	11%	12%	5%	9%

four columns of data, which include the percentage of response from all the consumers (1,018) who participated in a telephone survey and three subgroups of 100 interviews each from the first, middle, and last 100 interviews (each subgroup was also a random sample).

Regardless of which column is examined, "Material C" is the winner and most consumers think that it has the most modern or high-tech image, even though the last three columns have only one-tenth the number of interviews as the first column. A snapshot survey of 100 consumers would have produced the same results as the entire sample, in terms of selecting the overall "winner," Material C.

If you look carefully at this chart, however, you'll notice that the second highest answer, Material B, flips with Material A in Sample 1, but mirrors the percentages for All Consumers in Samples 2 and 3. This illustrates the snapshot survey's principle weakness: sorting out differences when the percentage of responses to a question category are close together.

To fully understand this weakness, you have to understand the concept of margin of error, or how accurate the survey findings are compared with the results if everyone in the population were interviewed. Because most companies can't afford to talk with everyone, they attempt to take a representative sample of those individuals. Depending on how they selected their sample (it was actually random) and how many people they talked to, they can be "confident" within a certain number of percentage points that the numbers they found in their survey actually represent what most people are thinking.

In many polls, you'll read something like "Some 1,000 consumers were interviewed for a margin of error of plus or minus three percentage points." Basically, this means that in our example if everyone in the United States were interviewed and asked this question, the percentage

FIGURE 1.3

Margin of error

SIZE OF SAMPLE	10%	20%	30%	40%	50%	60%	70%	80%	90%
100	6	8	9	10	10	10	9	8	6
200	4	6	7	7	7	7	7	6	4
300	4	5	5	6	6	6	5	5	4
400	3	4	5	5	5	5	5	4	3
500	3	4	4	4	5	4	4	4	3
600	2	3	4	4	4	4	4	3	2
700	2	3	4	4	4	4	4	3	2
800	2	3	3	3	3	3	3	3	2
900	2	3	3	3	3	3	3	3	2
1,000	2	3	3	3	3	3	3	3	2
1,500	2	2	2	3	3	3	2	2	2
3,000	1	2	2	2	2	2	2	2	1

stating Material C would be somewhere between 56 percent (three points lower than 59 percent) to 62 percent (three points higher than 59 percent). For 100 interviews, the margin of error is much larger and is plus or minus 10 percentage points, or 48 percent to 68 percent for Sample 1. In other words, the more interviews you do, the more confident the number you find in your survey represents a larger population.

Figure 1.3 lists a table for calculating the margin of error at the 95 percent confidence interval, which means that in 19 out of 20 times the findings in your survey results should be within a plus or minus range listed in the table (if you indeed interviewed everyone in the population). However, in 1 time out of 20, you might find percentages that are completely different. It is only a sampling after all.

To read the table in Figure 1.3, you need to know two things: how many interviews you conducted (listed on the far left column) and what percentage response you received to any specific question (listed across the top). Simply connect these two numbers and find the percentage, which represents your plus or minus margin of error. For example, if 300 interviews were completed and you had a response of 50 percent, the margin of error would be plus or minus 6 percentage points.

The statistical formula to calculate the margin of error is "1 divided by the square root of the number of people in the sample." If you surveyed 300 people, your margin of error would be 1 divided by 17.320508 (square root of 300), which equals 0.0577735, or 6 percent.

Notice that this is the number you would get in the 50 percent column, which is where the margin of error is largest.

To calculate the rest of the numbers in Figure 1.3, you need a slightly more advanced formula:

$$\text{Margin of error} = \sqrt{\frac{(\text{percentage}) \times (1 - \text{percentage})}{\text{sample size}}} \times 1.96$$

In this formula, you take the percentage you got to a specific question and multiply it by 1 minus that percentage. Then divide it by your sample size. Take the square root of that number and multiply it by 1.96 (which is two standard deviations). Let's say that you surveyed 300 people and you found that 80 percent liked your concept for a new product. The margin of error for this finding would be plus or minus 5 percent:

$$\text{Margin of error} = \sqrt{\frac{(.80) \times (1 - .80)}{300}} \times 1.96 = .0452626$$

There are five important things to keep in mind about the margin of error:

1. The margin of error works only for *random* samples (everyone has an equal chance of being selected). If you have a nonrandom sample, you can never say that it has a margin of error, because it doesn't apply. Therefore, even if you've interviewed 300 people who came through your store, you would not be able to say that the results had a margin of error of plus or minus 6 percentage points. This is why you'll see some reader or TV viewer response polls of 10,000 to 20,000 people that are sometimes described as "nonscientific." It's not about how many interviews you do, it's about whether those interviews were collected using a random-sampling technique.

2. The margin of error for an entire survey—like you would read in a survey report or would be included in a news story describing the results of a political poll—is always reported at the 50 percent level or the highest percentage for your sample size.

3. The margin of error of every question on your survey is actually different (you have to refer to Figure 1.3). With the previous ma-

terials example, when 13 percent was found in a 100-person sample, the actual margin of error for this question would be plus or minus 6 percentage points or 7 percent to 19 percent if everyone were interviewed. This is because 13 percent is closest to 10 percent, and if 100 and 10 percent are connected, the number is plus or minus 6 points.

4. After about 750 random interviews, you have to conduct another 1,250 interviews to pick up another point (the margin of error is plus or minus 3 percent for 750 interviews and 2 percent for 2,000)—then it never gets any better. This is why you'll see more 750 to 1,000 sample sizes in polls. Conducting 3,000 or more random interviews is a waste of money.

5. If you're going to look at a subgroup within your sample (e.g., only women), the margin of error for this group will be higher than the total margin of error for the entire study (because you have a smaller sample and you are, therefore, less statistically confident of your results).

The snapshot survey is strongest when identifying a majority of responses, which is typically the desired focus of most marketing and management questions that can be answered through marketing research. In many respects, the snapshot survey is like an electronic screwdriver. Once you have one, you lose almost all desire to tighten screws manually. It is a handy tool that is used frequently. However, it won't work in every situation. Sometimes you'll need a hammer.

HOW THE SNAPSHOT SURVEY STACKS UP TO OTHER MARKETING RESEARCH TOOLS

If you are already familiar with the assorted marketing research tools I've included in this section, you may want to skip ahead to the next chapter. If not, it's important to understand how the snapshot survey is similar and different from each of the more common research tools you can use to manage your business.

Figure 1.4 plots the four basic types of marketing research classifications: primary (any new research you conduct) versus secondary (any existing research, conducted by someone else) and qualitative (primarily words gathered through open-ended questions, observations, etc.) versus quantitative (primarily numbers, such as percentages, means, and other statistics).

FIGURE 1.4
Research classifications

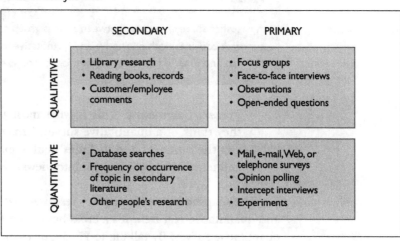

- *Secondary/Qualitative.* This type of research would include informal data gathering by looking at library research, sorting through records, reading customer comments, and the like. I strongly suggest that you become more acquainted with your local librarian. These professionals can almost always help you find data, resources, and other information, typically in a few minutes. (I believe so strongly in this point that I married a librarian. By asking her a couple of quick questions, I've been able to help dozens of clients find out what's already available before commissioning a new survey.)

- *Secondary/Quantitative.* Database searches, how often something is cited in the literature, and other people's research make up this category. It is often highly valuable—if you can find something that actually fits your particular situation. You can learn a lot by what other people are talking—or not talking—about. Sometimes, this type of research does little more than provide background perspective. It rarely answers something specific you need to know for your business.

- *Primary/Qualitative.* This is research that you either do yourself or commission someone else to do on your behalf. It includes things like focus groups, face-to-face interviews, observations, open-ended questions, and the like. This can be a highly valuable form of research, and examples of how and when to use each type are listed in a following section.

F *l a s h* **# 4**

A snapshot survey is a cross between a focus group and a large quantitative survey. It provides both qualitative and quantitative insights, at a fraction of the cost and time of conducting either focus groups or a full-scale study.

- *Primary/Quantitative.* This is what most people think of when they think of a quantitative survey. This type of research gives you the numbers and includes mail, e-mail, and Web surveys, and telephone and intercept interviews.

The snapshot survey is primary research that is a mix of qualitative and quantitative research. It's a cross between a focus group and large quantitative survey. By talking to 25, 50, or even 100 members of your target audience—instead of 300, 500, or even 1,000 of them—you can still obtain valuable insights. To see how, let's review seven of the basic research tools.

I. Focus Groups

When you bring a group of your target audience together to ask them questions, this is called a focus group—an organized discussion led by a moderator with the following characteristics:

- Typically, a group includes 8 to 12 participants, meeting for 1 to 2 hours.
- This is a good tool for consumer, customer, employee, business leader, and other audiences who are willing to give up some of their time for snacks, a meal, or a financial incentive (generally $50 to $70 for consumers and more for technical audiences).
- Focus group facilities include a one-way mirror for private viewing and also audio and video recording. If you're going to observe the group, try to listen for the general overall trends and themes. Don't fixate on any one participant and let his or her comments overwhelm your thinking.
- Conference and hotel rooms serve as excellent focus group rooms. All you need is a conference table and some seats. Ask the observers to sit on the sides and to tell the participants they are helping you take notes.

- Most focus groups include participants who are recruited through telephone interviews and other means. If they qualify (age range, experiences, gender, etc.), they are invited to participate.

2. Telephone Surveys

While a snapshot survey can certainly be conducted by telephone, the primary difference is that telephone surveys typically include more completed interviews and sometimes more complicated questionnaires. You guessed it, the researcher collects data by calling people on the phone. This type of research is most effective when:

- Your concept/topic can be described easily.
- You have a limited amount of time (5 to 15 minutes per interview).
- Your research is clearly focused and relatively specific.

To complete 300 telephone interviews, you might have to call between 1,000 to 3,000 people, depending on who is available and how sensitive your topic is. Telephone surveys are one of the most popular forms of research, because they afford a lot of control over the research process—and most people own a phone. If you don't reach someone the first time you call, you can call them back two or three times. If you're careful with your calling list, you can work small portions of it (50 numbers or so) multiple times before moving on to your next portion. Techniques like these ensure you're getting a representative sample (as long as you're working from a random sample).

Telephone surveys are used frequently for tracking surveys where you're trying to determine if any changes in attitudes or perceptions have occurred over time. Because typically it takes a lot of energy to get people's attention and persuade them—especially if you have a limited budget—many marketers expect to see only slight changes in perception over time. Because larger surveys have smaller margins of error, samples of 1,000-participant surveys conducted yearly are typical. While I've used the snapshot survey in some tracking situations, generally I'd recommend you hold more interviews. The only time a snapshot survey would pick up a change in perceptions is when that change was very dramatic, like no one knowing about your product or service to half the country seeing it—highly unlikely in most cases.

F *l a s h #* **5**

Telephone interviews, e-mail surveys, intercept interviews, and other data-collection methods can all be used to conduct a snapshot survey. The difference is in how these tools are applied to obtain fast, focused feedback.

3. Mail Surveys

With the onslaught of e-mail and other electronic communications, many people are overlooking the value of mail. In fact, it's getting easier and easier for your piece of mail to stand out. How? Put a real stamp on your letter, and personally address your envelope and cover letter (which should be signed by you in blue ink)—all techniques for dramatically increasing your response rates. With this type of research, the researcher sends questions to the target audience and hopes to receive responses through the mail (if you include a postage-paid return envelope, this is usually sufficient). This type of research is most effective when:

- A target audience is likely to respond (membership, employees, sometimes customers). Basically, the more someone knows you and the more they care about you, the more likely they will take the time to fill out and return your survey. If they don't know you (prospects), you should expect a much lower response rate (1 percent to 5 percent). A typical customer response rate is usually higher and closer to 20 percent to 25 percent. Member surveys can be even higher, and employee surveys often range between 50 percent to 75 percent, depending on what's going on within the organization and how suspicious the employees are.
- Mailing address information can be created easily and managed in software that is probably already on your computer.
- You have long lists of questions or complicated categories. This type of research can work very well, because respondents simply read your responses and check which ones best describe them.

To boost your response rate, send out a brightly colored reminder postcard about a week after your survey goes out, saying something like, "If you filled out your survey, thanks. If not, would you please take a moment to do so?" With this technique you generally will receive an additional 50 percent response (if you received 100 from your first mailing, you will typically get another 50, for a total of 150). Some people like to send out a third mailing that looks like the first mailing (cover letter, survey, and business reply envelope), but with a modified cover letter that begins, "Recently we sent you a survey. . . . "

Over the years, I've conducted a few snapshot surveys through the mail, but because of the amount of time it takes to get responses, I don't recommend this approach. The phone and other techniques are often faster.

4. Intercept Surveys

For intercept surveys, the researcher goes to the target audience and asks for feedback. Researchers contact targets in person where they are shopping or eating, visiting a trade show, or at other places. This is a terrific tool, because sometimes very difficult to reach audiences all show up at the same event or meeting and you can gather a lot of feedback quickly. This type of research is most effective when:

- The target audience is classified but you can't buy a list of them. I once sold a survey to interview temporary employees and later found out that I couldn't buy a list of these individuals. Instead, I had to conduct intercept interviews and ask people if they had worked as a temp within the past two years before inviting them to participate in the survey. It would have taken much, much longer to carry on this type of research by phone. Welfare recipients are also difficult to reach. Intercepting people on the street near the welfare office could be a way of reaching this audience.
- A good cross section of the audience is likely to be in one place (college students, conferences, sporting events, shopping malls).
- If you're interviewing outside, do it when the weather forecast is good. I participated in an intercept interview while trout fishing one day in the middle of a stream in a remote section of a state park. I later learned that one of my clients, the United States Department of Agriculture Forest Service, had sponsored this research to learn how people used the park and the economic impact fishing was having on the local economy.

I've carried out many snapshot surveys using the intercept interview format. Within a couple of days—and sometimes a couple of hours—you can get valuable feedback if you can find enough of your target audience in one location. For example, a client wanted to run a survey over the weekend of younger consumers 20 to 25 years old and what they preferred when purchasing coffee. Because it was summertime and there happened to be a block party happy hour, I sent a team of interviewers to the event. Within a couple of hours, we had interviewed more than 100 people. And because everyone had to have their ID checked before they got in (they were serving alcohol), we knew they met the minimum-age requirement. All we had to do was ask them their age before completing the survey (and make sure they hadn't consumed too much libation before answering our questions).

5. Face-to-Face Interviews

The best way to conduct executive or other important interviews is face-to-face—the researcher questions one person, typically in an office or private conference room. Most of the questions you'll ask should be open-ended. This technique works best when:

- You ask your open-ended question, but spend most of your energy probing and asking follow-up questions to get examples and find the "truth."
- The best information often comes after the "formal interview" as you are "heading toward the door." It always amazes me that when people think the formal interview is over, they begin to offer their valuable insights.
- Make sure you take sparse notes on key themes during the interview. Then, immediately after the interview, complete your notes and relevant quotes. Don't wait two or three days or longer to try to remember what was said. You'll forget it too quickly and won't remember who said what.

Face-to-face interviews work well with the snapshot survey, especially if most of your target audience is in the same place (same office or location). If not, they can be very tiring and a lot of work. I once did 20 face-to-face customer interviews for one of the country's largest benefits software companies. This involved flying to 20 different cities during a couple of weeks. Some of the locations also included long drives to reach the customers' offices. The customers were quite impressed that the company cared that much about their opinions that it would send a professional interviewer to spend a couple of hours with them. This type of interviewing is very tiring and time-consuming. I perked up quickly, however, as I deposited a nice size check for completing the project.

6. Experiments

Experiments aren't all that common in many marketing research situations, but they are worth mentioning. In this type of study, the researcher controls variables to test outcomes and reactions. They usually include the following elements:

- The researcher typically asks a series of questions of one respondent.
- Intercept interview forms, videotape, handouts, and other tools are often used to record the responses.

I used an experimental format one time to help a gift box manufacturer test some new design concepts. We interviewed women who were between the ages of 25 to 54 (the primary shopper) about what they thought of different package sizes, price points, designs, whether the boxes were manufactured in the United States, and other factors. By trying to change only one variable at a time (e.g., different size boxes for the same price), we were able to gather some interesting insights into what they liked best and why. As an incentive, we offered participants a $2 bill for completing the experiment. That's all. We had a tight budget and this unusual incentive worked in this case. I flew with the client to Detroit to visit a buyer from K-mart to present the findings and try to convince him to buy what the consumers liked the best.

7. New Media Research (E-mail and Web-based Surveys)

When the Internet was first getting hot, I made a fortune helping companies figure out what to include on their sites. It was just like the gold rush days—the only people making money were the ones selling the tents and supplies, not the miners who were digging for gold. At that time, I don't think anyone was even thinking about using the Internet to collect data, but they are now. Many inexpensive programs are now available to conduct these online surveys and more and more people are getting online, so this is an emerging research tool.

I suggest you consider this type of research as similar to mail surveys—the stronger the relationship between the company who is asking for feedback and the potential respondents, the greater the response. If someone knows and likes you, this is a great tool. If not, you'll get a low response rate, and sometimes it's difficult to tell who actually responded to your survey.

A number of paid online services as well as software are available for processing the data, but all of them seem to calculate your responses based on the number of people who answered a question—not on the number of people in your survey. This isn't a big issue unless half the people left a question blank. Make sure you pay attention to how many people answered each question as you're interpreting your data. You may have to spend some extra time recalculating the software's findings once your survey is finished.

Be careful how you distribute your survey. I once had a client distribute a survey through its e-mail system. Someone hacked into the distribution list and sent everyone a virus. Fortunately, we had already received a lot of responses, but the company had to stop the survey and send out an apology letter with directions on how to fix the problem. Granted, this is a rare example, but it's always best to protect yourself and your respondents.

I've found it's better to send a short e-mail with a link to a Web site that contains your survey. All people have to do is click your link, fill out the questions, and submit the response. Most programs perform the data coding and provide an overall summary of the responses (very nice if you don't want to do a lot of analysis).

Keep all your questions to one page. Trust me on this one. One option most programs give you is to ask only two or three questions at a time before having to click another button to go to the next page. In all the usability testing I've conducted over the years to see what people like and don't like about Web sites, no one minds scrolling down, but everyone hates to scroll sideways or click extra buttons to move to the next section. Just because the technology is available doesn't mean that it helps you gather better feedback.

I've used e-mail and Web surveys many times to conduct snapshot surveys. They are especially nice tools for gathering feedback quickly; you'll get most of your responses the first time people read their e-mail. I recently completed a survey for a trade association that had more than 8,000 members. We received about 2,500 responses within a week or so. There's no way we could have gotten that many surveys as quickly by mail, and it would have cost a fortune to do the same survey by phone.

If you'd like to find out how you can conduct your own snapshot survey from start to finish, as well as how to use this tool to ask questions about the most common marketing challenges most businesses face, please turn the page.

2

BOOT CAMP

How to Run Your Own Snapshot Survey

If we knew what it was we were doing,
it would not be called research, would it?
Albert Einstein

To conduct your own snapshot survey, you
will need some basic training on what to do and when to do it. While
the concept of a snapshot survey is intuitive and easy to grasp, the process of running your survey from start to finish is not so obvious or
straightforward. The subtle decisions you need to make can greatly influence the quality of your survey. It's easy to get off track and waste
time, energy, and money.

In this chapter, you'll walk through a snapshot survey project from
start to finish—beginning with the actual proposal used to sell the
project, to creating the survey questions, collecting the feedback, analyzing the findings, and finally summarizing the results.

This particular snapshot survey focused on suppliers or companies who provided a range of products that my customer used in its
operations and sometimes resold. It was one of several surveys I ran in
this project (which should be a hint to the consultants reading this
book that like so many products and services it is just as easy to sell
several snapshot surveys at the same time as it is to sell only one). Telephone interviews were completed with 25 suppliers over a 3-day period based on a list of about 50 companies given to me. Just like in the
TV show *Dragnet,* the customer's name and data were changed to
prot ect the innocent.

SELLING YOUR SNAPSHOT SURVEY

You can use a snapshot survey in your business or organization in many ways, including:

- For making decisions for your own company
- To help the associations, professional societies, and social organizations that you belong to determine ways they can operate more effectively
- As a specific product or service you sell to your customers to help them improve their operations and, perhaps, to help convince them to buy additional services from you to solve the problems you identify

Even if you are the boss and are spending your own money, taking a few minutes to articulate *why* you want to run a snapshot survey is extremely valuable. If you are not the boss or plan on using someone else's money, spelling out the focus of your survey and what you plan to do with the information you collect is invaluable.

Before you even think about what questions you should ask or who you should talk to, you must become crystal clear about two key questions:

1. *What do you want to learn?* Do you want to understand how customers and prospects see your company and its reputation? Do you want to pick the best name for a new product? What about finding out what your employees think of your new benefits program? Questions like these help you focus the purpose of your snapshot survey; they can get you on track quickly and keep you there. The more specific your focus and goals, the easier it is to run a snapshot survey.

2. *How do you want to use it?* Do you want to create a new brochure? Do you want to convince your board to invest in a new manufacturing facility? What about developing a strategy to increase sales? In my opinion, these are the more important questions. Here's why: Knowing where you want to end up will dramatically impact what questions you ask, who you talk with, how many interviews you decide to do, and whether you use the phone or an e-mail survey to collect your data.

F *l a s h* **# 6**

Running a snapshot survey is a lot like printing—you need to do many things right to produce a good product. You can have the best printing quality, but if your brochure is loaded with typos, it's worth nothing. Likewise, you can write and design a great piece, but if it's printed on a low-quality home printer, it won't be as impressive as it could be. The trick to running your own snapshot survey is to do each step right all the way through—the first time.

A manufacturing customer of mine decided against running a company-wide employee survey as part of an overall branding initiative that also included customer feedback and a competitive assessment. In addition to its perspectives about the strengths of the organization, my client was worried that issues such as the current benefits package, dissatisfaction with management, and other "nonmarketing" problems would be uncovered as part of the findings. The manufacturer ultimately wanted to focus on new marketing initiatives (brochure, Web site, trade show booth, brand image), so even though the employee feedback would have been nice to have, it was seen as a risk that could potentially derail the entire project. My customer decided not to ask questions that the company really did not want the answers to. Instead, I completed a handful of face-to-face interviews with sales and marketing employees who interacted with customers on a regular basis. I was able to get the employee perspectives I needed, but avoided uncovering a larger, peskier problem that really wasn't related to the task at hand.

Once you have a good idea of what you want to learn and how you want to use it, it's time to put those ideas on paper in the form of a proposal. Over the years, I've sold snapshot surveys with as little as a paragraph or two in an e-mail or as a narrative document that outlines the current problem and suggests how I'm going to run the survey in five to ten pages. The exact number of pages depends on the customer, but most snapshot survey proposals I write are two or three pages. I also typically include some standard background information such as my biography, a list of recent clients who faced similar circumstances, and the investment required to complete the project. Notice I didn't use the term *budget,* which implies that customers will have to "spend" money and view the project as a "cost." Instead, investment is a much more positive word and focuses the prospect on how it will be better off as a result of completing the survey. Investing means the prospect will get back what it spent, plus some—which is typically the case with a snapshot survey.

Here's what I wrote in a proposal to sell a supplier a snapshot survey, which was actually only one of several surveys and other consulting work I sold to a manufacturer to help it determine its current brand image. All told, my customer invested about $40,000 in the entire project, with about $4,000 dedicated to the supplier snapshot survey. Green Manufacturing is a name I made up to explain how you might run your own snapshot survey from start to finish. I've also changed most of the questions in the company's survey, the specific findings, and other data that is presented in the rest of this chapter.

GREEN MANUFACTURING SNAPSHOT SURVEY PROPOSAL

Background

Based on a strategic planning process completed earlier this year, Green Manufacturing has begun focusing on multiple initiatives designed to move the organization forward, establish awareness, and provide better customer service and solutions.

One primary goal of the strategic plan is to improve Green Manufacturing's customer focus and market intelligence. A working committee with representatives from each of the organization's five business units has begun exploring approaches for defining and promoting the new value propositions, completing market research (customer, prospect, distributor, employee, and supplier), and creating a strategic branding plan.

We are pleased to provide the following recommendations for conducting primary marketing research and finalizing the plan. These recommendations are based on input from the branding committee, strategic plan summary, past customer and distributor research, knowledge of Green Manufacturing, and follow-up conversations. We are also cognizant of budget issues and have recommended alternative approaches Green Manufacturing might use to complete this research.

Current Situation

While the Green Manufacturing Group has enjoyed tremendous success over the years, the company now realizes that a stronger brand image in the marketplace could help the organization achieve its new performance goals and help overcome these challenges:

- *Shorten sales cycles.* By reducing the sales cycles, the Green Manufacturing Group could devote fewer resources to the sales process and therefore expand its sales efforts with its existing staff. Long-term, corporate growth would occur at a faster rate.

- *Increase sales volume.* A stronger brand image would help Green Manufacturing differentiate itself from competitors and reduce the tendency for customers to buy based on "price."

- *Create a stronger reputation in the marketplace.* As the Green Manufacturing Group gains industry recognition as a leading, innovative company with exceptional customer service, it will be easier to set appointments, generate referrals, and market new products and services.

- *Position the Green Manufacturing Group for long-term growth.* Once Green Manufacturing attains a stronger brand image and reputation, sustaining growth should become easier because of a broader customer base and a recognized company image and focus.

Why Marketing Research Is Needed

Based on our initial meeting with the branding team, a number of important reasons were reviewed about why conducting marketing research will help the Green Manufacturing Group identify, focus, and implement its strategic branding plan. These include:

- To learn customer/prospect perceptions and insights about each business unit's strengths and weaknesses so that meaningful value propositions can be created and used in marketing materials.

- To determine how well Green Manufacturing brands stack up against key competitors and what the company must do to maintain its leadership position and/or close gaps.

- To identify effective communications channels that could be used to brand Green Manufacturing and its business units.

- To understand employee perceptions and the extent to which they are in sync with the external marketplace.

- To determine the potential for cross-selling services to customers who traditionally work with one business unit.

- To establish a baseline from which future branding and marketing efforts can be measured and tracked over time.

- Depending on the final structure of the research instruments, to include research questions regarding customers' and prospects' current awareness of each business unit's services and customers' interest in learning more about any specific service. If appropriate, questions that requested referrals may be added. (Note: While the primary goal of the research would be to better understand customers' perceptions, a secondary benefit could be as a marketing, public relations, and sales tool.)

Marketing Research Recommendations

To gather valuable insights regarding customer, prospect, distributor, and employee perceptions, we recommend the following research components:

- *Key customer and prospect telephone survey.* A total of 250 telephone interviews would be completed, with approximately 50 interviews completed for each business unit (25 customers and 25 prospects). We would use a Snapshot Survey™ methodology to provide directional feedback. The top 50 to 100 customers and prospects for each division would be used as a contact lists.

A "blind" survey would be conducted (so that customers would not be aware that Green Manufacturing is sponsoring the research). Similar questions to each audience and some unique questions would be added as needed for each business unit.

- *Competitor strategic branding assessment.* To learn how competitors are positioning themselves through advertisements, taglines, and other techniques, a review of secondary sources would be completed. These sources could include Web sites, trade publications, literature, and other resources. This insight would help ensure that the Green Manufacturing Group does not inadvertently attempt to stake out a branding platform that is already claimed—and perhaps owned—by a competitor.

- *Distributor telephone survey.* We recommend completing 25 interviews with a cross section of distributors to better understand their perceptions of this business unit and key competitors. We anticipate that this survey will be unique and help provide additional insight into this business unit's long-term strategy and decision to maintain a distributor network.

- *Employee survey.* An employee survey that contains questions that mirror the question topics of the customer and prospect survey would be distributed internally at Green Manufacturing and returned to a P.O. Box. Employees would be guaranteed complete confidentiality. To determine differences in perception between business units, key demographic questions would be included to provide additional insights and recommendations.

- *Supplier survey.* A total of 25 suppliers will be interviewed to learn their perspectives about Green Manufacturing. Where applicable, questions similar to those asked of customers and prospects will be identical so that differences in perception between the target audiences can be better understood.

Workflow

All marketing research surveys and telephone interviews will follow these primary steps:

- *Create a questionnaire.* We will prepare questionnaires based on the input received to date and on follow-up conversations with each business unit. Most survey instruments can be finalized in one to three drafts.

- *Obtain the contact lists.* Green Manufacturing will provide the customer, prospect, distributor, employee, and supplier contact lists. These lists should be verified prior to launching the research to ensure that the information is accurate.

- *Administer the survey.* Senior researchers who have completed numerous similar projects will complete the telephone interviews. The employee survey will be distributed internally.

- *Analyze the results.* Once the interviews are completed or the surveys are returned, we will code and analyze the results using a statistical software package. In addition to a set of crosstab tables (every question asked on the survey compared by key demographic variables), all appropriate statistical tests will be completed to uncover insights and trends from the data.

- *Present the results.* We will deliver a presentation of the results with key recommendations. We anticipate that a narrative summary (detailed findings including charts, graphs, selected comments, and other data) and a PowerPoint presentation (that highlights the key findings) will be prepared and delivered to Green Manufacturing's branding committee.

- *Application of the marketing research.* If desired, we will assist Green Manufacturing in exploring how the research results can be used to shape the final branding strategy and plan. We would be prepared to facilitate a half-day meeting that would result in an outline of the branding plan and most likely include insights regarding the plan's objectives, strategies, key messages, tactics, time-table, marketing ROI measures, and budget.

Timing

We anticipate that it will take four to six weeks to complete the entire project, depending on efficient turnaround on survey drafts, contact lists, and other materials. We expect that each snapshot survey will take three to five days to complete.

FIVE STEPS TO RUNNING YOUR OWN SNAPSHOT SURVEY

Once you "sell" your snapshot survey proposal, you have to start doing the work. While every snapshot survey is unique, each survey follows five basic steps as diagrammed in Figure 2.1. Essentially, you need to get a set of questions together, ask those questions to a limited sample of your target audience using some research approach (such as a phone or e-mail survey), analyze your data, and summarize your results.

1. Asking the Right Questions

If you want to obtain good information, you need to start by asking the right questions. The problem is that the right questions are never immediately obvious. It takes thinking and time to bring them into focus.

The fastest way to bring questions into focus is to review the snapshot surveys and situations featured throughout this book, as well as any other questionnaires you may have access to. Nothing beats a good example survey you can quickly modify.

Another technique I like to use to shorten the time it takes to discover which questions to ask in a snapshot survey is storyboarding or a visual way to brainstorm ideas that are written on index cards and pinned

FIGURE 2.1

Key steps for running your own snapshot survey

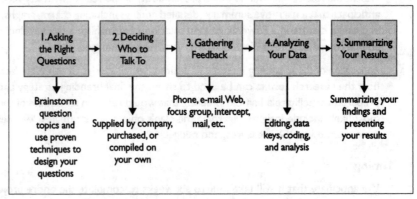

to a wall or a storyboard (foam core board). You may be familiar with how Hollywood movies are planned prior to filming. Long before the actors, camera operators, and other professionals arrive, every scene, line, and camera angle are mapped out and visually posted on a wall or storyboard.

This is the same concept that can be used to quickly develop your snapshot survey. It works best if you can round up one or two colleagues who can help you brainstorm which topics make sense for your survey. Get a stack of index cards and a marker. As a question topic comes up, write the topic on a card and pin it to the wall, lay it on the table, or place it on the floor—put it in a place that is easy to see. After 10 to 15 minutes of brainstorming, you should have a pretty good idea of the kinds of things you could ask in your survey.

Next, with the help of your colleagues, it's time to prioritize your ideas and create an initial outline for your survey. Start by gathering all the demographic questions together, such as age, income, gender, type of customer, or any other classification category you came up with. In most cases, you'll want to ask these questions in the last section of your survey and ask them in order from easiest to most difficult. For example, it's easier to ask someone what his or her highest level of education is than what his or her total household income is. If you meet someone for the first time at a party and the first question they ask you is "How much did you make last year?" or "How much do you weigh?" would you be put off? Of course you would, so why would you do the same thing to the people you meet in your survey? Coax them into the survey by asking for their opinions about your questions. Save the classification questions for the end of your survey.

With the rest of the cards, group them into natural categories or themes, ranging from the general to the specific. I call this the "funnel" technique. It's always easier to start with the broader questions ("What's your overall opinion of our product?") and move to the more specific ("If we added this new feature, what would your reaction be?"). Organizing your entire survey in this manner will serve you well.

The cards you end up with—and the order you've placed them in—will serve as a starting point for developing the wording of each question. Now the fun starts.

Ten ways to write high-impact questions. In writing more than 1,000 surveys, I've found the following 10 principles particularly helpful in transforming your thoughts into questions that respondents can easily understand and answer:

1. *Plan to use a mix of closed and open-ended questions.* A closed question has a fixed number of responses, such as "During the past week, how many times did you use our service?" These are terrific for getting feedback you can quantify and that is easy to process during your data-analysis stage. With open-ended questions, there is no definite answer. Instead, you often get a range of opinions and can hear how people talk in their own words— something that is highly valuable if you're planning to develop a brochure, advertisements, or sales literature. If you're going to ask 15 questions in your survey, I suggest you include at least 2 or 3 open-ended ones. The comments you hear often describe the feelings behind the numbers. Your survey will be stronger if it uses a mix of open-ended and closed questions, rather than only open-ended or only closed ones.

2. *Ask exactly what is needed and only what is needed.* The snapshot survey is about staying focused. Pick a topic and stick to it. Avoid the temptation to try to answer too many questions about too many topics in the same survey. Instead, plan a follow-up survey.

3. *Keep your wording simple.* A typical question should be 10 to 15 words long, or 1 or 2 lines of typed text. Use shorter syllable words wherever you can. It is more difficult to write a tightly worded, short question than a longer one.

4. *Use exact time references.* Change "during the past year" to "during the past 12 months." Twelve months is precise. The past year could mean anything from the current year, which you may only be into for 6 months or so, to the end of last year

minus the last couple months of the year. (I'm getting confused just trying to explain it.)

5. *Make your question categories exclusive (don't let them overlap).* If you asked someone, "How much would you be willing to spend on this product?" and your answers were $0 to $5.00, $5.00 to $10.00, and $10.00 to $15.00, which category should they pick if the respondent answered "$5.00"? Obviously, $5.00 is in the first and second category. So change your categories to $0 to $4.99, $5.00 to $9.99, and $10.00 to $14.99.

6. *Keep the "low" and "high" ends of rating scales pointing in the same direction.* Be careful that you don't trick your respondents by shifting your rating scales, making the "lows" or "bad" scores the low numbers on one question and later making them the high numbers. For example, if you have a 1 to 5 rating in a question that goes from poor (1) to excellent (5), don't change them in a follow-up question to exceeding my expectations (1) to not meeting my expectations (5). "Excellent" is like "exceeding my expectations" and both are positive. Either make them always the high number or always the low number, but don't mix them in the same survey.

7. *Use "skip to" questions sparingly.* At times, you may not want everyone to answer every question. For example, if someone has tried a product or service, you may want to ask only those individuals what they thought of the product and whether they would recommend it to someone else (pretty tough to do if they never tried it). In this case, you would start with a "skip to question" that asks, "Have you tried this product?" If they answer "yes," you ask the follow-up questions. If they answer "no," you skip to the next question or section. The problem is, because you typically don't have very many people in a snapshot survey, skipping a portion of them for a question can weaken that question. I always suggest that you keep as many people as possible in every question of your survey, because your statistics will be stronger.

8. *Include instructions for every question.* Should respondents check, mark, or click "one" or "all that apply"? Do you want them to "explain" their responses with a few sentences or simply give a "one-word" answer? This may seem like overkill if this is your first questionnaire, but it will make it easier on the people answering your questions and simplify your data analysis (because "check one" means you have one variable or response, while "check all that apply" means you could have several variables or responses).

9. *Ask one question at a time.* "Do you understand and like our new return policy?" Someone might understand it, but not like it. This question is really two questions and should be presented as such.

10. *Avoid loaded words and phrases.* "The company should continue its excellent fringe benefits program." "Excellent" is too much selling and not enough asking. In this case, excellent is a loaded word that will likely bias the results.

This ten-question design technique is the same one I used to develop the following snapshot survey questions for Green Manufacturing. Notice that I identified Green Manufacturing at the start of this survey (in the introduction), because I wanted suppliers to know who was sponsoring the research. I also told them that their responses were confidential, which means that no single person would ever be identified with a specific answer or quote in any of the questions. Each of the questions is in bold (because this is what was to be read to each supplier) and the directions to each question are in ALL CAPITALS (which are not to be read but help ensure an accurate response to each question). Finally, in question 5a, notice that the responses to the questions go "down" the column before moving to the next row, because this is how most people read and think (instead of going across columns before moving down to the next line). Like so many question-writing techniques, this may seem like overkill, but it will dramatically simplify your data analysis and make sure that you are not mixing up answers and drawing the wrong conclusions because of sloppiness.

GREEN MANUFACTURING SNAPSHOT SURVEY QUESTIONS

Hello. This is _____ calling from CorCom, Inc. We are contacting Green Manufacturing suppliers to learn your opinions about customer service and other issues. Your responses will be kept strictly confidential. Would you mind answering a few questions? (IF INCONVENIENT TIME, SCHEDULE A CALL-BACK TIME.)

1. **What is your overall impression of Green Manufacturing?** (PROBE. RECORD VERBATIM RESPONSE.)

2. **What are Green Manufacturing's greatest strengths?** (PROBE. RECORD VERBATIM RESPONSE.

3. **What are its weaknesses or challenges?** (PROBE. RECORD VERBATIM RESPONSE.)

4. **How would you rate Green Manufacturing on its _____ (INSERT ATTRIBUTE) on a 1 to 10 scale where 1 is "poor" and 10 is "excellent"?** (MARK ONE FOR EACH.)

    a. Accountability—does what it promised, when it promised   ____
    b. Creativity—offers innovative products, services, and solutions   ____
    c. Growth—establishes relationships that help all stakeholders grow and prosper   ____
    d. Industry leadership—number 1, lots of people use and like the company, favorite of many people   ____
    e. Integrity—ethical in dealings, you can rely on the company, shows integrity   ____
    f. Offer value—provides services and ideas that can't be easily found in other places   ____
    h. Respect—demonstrates concern and understands customers' situations   ____
    i. Satisfaction—works hard at keeping its stakeholders satisfied   ____
    j. Technology—introduces new and improved products and services   ____

5a. **How effective are communications with Green Manufacturing?** (READ. MARK ONE.)

    1   Very effective   3   Not at all effective
    2   Somewhat effective   4   Don't Know/No Response (DK/NR)

5b. **How might they be improved?** (PROBE. RECORD VERBATIM RESPONSE.)

6. **Who are the industry's top distributors and why?** (LIST. PROBE. RECORD VERBATIM RESPONSE.)

7. **Which distributor(s) promotes your products the best?** (PROBE. RECORD VERBATIM RESPONSE.)

8. **Who is most innovative and why?** (PROBE. RECORD VERBATIM RESPONSE.)

9. **How does Green Manufacturing stack up against these top distributors?** (PROBE. RECORD VERBATIM RESPONSE.)

10. **How can Green Manufacturing do a better job?** (PROBE. RECORD VERBATIM RESPONSE.)

11. **In the next two or three years, what do you think will be the greatest changes or trends in the area of distribution?** (PROBE. RECORD VERBATIM RESPONSE.)

12. **From your perspective, what is the value in distribution compared to other sales or marketing channels?** (PROBE. RECORD VERBATIM RESPONSE.)

13. **What role do you think distributors fill?** (PROBE. RECORD VERBATIM RESPONSE.)

14. **What kinds of accounts are best served by distributors?** (PROBE FOR SMALL, MEDIUM, LARGE; NATIONAL, REGIONAL, MOMS & POPS. RECORD VERBATIM RESPONSE.)

> **F** *l a s h* **# 7**
>
> Fortunately, marketing research like the snapshot survey is exempt from consumer "do not call" lists, but when buying these lists you may be asked to submit a list of questions and sign an affidavit. Frankly, a lot of consumers are sick and tired of telemarketing and many see phone interviews as a nuisance. That's why you'll need to pour on the charm whenever you start dialing.

2. Deciding Who to Talk To

Next, you need to decide who you are going to talk to. Who are they? Where do they hang out? What's the most effective way to reach them (phone, e-mail, mail, intercept, etc.)? This is often the most difficult and frustrating of the five steps to running your own snapshot survey. I can't tell you the number of times my customers have claimed that they have "great contact information," only to soon find out that they are missing phone numbers, only have addresses for the billing or delivery of shipments (not the specific person who makes the buying decision), they didn't realize there's been turnover, or a number of other problems exist.

If you (or your customer) don't already have a list, there are many ways to create or buy one. I typically start with one of the many list houses. These companies often can provide both general and specific lists, which are created from many sources, such as government classifications (Standard Industrial Code or North American Industrial Code), magazine subscriptions, membership rosters, and other sources. Typically, you can buy a list for several hundred dollars, depending on who's selling it and how difficult it was to create. Some list houses will also sell you consumer information that is linked to U.S. Census data. For example, I recently completed a survey for a university that wanted to contact parents of high school students. This list included a random selection of households that were likely to have high school children living there. Buying this list was a lot more economical and efficient than trying to call a random sample of households and asking if they had any high school students living there.

Sometimes you can buy lists that were created from other lists. The private banking division of one of the nation's largest banks asked me to conduct a survey of "millionaires" to find out their preferences for making investments. Because most millionaires don't readily identify themselves, I found a list company who created these lists by finding the names of people who purchased five or more big-ticket items, such as a yacht, Rolls-Royce, or home for more than $500,000. If the individual purchases were more than $1,000,000, then that person would have to be a millionaire and included in the contact list.

If you don't want to pay for a list, you can try the Internet. Many local chapters of associations list the names and phone numbers of their members. If you're a member of a large chat room, you might try posting your Web survey on the site, but expect to be harassed if you aren't a regular member and you're just using the site to get feedback. In cases where you can find a few names to get started, I like to ask the respondents "who else" they know who I could interview. This snowball technique works great for finding people who aren't accessible through lists.

Make sure that you can actually get a list of the people you want to talk with before selling your survey. Early in my career, I sold a survey that would involve 200 telephone interviews with consumers who worked as temporary employees during the past two years. When I got back to my office and started mapping out the project, I quickly found that employment records are confidential and that no one had or would sell me a list of people who worked as temporary employees. To complete this project, I would need to make hundreds—maybe even thousands—of telephone calls to find people who met the criteria I needed. So, with my hat in hand, I went back to my customer and asked him if I could switch the methodology from a telephone survey to an intercept interview. Fortunately, he agreed. I sent an interviewing team to a local parade and they walked up and down both sides of the street asking everyone, "Have you worked as a temporary employee during the past two years?" Those who said yes were asked to participate in the survey. Since then, I always make sure I can get a list before I quote a price for a survey.

F *l a s h* **# 8**

If you're making business-to-business calls, leave messages and talk with administrative support personnel and other staff members to find out the best time to reach the person you're calling. You'll be surprised that with a little effort, you can increase the productivity of your contact list and save yourself time and energy.

In the Green Manufacturing supplier survey, my customer was able to gather 50 names in a few days. It also alerted each supplier through e-mail and some phone follow-up that someone from my office may be contacting them for a survey. We wanted to make sure that the suppliers didn't think we were working for competitors and fishing for information, and the advanced notice helped make completing the interviews easier.

3. Gathering Feedback

If you're gathering feedback over the phone or in person, your tone, body language, listening skills, and a host of other issues come into play. In my opinion, effective interviewing skills are a learned art. With practice, you should get better and better at it. Here are eight basic tips I tell my interview staff to help them improve their skills:

1. Be yourself, unless you are naturally grumpy. Smile.
2. Try to sound natural instead of sounding like you are reading.
3. Be polite. Some people will be rude to you, but remember that you are representing our company and our clients.
4. Don't take rudeness to heart. Some people are just having a bad day. They are rejecting the "role" (as an interviewer) you are playing, not you as a person. Likewise, if you're having a bad day, don't take it out on the people you are calling or interviewing.
5. Be enthusiastic. You'll get more results when your positive attitude shows through.
6. Listen to what they are saying. Write quotes down verbatim (not, "She thinks . . ."). It's better to take a few notes during the interview, then immediately go back and fill in what they said rather than to try to write down each word as they are saying it. Chances are, you'll miss key information or forget what they said—especially if you wait several hours or days to finish completing your questionnaires.
7. Take your time with the questions so the interviewee doesn't feel rushed. At the same time, make sure that you read each question in its entirety as it is written on the survey. Our process is scientific, so we need to ensure we are collecting data accurately and in the same way between interviews. Occasionally, some people will be lonely and want to talk to you for a long time. In these situations, keep the survey moving. Be polite, but always focus on production.

8. Write neatly. If you can't read the responses, why did you bother to ask the questions?

If you're using a Web-based, mail, or other visual survey, the graphic design you select matters. Basically, the more professional looking your survey, the more credibility it will have. I often hire a professional graphic designer to create survey forms from the questions I write for mail surveys.

Regardless of whether you're creating a spoken (telephone, intercept, etc.) or printed (mail, Web, etc.) snapshot survey, make sure you test it. Give it to a handful of people and ask them to try to fill it out or answer the questions. If they have any trouble and don't understand what a question means or where they should mark a response, or there's any other problem, fix it before you start your actual survey. If you're only conducting 50 interviews for your snapshot survey, why let 5 to 10 surveys get messed up. With Web- or e-mail-based surveys, I typically fill out 4 or 5 fake surveys, putting all #1 responses for one survey, #2 for the second survey, etc. Then I check the data file to make sure that every question is loading properly. I've been burned before with responses coming back missing crucial categories, forcing me to throw out the data for that question.

After you conduct several surveys, you'll get smarter about how you invite people to participate. For example, some people will say, "How long will this take?" Don't tell them 15 to 20 minutes, because you'll never get to talk to anyone. Instead, say a "couple of minutes." If you're conducting business-to-business interviews, it may make sense to schedule phone appointments with respondents and ask them to block out 15 minutes of time. People will always spend more time on the phone once the interview is started.

Over the years, I've had the pleasure of working with some great interviewers who gathered accurate feedback and didn't waste a lot of time collecting it. I overheard some great one-liners, including two of my favorites:

- "Hi. My name is Adam and I'm just working my way through college." Who can hang up on a hard-working college student?
- "We're conducting a national poll tonight and I'm calling people on the West Coast. Actually, I'm finding the farther west I go, the more intelligent and interesting people seem to be. So, that's why I'd like to talk with you tonight." Talk about a compliment!

I even had an employee find true love while interviewing. After finishing a call one evening, the man on the other end wanted to ask her a couple of questions. They struck up a friendship and got to know each other over several months. She eventually visited Kansas where he lived. I remember the day she told me she was quitting to move west to get married. I was happy for her. Surveys have always been a lot more than just about research.

4. Analyzing Your Data

A stack of surveys is only a stack of surveys until you interpret them. Whether you hand count your responses or plug them into a spreadsheet and let your software tally the results, you need a disciplined process for handling each question on your survey and every response to those questions. So, how do you get started?

Editing your surveys.   Before you try to analyze your feedback, you need to spend a few minutes making sure your surveys were filled out properly, because it will keep you from entering bad data that has to be cleaned up later. Take each survey and look at the responses:

- Was every question answered?
- Was every question answered properly? If you had "skip to" questions, were the questions skipped properly or did someone answer questions they should not have? For example, if only the "yes" responses were supposed to have follow-up questions, you may have to either change the first "yes" to a "no" or disregard the follow-up questions.
- Number your surveys. I like to use the top left corner of the first page. This tells me how many surveys I have and if there's a problem with any of my data, I can quickly find the survey I need and not have to sort through the entire pile.

The easiest approach: hand-tally your results.   Because only 25 to 50 respondents are involved in most snapshot surveys, it is often quickest to hand-tally the results using one of these techniques:

- Stack the surveys in piles based on how the respondents answered each question. For example, if you have a "yes," "no," and "don't know" question, you'll need three piles. Sort all the surveys on only that question. Then simply add up the responses to each category and record them on a blank survey. Repeat the process for every question. Once you're finished, change your raw numbers into percentages by dividing the number of people who answered each category by the number of people who should have answered the question. For example, if 15 of the 25 people said yes, then the percentage would be 60 percent.

- Take out a blank sheet of paper and create and number the left-hand column, using one number for each question. Across the top, list the categories for each question. Under each question category, place Roman numerals for each person who gave a response. Like the last approach, transform the raw numbers into percentages. An easy way to add some depth to your analysis is to select one demographic question to sort all of the responses into, such as "customers" and "prospects." For each survey from a customer, place a Roman numeral mark under that category and use the same process for prospects. Using this technique will help you create a rudimentary "crosstab" or cross-tabulation table and give you insight about how similar or different the scores are from each group.

Both of these approaches work for "closed" questions where you should have included the question directions "check one" or "check all that apply." They do not work for open-ended questions where you can have a variety of statements unless you develop several categories of response. To classify your open-ended questions, you need to first make a list of topics that the majority of your answers fall under. I like to take a handful of surveys, read over the responses to an open-ended question, then start writing down key words or ideas. You can use the Roman numeral system to help by creating a quick hand-tally of the top four or five responses to each open-ended question. Then all you have do is include the answers to these open-ended questions as part of your findings.

F l a s h # 9

_____

An easy way to boost the impact of your snapshot survey and report is to include specific recommendations. Don't be satisfied with simply finding the "numbers." Instead, take the lead on determining what the numbers mean and how they should be used—starting today!

In the Green Manufacturing survey, the second question asked, "What are Green Manufacturing's greatest strengths?" Reading over the responses, five themes came up and were used to classify the responses: (1) good customer service, (2) the people, (3) communications with suppliers, (4) willingness to partner, and (5) the purchasing department.

Sometimes, your responses to open-ended questions are so scattered or varied that it doesn't make sense to tally them. In these cases, I like to simply list them as bulleted comments. If you have a lot of them, pick 10 to 15 that represent what people were saying. You'll find that these quotes can add life and drama to the numbers you find.

If you've included some 1 to 5 scales, such as strongly disagree to strongly agree, it might make sense to calculate the mean for these questions. Let's say you found these raw numbers to a 1 to 5 scale of a snapshot survey of 25 people:

Strongly Disagree (1)	Disagree (2)	Neither Agree Nor Disagree (3)	Agree (4)	Strongly Agree (5)
6	5	3	4	7

To calculate the mean, you simply multiply the number of people who answered each statement by the numerical value of that statement and add them together ($[6 \times 1] + [5 \times 2] + [3 \times 3] + [4 \times 4] + [7 \times 5]$), then divide your total number (76) by the number of people in your survey (25). In this example, your mean is 3.04, or 3.0 if you're rounding your numbers to the nearest tenth.

The advanced approach: use a software program to analyze your data. If your surveys contain a lot of questions or if you want to perform more sophisticated analyses, you need to use a software program.

To get started, you'll employ a process I call "coding." To keep things simple, you are creating a database file where:

- Every row (across the spreadsheet from left to right) is one survey (or one person's responses).
- Every column (down the page from top to bottom) equals all the answers to one question (or variable).

To figure out what to place where, you need to create what I call a data "key," which says exactly where each answer is to go in your data file. You must assign a number to each of the responses you received in your survey. For example, a "yes" or "no" question could be assigned a "1" for the yeses and a "2" for the nos. If you looked down your column and counted all the 1s and all the 2s, you would have the total response for that question. If you have 1 to 5 or 1 to 10 rating scales, simply use those numbers. If you have a "check all that apply" question, you really have several questions in one, so I use a "1" if it was checked (a "yes" response) and a "2" if it wasn't checked (a "no" response).

Let's take a look at the data key and data file for Green Manufacturing and the specific coding using only two of the questions on the survey that asked about how effective communications with the company were.

5a. How effective are communications with Green Manufacturing? (READ. MARK ONE.)

1 Very effective

2 Somewhat effective

3 Not at all effective

4 Don't know/no response

5b. How might they be improved? (PROBE. RECORD VERBATIM RESPONSE.)

1 No improvement

2 Get to know sales reps better

3 One contact person

4 Always room for improvement

5 24-hour hotline

6 Call us with new ideas

9 Don't know/no response

Question 5a already had numbers placed in front of the responses as the questionnaire was developed, so we can simply use them to code in the responses. Questions 5b was an open-ended question that was classified into seven categories. Responses 1 to 6 were the themes that most people chose. Those who left the question blank or said they didn't know were given a "9," which I use because it typically stands out from the other numbers on the list. Questions 5a and 5b appear bold in the data list that follows. The other numbers in this file go with other questions on the survey.

```
01111  0708070708990503051 12  1101  1111222222
02112  9908070909090908081 29  2202  2212222122
03211  0507080907060805071 31  2303  3311222222
04423  09100910101005101011 2  2404  8211111122
```

```
05111  08101010081008091011 2  2405  3322221122
06311  07080909080909070811 2  2506  1411222222
07431  99999999999999999991 49  9603  4412222222
08112  08080808070707060614 9  2207  2122122222
09441  99101010101007089911 2  2407  1511111122
10141  08101010991009090911 2  9699  9912222222
11432  07101010080908080811 2  3605  3051112222
12124  08100809080899999111 2  2607  9412222122
13519  09080809090810090911 9  2609  9612122222
14345  08100908080899060719 9  9808  5312222222
15442  08080908070710100925 9  3299  4412222222
16341  08080809100908080815 2  4388  9311111122
17145  07080909080809090926 2  4107  4311111122
18141  08101010101010101011 8  4609  9111111122
19143  08100809091008080915 2  4205  4111111122
20432  09101010100910101011 2  4201  5912222222
21141  08080809091009099911 9  4402  4612222222
22151  08990808090808089919 9  2299  5911111122
23441  99080809090999080819 9  1699  2612222222
24311  09101010091009090919 2  2401  2612222222
25348  08090809080808990912 9  2601  5511222222
```

If you count the numbers in the first bold column, you see that 23 of them are "1s," or "very effective," and there are two "2s," or "somewhat effective." If you count the second column, you get:

- twelve "1s," or "no improvement needed"
- two "2s," or "get to know sales rep better"
- one "3," or "one contact person"
- two "4s," or "always room for improvement"
- three "5s," or "24-hour hotline"
- one "6," or "call us with new ideas"
- four "9s," or "don't know/no response"

In addition to the two bold columns of numbers in this file, notice that the first two digits in each row is the survey identification number, from 1 to 25 (01–25). This file was coded in Microsoft Notepad, which creates basis text files that can be imported into virtually every data-analysis program. To keep the coding simple, I included a space at the end of each page on the survey (which was four pages long when I left enough space to write the answers to each open-ended question). If I mess up a line of coding, I don't have to redo the entire survey, just the page I'm on. The entire survey could have easily been coded directly into a processing program, such as Excel. Because most database programs use cells for numbers, I wouldn't need to add a space at the end of each page, for the lines from each cell would keep things lined up.

If you have only a handful of surveys and a limited number of questions, it is easiest to code directly into a database or statistical software program. If you have a lot of surveys, I like to use Notepad, because it requires half the key strokes to enter the same data (in the database programs you have to use the right arrow key to move to the next cell, while in Notepad, you just type it in). Try coding 1,000 surveys sometimes and you'll be glad you used Notepad.

Once these numbers were merged into a database file or statistical program, you could use the program commands to calculate these same values you just determined by visually inspecting your data file. You can also compare responses from one question to another one and calculate statistics very quickly and easily.

5. Summarizing Your Results

Once you've asked the questions, found enough of the right people to talk with, and gathered their feedback and analyzed it, you need to put it all together in a simple summary and present it in a way that you can communicate your findings clearly.

While findings can be reported in numerous ways, I like to use a "top line report" that includes a few verbatim comments. All you need to do is save a copy of your original survey file and enter your percentages, quotes, and other data right in this form. If you like, include a brief summary with a sentence or two about how you conducted your snapshot survey (e.g., number of people you interviewed, when you interviewed them, etc.).

Let's take a look at the report from Green Manufacturing. Notice that it starts with a sentence about the methods and a brief statement about the overall findings then continues by listing the answers to every question in the survey. Many of the percentages to each question are ranked from highest to lowest scores to make the report easier to read. I've also listed the "base" under each question, or the number of people who responded to the question. If you are using "skip to" questions, your base will be lower for some questions (and your percentages will also be calculated on those smaller numbers than on the total number of people in your survey).

GREEN MANUFACTURING
Supplier Survey Top Line Report

A total of 25 interviews were completed with Green Manufacturing suppliers between January 16 and January 19.

The overall conclusion of this research is that suppliers have a positive impression of Green Manufacturing and find it to be "a good company" (44%) and "a good company to work with" (28%). Suppliers also see Green Manufacturing as "very professional" (20%), "effective" (4%), and "very positive" (4%).

1. **What is your overall impression of Green Manufacturing?** (PROBE. RECORD VERBATIM RESPONSE.)

   Base: 25

44%	Good company	4%	Effective
28%	Good to work with	4%	Very positive
20%	Very professional		

2. **What are Green Manufacturing's greatest strengths?** (PROBE. RECORD VERBATIM RESPONSE.)

   Base: 25

44%	Good customer service	8%	Willingness to partner
32%	The people	4%	Purchasing department
12%	Communications		

3. **What are its weaknesses?** (PROBE. RECORD VERBATIM RESPONSE.)

   Base: 25

52%	No weakness	4%	Not enough lead time
20%	Too much overlap	4%	Other
8%	Need more national coverage	4%	Don't know/no response
8%	Back orders		

4. **How would you rate Green Manufacturing on its _____ (INSERT ATTRIBUTE) on a 1 to 10 scale where 1 is "poor" and 10 is "excellent"?** (MARK ONE FOR EACH.)

Base: 25	Mean
Integrity—ethical in dealings, you can rely on the company, shows integrity	9.1
Respect—demonstrates concern and understands customers' situations	9.0
Satisfaction—works hard at keeping its stakeholders satisfied	8.8
Accountability—does what it promised, when it promised	8.7
Growth—establishes relationships that help all stakeholders grow and prosper	8.6
Offer value—provides services and ideas that can't be easily found in other places	8.4

	Mean
Industry leadership—number 1, lots of people use and like the company, favorite of many people	8.3
Technology—introduces new and improved products and services	8.1
Creativity—offers innovative products, services, and solutions	7.9

5a. How effective are communications with Green Manufacturing? (READ. MARK ONE.)

Base: 25

92%	Very effective	0%	Not at all effective
8%	Somewhat effective	0%	Don't know/no response

5b. How might they be improved? (PROBE. RECORD VERBATIM RESPONSE.)

Base: 25

48%	No improvement	4%	24-hour hotline
12%	Get to know sales reps better	4%	Call us with new ideas
8%	One contact person	16%	Don't know/no response
8%	Always room for improvement		

6. Who are the industry's top distributors and why? (LIST. PROBE. RECORD VERBATIM RESPONSE.)

Selected Comments:

- "Blue and Red. They are big and national."
- "Blue and Red are everywhere."
- "Blue and Red are the biggest in the business."
- "Green Manufacturing. It has the best customer service."
- "There are too many that are all the same."
- "Blue and Red are so big."
- "Green Manufacturing and Red. They are all over the place."
- "Blue and Green Manufacturing have the most customers."
- "Green Manufacturing makes the best products."
- "Hard to say. Probably Green Manufacturing and Red."

7. Which distributor(s) promotes your products the best? (PROBE. RECORD VERBATIM RESPONSE.)

Base: 25

52%	Green Manufacturing	4%	Other
4%	Red	40%	Don't know/no response

8. **Who is most innovative and why?** (PROBE. RECORD VERBATIM RESPONSE.)

   Selected comments:
   - "Blue and Red have great design centers."
   - "Blue. They offer more opportunities."
   - "Red has the finest design department."
   - "Green Manufacturing. Great products."
   - "Red. It's approach is so much different."
   - "Blue has the most innovative design concepts."
   - "Green Manufacturing. It offers the best product."
   - "Blue. It's known nationally."
   - "Green Manufacturing has the biggest selection."
   - "Green Manufacturing. The company doesn't push, it just does things by itself."

9. **How does Green Manufacturing stack up against these top distributors?** (PROBE. RECORD VERBATIM RESPONSE.)

   Base: 25

48% Very well	8% Working toward the top
24% Green Manufacturing is the best	12% Don't know/no response
8% Have not seen	

10. **How can Green Manufacturing do a better job?** (PROBE. RECORD VERBATIM RESPONSE.)

    Base: 25

32% Cannot do a better job	8% Educate more in the product line
24% Better communication	4% More inventory
20% Buy more	4% Other
8% More competitive	

11. **In the next two or three years, what do you think will be the greatest changes or trends in the area of distribution?** (PROBE. RECORD VERBATIM RESPONSE.)

    Base: 25

16% Industry is growing	4% Depth of partnering
16% Better technology	4% Reduction of inventory
12% More involvement with user	4% More warehousing
8% More products	4% Other
8% Consolidation	16% Don't know/no response
8% Different materials	

12. **From your perspective, what is the value in distribution compared to other sales or marketing channels?** (PROBE. RECORD VERBATIM RESPONSE.)

Base: 25

20%	Time-saving	12%	Sales force
16%	Cost-saving	4%	Other
16%	Smaller quantities	20%	Don't know/no response
12%	Local reps		

13. **What role do you think distributors fill?** (PROBE. RECORD VERBATIM RESPONSE.)

Base: 25

20%	Partner in manufacturing	8%	Warehouse products
20%	Contact with end users	8%	New business
16%	Middlemen	12%	Don't know/no response
16%	Service smaller companies		

14. **What kinds of accounts are best served by distributors?** (PROBE FOR SMALL, MEDIUM, LARGE; NATIONAL, REGIONAL, MOM-and-POPS. RECORD VERBATIM RESPONSE.)

Base: 25

92%	Small	32%	Regional
48%	Midsize	32%	National
40%	Large	0%	Other
40%	Mom-and-Pop	0%	Don't know/no response

After you've created your summary report, you may need to communicate your findings to colleagues, your boss, customers, or other audiences. It's important to keep these thoughts in mind as you prepare your presentation:

- Multiple audiences (current and future) may see your report. Once you publish it, it seems to take on a life of its own. So make sure your data is correct and your findings and recommendations are precise. It's impossible to take it back once it leaves your office.
- The more common ground (shared history with different members of your audience) you have, the easier it will be to present your findings. If there are people who are not familiar with your company, product, or service, you may want to spend a few min-

F *l a s h* **# I 0**

The more controversial your topic or recommendations, the more "enemies" you're likely to face. Depending on your political climate, you may find that some people challenge your findings. If this happens, protect your "methodology" first. Don't let them say that you sampled the wrong people or asked biased questions. If they convince others there's something wrong with how you collected your data, all your findings may be dismissed. Instead, get them to debate about the best way to apply the findings or how they might see using them.

utes in your presentation setting the context and explaining why you decided to conduct your research.

- Watch out for "fake questions," which are really someone else's opinion phrased as a question. They sound like, "Wouldn't it better if . . . ?" or "Don't you think that . . . ?" These are not real questions, so don't answer them. Instead, say something like, "That's an interesting opinion, but we didn't find any data in this survey to support that idea."

Now that you know the basics of how to conduct your own snapshot survey from start to finish, let's talk about some of the specific marketing, communication, branding, and challenges most companies face and how you can use the snapshot survey to improve your results and build your bottom line.

Part Two

BASIC APPLICATIONS

3

SIZING UP THE COMPETITION

*How to Drill Deep Enough to Discover Your
Organization's True Image and Reputation in
the Marketplace*

The secret of success is to know something nobody else knows.

Aristotle Onassis

Your customers are your competitors' prospects. Whether you're aware of it or not, your competitors are desperately trying to lure your customers away from you—especially the big ones you've built the strongest bonds with and worked the hardest to keep. By offering a better price, promising faster delivery, presenting more professional-looking marketing literature, or exploiting some other weakness they see in you, their goal is to win business from the same people who have been keeping you *in* business.

The snapshot survey is an excellent tool for helping you better understand how you stack up against your competitors and which ones pose the greatest and most immediate threats to your business. When you ask your customers, prospects, and others what they think of you and your competitors' products and services, you obtain a clearer picture of your true image and reputation in the marketplace. You start to find very specific insights that you can use to differentiate your products and services or set priorities for improvement.

> **F l a s h   # 1 1**
>
> ___
>
> If you consistently underestimate your competition, you may soon be working for them. Markets may be dynamic, but customer relationships are fragile and take constant work and care to maintain. The more you know about your competitors—and their sneaky approaches—the better you'll be able to fend off their attacks and keep the customers you already have.

WHY YOU HAVE AS MUCH COMPETITION AS YOU DESERVE

Let's clear up one thing right away. Every business has competitors, even the ones you might not think of initially, such as monopolies, governments, and nonprofits. For example, consider the deregulation of electric, gas, and other utilities. For years, consumers had only one choice; now there are many. Governments are privatizing services, reorganizing themselves, and in some cases merging. Even after-school programs face stiff competition from organized sports, dance, and other programs that all compete for the same young adults (not to mention the financial and emotional support of their parents).

The exact number and type of competitors that you have depends on many factors, including:

- *The number of markets, products, and services you're focused on.* The more you've spread out your business and your product and service offerings, the more competitors you are likely to have.
- *The perceived profitability of your products and services.* The more successful everyone thinks you are, the more they'll want a piece of your action.
- *The maturity of your offerings and/or market.* Older products and services usually have more competitors, unless the price pressure has become so fierce that it is driving competitors away or innovation is redefining the playing field.
- *Your image and reputation.* If you have a strong, trusted brand, this can be a huge advantage in thwarting attempts by competitors to enter your markets.
- *The effectiveness of your marketing efforts.*
- *How much it costs to get into and out of a particular market.*

- *How transparent the sales or bidding process is in your industry.* Of course, you'll have a lot more competitors if you're responding to public requests for proposals than if you happen to be talking in private to a decision maker who's ready to solve a problem he or she's been struggling with.
- *How successful you have been at getting one of your products specified in bid documents* (e.g., architectural plans calling for a specific brand of roofing material).
- *How difficult it is to gain, purchase, or hire expertise, knowledge, and credibility in your field.* Are you in a business where your assets go home every night? Most professional service firms are. The more difficult it is to acquire your specialized knowledge, the fewer competitors you're likely to have, unless your customers and prospects don't fully comprehend what you do. If that's the case, they will lump you into categories with other firms that may not have your level of expertise or experience, but who still get a shot at winning the business.
- *The number of former employees who have started their own companies.* A major problem for many professional service firms is that when their employees leave, they often become competitors (noncompete contracts eventually run out).
- *How good you are at keeping3 customers happy.* In the advertising industry, a popular marketing tactic is to keep track of the companies who have changed agencies. After about six months, it's wise to start prospecting those firms, because many of them turn over quickly and you'll want to be invited for the next pitch.
- *How much you know (or don't know) about your competitors and what they're doing.*
- *What your customers think of your competitors,* especially in terms of how they compare to you.

Some of these factors are outside of your control and your only option is to respond to them as best you can. Others are the direct result of the decisions you and others have made about your business up to this point. They can be changed and the snapshot survey is a great tool for figuring out how to do so.

SCRATCHING THE SURFACE: BASIC TECHNIQUES FOR LEARNING ABOUT YOUR COMPETITORS

If you want to know how well you stack up against your competitors, start by learning as much as you can about what they are doing or not doing. Once you start digging, you will find plenty of clues.

- *Begin by taking a look at their Web sites from both a potential customer's and a professional marketer's point of view.* What are they offering? What do they say are the benefits of using them versus someone else? What are the slogans and other words they're using to describe what they do? About the most worn-out term I've seen is the word *solution* and all its variations (*solutions provider, problem solver, integrated solutions,* etc.). In many industries, you could easily switch the masthead from one competitor's site with another and not notice any appreciable difference in how they are positioning themselves. This is especially true in markets where there's a lot of competition and price pressure.
- *Take a look at the site's design, layout, and content.* If it says the company "consults" with customers to find customized solutions, does the site include white papers or other valuable free information a prospect could use to better understand the situation (in other words, does it look like a consulting Web site or is it just a big commercial)?
- *Search the Internet for your competitors' names (as well as their product and service names), key executives, and other terms that closely identify them.* Stay away from search terms that are too vague and could apply to many businesses; otherwise, you'll simply waste your time with a lot of unproductive digging. The information you find will give you an initial overview of the kind of media coverage they are receiving and how pervasive they seem to be.
- *Depending on what you're selling, don't forget to check out sites with chat rooms that may contain dialogue about how people are making their decisions to select a specific product or supplier.* It's always interesting to learn which of your competitors are being talked about the most and why.
- *Sometimes, you can find analyst reports, as well as trade or industry papers, that describe trends or predictions within your marketplace.* Depending on the resources at your local library, you may have

---

F *l a s h* **# 1 2**

You may be surprised to find out that your customers know a lot more about your competitors than you think. After all, your competitors will undoubtedly attempt to lure them. Not only do your customers have firsthand insights about how your competitors market (and do business), they have one of the best seats in the house for viewing both of your performances.

---

access to more sophisticated databases that search more publications.

- *Trade publications that contain sample ads from your competitors can be a treasure trove of information,* especially if you pin these ads next to each other on a wall. I used this technique once as part of an image audit for a hospital. The CEO walked around the room and commented, "These ads all look alike," which was my point exactly. No wonder this hospital wasn't standing out from its competitors. It was swimming in a sea of sameness and needed a marketing campaign to sharpen the differences between it and its competitors.

- *Find other information about your competitors through the literature you've picked up at trade shows, bid results, copies of quotes or proposals, or even employees you've hired away from them.* This will allow you to possess additional insights into how your competitors are marketing and positioning themselves.

Certainly, this list is not exhaustive, but you get the point. You can go to plenty of places to find out more about what each of your competitors is doing and saying about itself.

GOING DEEPER: HOW TO DISCOVER STRENGTHS AND WEAKNESSES

After you find out as much as you can about "what" your competitors are doing, the next step is to see if what they're doing is having any impact. What do your customers *think* about your competitors, especially in terms of your company and its products and services? Who has the best price, value, service, or delivery? You can use the snapshot survey to gauge how your customers see your competitors, because some of your customers may be buying from your competitors. These customers will possess insights that are not easily found through other sources.

A note of caution: If you come straight out and ask your customers what they think of your competitors, most are only going to tell you what they think you want to hear, not what they really think. Some probably won't even answer your questions. If they do, they will sugarcoat their answers and try to say things delicately, when what you would rather have is an honest idea of how they feel.

To get around this problem, I like to use a "blind" questioning technique that shields the true identity of my customers. By asking everyone in the survey the same questions about each competitor, it is much more difficult to figure out who's sponsoring the survey. If you approach your snapshot survey as an "industry" study (where you're looking for feedback about a number of companies) instead of a "customer survey" (where you'd like to know how you're doing compared to your competitors), you often get more reliable and insightful results.

The typical questions you want to ask in a blind industry type of snapshot survey about your competitors include:

- *Who are the leaders in your industry and why?* This question helps you determine who is topmost in the minds of your industry heads and which firms get mentioned most of the time. Make sure you probe as deeply as you can on the "why" portion of the question. Then pay extra attention to the competitors who are mentioned by most of your customers. In all likelihood, it's these competitors who are doing the best job and may be contacting your customers more regularly than other competitors.

- *What are the biggest trends facing your industry in the next two or three years?* This helps determine where your customers think the market is headed. This information can be extremely helpful for strategic and other planning, product development, and other purposes.

- *How familiar are you with each company in this industry (aka, your competitors)?* This tells you who's on the radar screen and who's off. Ideally, it would be nice if your best customers knew very little about your competitors, but chances are they'll know a lot about them. You can make the answer to this question more sophisticated by including several categories for each answer, such as "very familiar," "somewhat familiar," and "not at all familiar." These categories can help you figure out how well each competitor is known (instead of simply asking if they have ever heard of them). You can also use these responses to compare the answers to other questions in your survey. For example, do the respondents who are very familiar with a particular competitor (versus only somewhat familiar) think differently about your competitor's level of service, quality, or some other factor?

- *What are the strengths and weaknesses of each firm?* Knowing what your customers think of your competitors' strengths gives you something to work toward. Knowing their weaknesses gives you something to exploit.
- *Have you transacted any business with any of these organizations?* This question will help you determine if your customers work solely with you or if you share them with your competitors, which is the case in many businesses. You can take this question a step further and ask the customer what percentage of its business it gives to each firm; this gives you a perspective on the amount of business you are currently doing. You may already be getting the lion's share of their work or only a small morsel. Of course, those firms who are buying a lot of services from your competitors should be at the top of your prospecting list.
- *What would it take for another company to win your business?* This is an excellent question to find out what you need to do to grow your business. I'm always surprised to hear the answers to this question from the snapshot surveys I conduct. A lot of times it's price, but not always. Many other problems drive customers nuts, like having to talk with someone different every time they call, feeling like they aren't that important to the business, or generally making their lives more complicated with bureaucratic procedures that benefit your company but not their companies.

F *l a s h* **# 1 3**

A customer satisfaction survey is a great tool for asking questions about your competitors. You don't have to limit your questions to service and product performance. All you have to do is add a few questions about which competitors your customers are familiar with and what they think of them. It takes guts to hear that some customers think more highly of your competitors than they think of you.

How a Professional Service Firm Asked about Its Competitors through a Customer Satisfaction Survey

A professional service firm grew from the two founding partners to more than 25 employees in just a few years, primarily by working on small, regional projects. After winning a couple of larger projects, the firm was convinced that it was ready to handle national projects by leveraging its reputation as a nimble and responsive alternative to the big, bureaucratic, expensive firms. The partners believed the young and talented staff was also ready for more. There was only one problem: They weren't winning as many big projects as they thought they should be and they were losing some of their longtime clients. They wanted to know why and what they should do about it.

Using a snapshot survey, I got feedback through telephone interviews with about 20 of their customers, prospects, and lost customers.

INTRODUCTION TALKING POINTS

- We are helping Company A with marketing efforts.

- Joe Smith asked me to call you to get your perspective.

- We're an independent firm.

- Your responses are confidential.

IMAGE AND PERCEPTIONS

1. What are your overall opinions of Company A?

2. How did you first find out about the company?

3. Other than through a referral from a friend or colleague, what other ways do you typically learn about expert witnesses, consultants, or other professionals you may engage as part of your counsel?

4. How much of an influence is (or was) location to your decision?

5. What are Company A's greatest strengths?

6. What are its weaknesses/challenges?

7. If you were going to describe Company A to a friend or colleague IN SIMPLE TERMS, what would you say it does?

8. What words (attributes) would you use to describe the company?

9. What's the greatest benefit Company A provides customers?

10. (If customer) What is your impression of Company A since you began working with (worked with) it?

11. What is your opinion about the current level of service you are receiving from Company A?

COMPETITORS

12. Who do you think are Company A's key competitors?

13. Have you worked with any of these firms/individuals? If so, what was your impression of them, especially compared to Company A?

14. In what ways is Company A better than its competitors?

15. In what ways are competitors stronger than Company A?

MARKETING

16. Would you recommend Company A? Why or why not?

17. From what you know of other cities or markets, do firms from those locations select consultants in essentially the same way or are there important differences Company A should consider?

18. What role does price (hourly rates) play in your decision to select a consultant similar to Company A?

19. Company A is thinking about preparing a seminar that offered CLE credits. Is this a good idea? If so, how should the company organize the seminars (public, internal, other)?

20. What additional advice would you give Company A in marketing, selling, and branding itself?

It didn't take long to find out what was really going on. Everyone loved the partners and thought the world of their work, but they didn't think that the younger staff was functioning at the same level as the partners were or that the younger staff was ready to manage their own projects. The survey also showed that some of the smaller customers were frustrated because they weren't receiving the individual attention from the partners that they had become accustomed to. In addition to hiring more senior staff and developing a mentoring program, the firm's primary marketing challenge was to find a better way to control how it presented itself to the marketplace. It needed one set of messages for the smaller, regional clients and another set for the larger, national projects.

USING ATTRIBUTE RATINGS AS YOUR YARDSTICK

Attributes are words and short phrases that describe qualities and characteristics of your company (or its products and services) and of your competitors. They help clarify the emotional feelings that people use to make business decisions, like what they are going to buy and from whom. More times than not, people buy from companies they know and like. They almost always describe those companies using positive attributes such as "great customer service," "friendly staff," "good product selection," or some similar terms. Knowing a little bit more about which attributes your customers might use to describe your company can crystallize the differences between you and your competitors.

If you're in one of the many industries that face stiff price competition, your products and services are often viewed as commodities that are easily interchanged or purchased from one company or another. If your customers don't see much difference between what you're offering and what your competitors are offering, what your customers are really saying is that the only true differentiating attribute is price. In this case, no one firm has demonstrated why an attribute other than price—such as service, delivery time, integrity, brand image, or something else—is *the* reason to buy from that firm.

Figure 3.1 contains ten attributes and a brief description of each that many of my customers have used in their snapshot surveys to find out exactly how they compare to their competitors. These attributes are universal and can describe virtually any company. Of course, you can

> **F** *l a s h* **# 1 4**
>
> The most valuable thing you'll ever own is your reputation. One of the best ways to find out more about your reputation is to ask customers to rate your company using a series of attributes or statements. When you ask them to rate these same attributes for your competitors, you start to get the sophisticated insight you need to position your company for long-term success.

FIGURE 3.1

Ten attributes to use to rate your company and your competitors

- *Traditional*—possesses strong traditions, heritage

- *Market leadership*—number 1, lots of people use and like the company, favorite of many people

- *Accessibility*—open and proactive in its external communications

- *Growth*—Increasing in size and expanding geographically

- *Trustworthy*—ethical in dealings, you can rely on it, shows integrity

- *Visionary*—possesses a strong vision for the future, forward-looking

- *Technology*—introduces new and improved products and services

- *Offer value*—provides services and ideas that can't be easily found in other places

- *Customer-service orientation*—works hard at keeping its customers satisfied

- *Efficient*—uses resources well, gets things done quickly with little waste

also modify them or add different ones to make them more specific to your company and current situation. One way to do this is to take a look at your mission statement and values (as long as your mission statement is unique and doesn't sound like everyone else's). If your company is striving to reach specific ideals, you can turn those ideals into attribute statements and ask customers to rate them in your survey.

In your snapshot survey, the best way to ask about these attribute statements in a question is to build them into a table. List the attributes down the left-hand column and your company and several of your competitors across the top. Each cell will be used to record the specific ratings from customers. I like to use a rating scale that goes from 1 to 5 or 1 to 10. The low numbers might be "poor" or "does not describe them," while the high numbers might be "excellent" or "completely describes them." Let's take a look at how we could modify the Green Manufacturing example survey in Chapter 2 to include competitor ratings. Notice that the attribute statements included in this list are modifications from our original list of ten attributes in Figure 3.1.

How would you rate _____ (INSERT COMPANY NAME) **on their**
_____ (INSERT ATTRIBUTE) **on a 1 to 10 scale where 1 is "poor" and 10 is**
"excellent"? (MARK ONE FOR EACH.)

	Green Manufacturing	Competitor #1	Competitor #2	Competitor #3
Accountability—does what it promised, when it promised	_____	_____	_____	_____
Creativity—offers innovative products, services, and solutions	_____	_____	_____	_____
Growth—establishes relationships that help all stakeholders grow and prosper	_____	_____	_____	_____
Industry leadership—number 1, lots of people use and like the company, favorite of many people	_____	_____	_____	_____
Integrity—ethical in dealings, you can rely on it, shows integrity	_____	_____	_____	_____
Offer value—provides services and ideas that can't be easily found in other places	_____	_____	_____	_____
Respect—demonstrates concern and understands customers' situations	_____	_____	_____	_____
Satisfaction—works hard at keeping its stakeholders satisfied	_____	_____	_____	_____
Technology—introduces new and improved products and services	_____	_____	_____	_____

HOW TO EVALUATE YOUR ATTRIBUTES

If you decide to ask a question that includes a list of attributes you want your customers to rate about you and your competitors, you'll need to spend a few extra minutes analyzing these findings before drawing any specific conclusions.

Because most of your ratings are on a "continuous" scale (1 to 10), you should take the mean of each rating. If you're going to do this by hand, refer to Chapter 2 for examples of how to do this. If you're going to use a software program, make sure you don't include the people who left a particular attribute blank. Depending on how you set up your survey, you might use a "99" or a "0" or some other number to represent the people who left a statement blank. If you include 99 as part of your mean score, you might find a mean score that is much higher than your rating range of 1 to 10 (e.g., 12.3, which is obviously wrong because your scale only goes to 10). Likewise, if you include "0s" when you shouldn't, you'll have a deflated score.

Depending on who rated each statement for you or your competitors, you can draw a number of false conclusions. So always use the number of people who answered each attribute for your base to each question. For example, if you have 50 people in your survey and 35 were familiar with one of your competitors, then use the 35 to calculate each mean score. However, if 5 people did not rate one of your attribute statements and left it blank (and you filled in some other number like "0" or "99"), divide only that attribute by 30 (or 35 [who were familiar with a competitor] – 5 [who left a specific attribute blank] = 30 [people who answered the question]).

Once you've calculated everything, you should build a table that looks something like Table 3.1.

Now you're ready to start figuring out what your responses mean. In this example, you might draw the following insights:

- When you look at all the scores, Green Manufacturing is somewhere in the middle, doing better than Competitor #1, about the same as Competitor #2, and a little behind Competitor #3.
- Green Manufacturing's highest mean score was for being an industry leader (8.8) and their lowest was for being technology oriented (8.5), a pretty tight spread. These findings suggest that most customers were giving the organization 10s, 9s, 8s, and a few 7s, but we could be sure if we looked at the frequency to each attribute and examined how many people gave high, medium, and low responses.
- Even though some differences do exist between competitors, customers seem to think highly of a number of companies. So, staying away from competitor put-downs and other negative comments when talking with your customers about competitors would be wise. Instead, focus on what you do well and how you do it.
- While Competitor #3 looks like it is doing a good job, only 24 customers were familiar enough with the company to rate it. You may want to take a closer look at the kinds of customers who were rating it. Is it your largest customers, smallest, or some combination of both? What percentage of your customers are also buying from that company? This competitor might be a blip on the radar

TABLE 3.1
Attribute ratings of competition

	ATTRIBUTE RATINGS *(50 Respondents in the Survey Using a 1 to 10 Scale, with 1 = Poor and 10 = Excellent)*			
	Green Manufacturing	**Competitor #1**	**Competitor #2**	**Competitor #3**
(Base)	(50)	(34)	(42)	(24)
Accountability—does what it promised, when it promised	8.7	7.0	8.5	9.3
Creativity—offers innovative products, services, and solutions	8.7	7.1	8.5	9.6
Growth—establishes relationships that help all stakeholders grow and prosper	8.6	6.8	8.8	9.3
Industry leadership—number 1, lots of people use and like the company, favorite of many people	8.8	7.0	8.6	9.4
Integrity—ethical in dealings, you can rely on it, shows integrity	8.5	6.7	8.4	9.2
Offer value—provides services and ideas that can't be easily found in other places	8.6	7.5	8.6	9.6
Respect—demonstrates concern and understands customers' situations	8.7	7.2	8.2	9.4
Satisfaction—works hard at keeping its stakeholders satisfied	8.7	8.1	8.3	8.6
Technology—introduces new and improved products and services	8.5	7.1	8.4	9.0

screen or it might be an up-and-coming challenger, poised to lure more of your customers away from you.

USING PERSONIFICATION QUESTIONS TO GET A GOOD SENSE OF YOUR COMPETITORS

Another technique for learning about the image of your company and your competitors is to ask your customers to personify your organization. I say to respondents, "Stretch with me on these next questions," then ask:

- If your company (your competitors) were a person, would it be a man or a woman?
- How old would he or she be?
- What kind of car would he or she drive?
- What kind of restaurants would he or she eat in?
- What kind of house would he or she live in?
- If the company (or your competitors) were a famous person, who would it be?

Not too long ago, I was delivering a seminar to public affairs officers from the U.S. Army. As an example of this technique, I asked them to personify a U.S. soldier. In a few moments, virtually everyone said the soldier would be a young man in his late teens or early 20s, from a small rural town, who drives a pickup. He would probably have a high school diploma, but not much college training. After the seminar, one of the participants came up to me and said he had just overseen a three-year, $18-million-dollar study that came up with the same conclusions. Even though I was happy to hear him validate the power of this personification technique, I couldn't help but ask myself, "I wonder if there was any way I could charge $18 million for a snapshot survey?"

Make sure you ask your customers why they are answering the way that they are. Some customers may start out slow and resist your attempts to answer these questions, but most will have fun with them. The input you get will help you better figure out exactly who you are.

Case History

Printing Company Competitive Assessment Survey

A small printer was experiencing significant growth after heavily investing in state-of-the-art printing technology and a new building. At the time, it was one of only a handful of printers that owned a ten-color press. The company wanted to grow even more quickly, but it didn't know what customers thought of it or its competitors.

The following "blind" snapshot survey was conducted with 25 customers and 25 prospects. Respondents were not aware of who was sponsoring the survey and were asked the same questions about each of the leading local printers.

This printer learned a lot about its competitors from this survey, namely that many of its customers were working with them. More important, many of the printer's customers liked working with those competitors and thought that they

Hello. This is _____ calling from _____ . We are contacting companies that purchase commercial printing services to learn their opinions about leading commercial printers. Your responses will be kept strictly confidential. Would you mind answering a few questions? (IF INCONVENIENT TIME, SCHEDULE A CALL-BACK TIME.)

1. **In your organization, are you the person (or one of the persons) responsible for deciding to purchase printing from a commercial printer?** (MARK ONE.)

   1 Yes
   2 No (ASK FOR OTHER, ELSE TERMINATE)
   3 DK/NR (ASK FOR OTHER, ELSE TERMINATE)

2. **What type of printing do you purchase?** (READ. MARK ALL THAT APPLY.)

   1 Short run (i.e., color, copies, print on demand)
   2 Medium to long run (i.e., sheeted and half-size web)
   3 Very long run (i.e., full-size web and gravure)
   4 Other: _____
   5 DK/NR

3. **Thinking about the commercial printers you're familiar with, who are the leaders and why?** (PROBE. RECORD VERBATIM RESPONSE.)

4a. **I'm going to read the names of some leading commercial printing companies. Tell me if you are very familiar, somewhat familiar, or not at all familiar with each of them.** (MARK ONE FOR EACH.)

		4a.			4b.	4c.
	Very familiar	Somewhat familiar	Not at all familiar	DK/NR	Purchased Printing	Performance Rating
a. Competitor 1	1	2	3	4	1	_____
b. Competitor 2	1	2	3	4	2	_____
c. Company B	1	2	3	4	3	_____
d. Competitor 3	1	2	3	4	4	_____
e. Competitor 4	1	2	3	4	5	_____
f. Competitor 5	1	2	3	4	6	_____
g. Competitor 6	1	2	3	4	7	_____

4b. (FOR EACH PRINTER PROSPECT IS "VERY" OR "SOMEWHAT" FAMILIAR WITH, ASK:) **During the past 12 months, have you purchased any printing from _____ ?** (RECORD ABOVE.)

4c. (FOR EACH PRINTER PROSPECT PURCHASED PRINTING FROM, ASK:) **Overall, how would you rate _____'s performance on a 1 to 10 scale, where 1 is "poor" and 10 is "excellent"?** (RECORD ABOVE.)

5. (FOR EACH PRINTER PROSPECT PURCHASED PRINTING FROM, ASK:) **Why did you purchase from _____ ?** (PROBE. RECORD VERBATIM RESPONSE.)

   a. Competitor 1 _____

   b. Competitor 2 _____

   c. Company B _____

   d. Competitor 3 _____

   e. Competitor 4 _____

   f. Competitor 5 _____

   g. Competitor 6 _____

6. (IF PROSPECT IS FAMILIAR WITH COMPANY B—AND DID NOT PURCHASE PRINTING, ASK:) **Have you asked Company B for a printing quote?** (MARK ONE.)

   1 Yes . . . **Why didn't you buy from Company B?** (PROBE. RECORD VERBATIM RESPONSE.)

   2 No . . . **Why not?** (PROBE. RECORD VERBATIM RESPONSE.)

   3 DK/NR

7. **Are you planning to ask Company B to bid on future projects?** (MARK ONE.)

   1 Yes . . . **Would you like someone from Company B to contact you?**

      1 Yes . . . **When?**

      2 No

      3 DK/NR

   2 No . . . **Why not?** (PROBE. RECORD VERBATIM RESPONSE.)

   3 DK/NR

8. **What could Company B printing do to win part of your printing business?** (PROBE. RECORD VERBATIM RESPONSE.)

9. **What are the best ways for you to find out about a commercial printing company's capabilities?** (DO NOT READ. MARK ALL THAT APPLY.)

1 Referral from friend/colleague	7 Advertisements
2 Direct mail	8 On-site visit
3 In-person sales call/presentation	9 Seminar
4 Telephone	88 Other: _____
5 Web page	99 DK/NR
6 News articles	

10. **What is your department's or company's annual commercial printing volume?**
    (READ. MARK ONE.)

1 Less than $100,000	4 $500,000 to $999,999
2 $100,000 to $249,999	5 $1,000,000 or more
3 $250,000 to $499,999	6 DK/NR

were good firms who provided quality products. Through redesigning its marketing literature, holding a series of on-site events, and other tactics, the printer continued to grow rapidly and better define itself now that it understood how the firm was coming across to customers and prospects.

TO SEE THE BIGGER PICTURE, ASK OTHER AUDIENCES WHAT THEY THINK

While customers are typically the most important audience to include in your snapshot survey, you may also want to hear from other groups who can offer additional perspectives about how well you're doing compared to your competitors. Figure 3.2 lists some of the audiences who typically offer valuable insights. To keep things simple, I've grouped them into external (outside of your company), internal (inside your company or closely connected to it), and opinion leader (everyone else).

Flash #15

While customers have valuable perceptions about you and your competitors' images and reputations, so do a lot of other folks such as prospects, employees, distributors, and the media. To get a more complete picture of how your company is seen in the marketplace, be sure to include them in your analysis.

FIGURE 3.2

Target audiences frequently included in image and reputation audits

External	Internal	Opinion Leader
Customers	Senior management	Media
Largest accounts	Midlevel managers	Consumer
Medium/smaller accounts	Employees	Business
Transactional	Office/plant locations	Trade
Prospects	Advisors (legal, financial)	Analysts
Lost customers	Board of Directors	Trade associations
Distributors		Community leaders
Suppliers		Government leaders
Other channel partners		
Community groups		

External

Your prospects are the most logical and valuable extension beyond customers. These people expressed some interest in your company, products, or services, but they haven't purchased anything. Even in a small snapshot survey, I like to include at least four or five prospects, because they often provide a valuable and fresh perspective you don't hear from customers. They tend to be a little more honest (and sometimes downright brutal) in their assessment of your strengths and weaknesses. Plus, if you've given them a proposal or a recent bid, but they didn't buy, you can ask them why. In a larger snapshot survey of 50 business-to-business interviews, I like to do about half of them with customers and the other half with prospects. It makes for a great compare-and-contrast type of analysis.

Lost customers are also an excellent source of perspectives. These are individuals who purchased from you—perhaps for several years—but started buying less and less to the point that they don't purchase from you anymore. Why did they leave? Are they happy with their new supplier? I've been amazed at how many of the customers who have stopped buying from me end up buying again. It usually comes down to the fact that I got lazy and stopped calling on them as much as I used to. It's the old "out of sight, out of mind" mentality. Some lost customers just need to see you once in a while to start buying again.

Distributors, suppliers, and other channel partners can also provide valuable perspectives. Distributors often have a lot to say about marketing materials, givebacks (deals, price breaks, etc.), and your competitors' marketing techniques. If you sell through distributors and they represent multiple manufacturers, ask them which manufacturer is doing the best job and why.

In general, suppliers tend to be more positive than distributors, mainly because they want to sell you more of their products and services. They can give you insights about whom else they are supplying to and what their impressions of the industry are.

Depending on how visible you are in your local community, gathering feedback from community groups, consumers, and others can be very helpful. Over the years, I've run a number of these community-perception snapshot surveys for banks, hospitals, universities, nonprofit organizations, professional sports teams, manufacturing firms, and others. Recently, I completed one of these studies for one of the world's largest aluminum producers. The company wanted to know what consumers who lived near its plants thought of the firm. Both local businesses and consumers were interviewed using a blind survey that asked similar questions about the aluminum producer as well as five other local companies with plants in the same community. The company used the results to evaluate its corporate giving program and ensure that its donations were keeping the company in good graces in the communities in which it operated. The feedback about the other manufacturers helped the firm gauge how well these companies were doing, for many of them had sparse community-sponsorship programs.

Internal

Feedback from sources outside of your company becomes even more valuable when you compare it to what people from inside your organization think. Executives and senior managers are among my favorite respondents to interview. I find that the time I spend with them is highly productive, enlightening, and energizing. They often have terrific insights not only about their own company and their competitors, but also about the leading trends within their industry. They typically read, think, and talk a lot more about what's going on in their industry than anyone else. I use their feedback to "get smart quickly." Knowing what senior management thinks is also very helpful in formulating questions to customers, employees, and other groups about the image and reputation of the organization. After all, they are the ones I'm working for and I'm going to present my findings to. Knowing all I can about them and what they care about ahead of time helps me do my best work.

I would classify board members in the same category as executives, because many of them are executives only with a slightly more external worldview. They can tell you how well they think the firm is doing compared to other industries or situations.

I almost always recommend that employees be included in image and perception research, because they are on the front lines and are often the ones who are going to make or break how customers feel about your organization. It's almost like a battle between your employees and your competitors' employees. Whoever is doing the better job will win. Either by phone, mail, pass-out, e-mail, focus group, face-to-face interviews, or some other technique, I like to include their perspectives. They pay a lot closer attention to what's going on with your company than you might think. And many have interesting perceptions about what your company and your competitors are doing.

Advisors, such as your legal counsel, accountant, banker, and others, also have terrific insights that can help you understand how well you're doing compared to competitors. Most of these individuals have advanced degrees and strong opinions. They are also less prone to give the "politically correct" responses, especially if you have someone from outside of your company conducting the interviews and you've guaranteed them confidentiality. Most have a knack for cutting to the real issues quickly, instead of beating around the bush.

Opinion Leaders

Opinion leaders are individuals who don't purchase or sell your products, nor are they directly connected to your company, but they can influence other people's perceptions about your company. The most obvious source of opinion leaders is the media—all forms of print, broadcast, and online—which can be focused on consumer, business, trade, or some other topic. I've included the media in many of the image and reputation audits I've run over the years. They provide an excellent perspective about your public image. Business and trade editors have terrific insights about the latest trends and often possess firsthand information about what strategies competitors are exploring. If you've had an antagonistic relationship with some reporters, make sure you work with an outside firm to do these interviews and use the blind interviewing technique so you can get an accurate read on your competitors. In most cases, however, reporters and editors are gracious individuals who are happy to share their perspectives (as long as they aren't under deadline). Whenever I'm running media interviews, the first thing I like to ask is, "Are you under deadline?" If they say yes, I try to schedule a time to call them back.

Any number of other opinion leaders and experts may be within your industry. You often stumble across them as you're doing your database searching. Sometimes simply including one or two interviews with these individuals can help round out the perceptions about you and your competitors.

WHY SIZE DOESN'T MATTER IF YOU'RE TALKING WITH THE RIGHT PEOPLE

The exact number of people you choose to interview can vary. Many of the snapshot surveys I've conducted for leading companies have included only a handful of interviews. But we interviewed the right people—the people the company really wanted to hear from. Consider these three examples:

Coordinating Company and Product Brand Names with Customer Feedback

A Fortune 50 company faced an interesting image and reputation challenge. Should it leverage its company name as an "umbrella" branding platform or let its various products continue to exist with their individual names and brands, especially those being sold in Europe. At issue was the fact that some division leaders felt the organization should market itself under one company name, while others remained unconvinced.

For almost four years, the company had invested in customer-satisfaction studies of its various product divisions. A meta-analysis of these studies was completed to determine, as a company, where the organization was strong and where improvements were needed.

Because little to no information was available from prospective customers and other key audiences, such as the media, telephone interviews were completed with the audiences who represented five locations where the organization had a presence: the United States, Great Britain, France, Germany, and Italy.

The results of the research were used to build an image campaign that repositioned and strengthened several product lines and helped key decision makers buy in to the new marketing strategy, which included listing the company name along with all product information.

Creating a More Entrepreneurial Image

A national health insurance provider that enjoyed a solid reputation and position as the market leader in recent years faced stiff competition from new competitors and local health systems (who were starting to offer their own health insurance). These new competitors forced the organization to examine its image and reputation in the marketplace, because it was losing customers.

To better understand the organization's image, we completed about 20 interviews with the media, business and community leaders, physicians, human resources executives, and senior management to better understand the insurance company's image and reputation. To add credibility to the findings, the interviews were conducted in a blind fashion (interviewees did not know who was sponsoring the survey) where each audience segment provided insight about the provider, as well as giving perspectives about the competitors.

The findings were used to recommend specific strategies and tactics designed to transform the company's image into a more entrepreneurial and customer-focused organization.

Building a Marketing Infrastructure Program

An engineering consulting firm that operates primarily in West Virginia, Virginia, and Maryland, assessed its image and those of its competitors by doing less than 20 interviews with customers. While the firm had achieved great success, it had done so with no formalized marketing program that was coordinated between its various office locations. As a result, management believed it was seen as a small, local firm, when, in fact, it had more than 200 employees and was listed as one of the 500 largest engineering firms in the United States.

The survey results were used to develop a marketing infrastructure program, designed to develop younger staff members' marketing and selling skills, as well as to redefine the image of the firm as the larger, more sophisticated organization that it actually was.

C *ase* **H** *istory*

Assessing the Damage Caused by Media Attacks

A few years ago a leading public television station came under fire by the local media. While the station was classified as nonprofit, it had developed successful syndicated programs and its executives were paid like the executives of a successful, for-profit organization.

The reporters started digging and began writing what the organization felt were negative stories. Before long, some members of the community became upset about how much the station was paying these executives. They were angry because they felt that too much money was going toward executive salaries and not enough toward buying and developing better programming for viewers. After all, they contended, it was the public who paid for the station through their financial donations. Why should a handful of executives profit personally from these contributions?

The media continued picking and digging. The negative stories kept coming out and started to impact the number of donors and the amount they were giving. Some contributors refused to renew their memberships. Employees were worried and tense about the station's future.

Because the station was my client, I suggested that instead of guessing how many people might care about the media coverage, we ask them directly through a snapshot survey. We completed a number of telephone interviews, with about half from existing financial donors and half with nondonors.

The results: Over the years, the organization had developed a very strong and positive image in the community. It had a reputation of developing and airing high-quality, educational programs that both the members and the nonmembers enjoyed. Interestingly, less than half of the members had even heard about or were aware of any of the negative news stories about the station and the pay of its executives.

This information was critical learning, because it suggested where to find the solution. Most people already had a positive image of the organization. The TV station needed to start reinforcing that image with the general community. Because the station tracked the names of individual donors and could easily generate a list of those who declined to renew, it was possible to launch a "we want you back" repair-building campaign with them. Letters and telephone calls were made. The organization admitted it had made a mistake and cared about what its donors thought. Changes were being made. The organization was serious about rebuilding the trust that was lost.

Eventually, the senior executives retired and new leadership came in and continued the process of repairing the station's image. In retrospect, it would have been better to avoid the media battle in the first place.

What saved this organization, however, were the years of goodwill that had been built up within the community and the station's supporters. The potential long-term consequences were not nearly so bad as the internal audiences had first feared.

STRIKING PAY DIRT: WHAT TO DO WHEN YOU FIND THE MOTHER LODE

Once you've completed your snapshot survey and received some feedback from customers and other audiences, you should be able to answer these questions about your company or its products and services:

- Do they know we exist? Are we topmost in their minds or did we have to prod everyone's memory to get them to mention the company's name?
- What do they know about us? Do they have a deep and comprehensive understanding of our offering, or is it shallow and superficial?
- What is our reputation? Are we seen as high quality, low price, a leader, a follower, or something else? Are we someone who can be trusted?
- How do we stack up against our competitors? What do they see as our strengths and weaknesses when comparing us against our competitors?
- Are everyone else's perceptions of our company in line with our own? Do they see what you see or are there substantial gaps? Are those gaps something we close with better communication and marketing or do they think we're something we're really not?

A good way to understand and apply the snapshot survey results you get back is to organize an internal meeting to talk about what you found and what it means. I frequently lead these types of meetings with my clients and I use the following topics to guide the discussion:

- What we learned from the research
- Key customer insights
- Key prospective customer insights

- Insights from employees, opinion leaders, and others we talked with
- Competitor insights
- Attributes we own
- Attributes we could own
- Attributes competitors can't easily copy
- How each attribute translates into a customer benefit
- We are different from our competitors because . . .
- Ways to capitalize on our differences
- Ways of communicating our uniqueness to the market

Knowing what your customers think about your competitors is a great start to differentiating your true value in the marketplace. Broadening the feedback to include your prospects, employees, and other audiences helps further define your image and reputation. Once you possess these insights, it's a whole lot easier to manage the rest of your marketing, communication, and management challenges.

4

CUSTOMER SATISFACTION, CUSTOMER LEADS

*How to Get Referrals, Create Loyalty, and
Develop Lifelong Partnerships*

*Because its purpose is to create a customer, the business has two—and only two—basic functions:
marketing and innovation. Marketing and innovation produce results; all the rest are costs.*

Peter Drucker

Detailed customer feedback about your quality, performance, and pricing allows you to make product and service changes that keep your customers coming back. When you find out what your customers really want and give it to them better than anyone else can, you've discovered the true meaning of customer satisfaction.

What most people don't realize, however, is that their customer satisfaction surveys could be working a lot harder than they currently are. Most companies limit their satisfaction surveys to a handful of customer-service and product-performance topics, then analyze those findings by slicing and dicing them with demographic questions such as when you made a purchase, how much you spent, and other facts about yourself (age, education, income, and so on) or your company (industry, size, length of relationship).

While these customer insights are enough for many firms, the snapshot survey can be much more powerful. It can do the heavy lifting on other important business and marketing goals, such as generating sales leads, discovering what customers really care about, and finding out the extent to which you're focused on what your customers want you to be focused on. When you get beyond the surface feedback, you can find out what it really takes to build relationships that last for a long time and mean lots of success, satisfaction, and money for your company.

> ### F l a s h # 1 6
>
> Customer satisfaction surveys can be easily transformed into marketing tools without violating the basic research premise of no selling. By adding questions about how aware customers are of your products and services, whether they want more information about any of those products or services, and if they would refer someone, you can get a good idea of how much additional business you might win from the customers who are already buying from you. Make sure you keep your survey and your selling separate. Don't offer additional information during the actual survey. That's only appropriate for a follow-up meeting with those customers who want it.

USING YOUR CUSTOMER SATISFACTION SURVEY TO PAY THE BILLS

Why limit your customer satisfaction survey to questions about products customers have already ordered or services already rendered? You can take your snapshot survey a step further and find out how much your customers know about your entire product line, which products they would like to learn more about, and who else they feel could use your product or service. By adding a few specific questions like these, you can not only find out how you did on your last sale, but you can also learn how to get started on your next one.

Some years ago, the partners of a sales training firm I worked for asked me an interesting question: "Is there a legitimate way to turn customer-satisfaction surveys into lead-generation tools?" I cringed. It would be easy to mix research and selling. It's called "bait and switch." This is the slimy prospecting strategy where someone starts off an interview pretending they are doing a survey, when it is really a sales call. It sounds like this:

Caller: "I'd like to ask you about some of the appliances in your home. Do you have a refrigerator?"

Homeowner: "Yes."

Caller: "Does your family eat meat?"

Homeowner: "Yes."

Caller: "Well, today is your lucky day. It just so happens that we have received an extra truckload of steaks and chicken and we are offering homeowners like yourself a 20 percent discount. Would you like to buy some meat today?"

Of course, this company isn't conducting a survey at all. They are simply using the good reputation that marketing researchers have worked decades to build as a hook to get you to talk with them. It sickens me and it's the last thing I wanted for the snapshot survey. So I proceeded with extreme caution.

But the more I thought about it, the more I realized that every question you ask in a customer-satisfaction survey is legitimate as long as it's focused on ways to better serve your customers. What's not always legitimate is how you handle or don't handle the results. It's not about the questions you ask; it's about what you do with the answers. For example, if you promise someone confidentiality and that only a group summary of the results will be presented to the company sponsoring the survey, then you had better not break that promise. Knowing exactly what each customer said and using it to create your sales strategy crosses the line.

To transform a customer-satisfaction survey into a lead-generation tool, I started adding three questions to a series of quality and customer-satisfaction surveys I was conducting for an electric motor repair division of a leading international manufacturer. Figure 4.1 lists these questions (with specific product and service names changed), which usually work best toward the end of the survey, after you've asked about product quality, delivery, service, and other topics. The three kinds of questions you want to add include:

1. *Awareness.* Which customers know about which products? How many of your customers know about everything you offer? Are there one or two products that might warrant a special promotion?
2. *More information.* Do any of your customers want more information about any of the products or services that you offer?
3. *Referral.* Do your customers know of anyone either inside their organization or at another company who might be interested in your products or services?

FIGURE 4.1

Awareness, more information, and referral questions added to a total quality and customer-satisfaction survey

Following are some of the different products and services that we offer.

1. Under the column entitled *Awareness*, please check if you were aware that we provide this product or service.

2. Under the column entitled *More Information*, place a check next to the products or services that you would like more information about.

	Awareness	More Information
Products		
AC and DC USEM electric motors	☐	☐
Johnson electric motors	☐	☐
Fairfield electric motors	☐	☐
USEM gear products (R.A. and Par.)	☐	☐
Industrial Air Machine (reciprocating air compressors)	☐	☐
Greater Division (rotary-screw air compressors)	☐	☐
C-X control (liquid level controls)	☐	☐
Services		
AC electric motor repair (up to 2500 HP)	☐	☐
Explosion-proof motor repair (U.L.)	☐	☐
DC electric motor repair (testing capability up to 250 HP)	☐	☐
Generator and welder repair	☐	☐
Air compressor repair (rotary-screw, rotary-vane, reciprocating)	☐	☐
Hoist repair	☐	☐
Rotating machinery balancing (in-house and field)	☐	☐
AC and DC armature rewinding and balancing	☐	☐
Machine shop	☐	☐
Press work (up to 200 tons)	☐	☐

3. Do you know anyone else who might need our products or services within your company or at another firm? (If so, please list their name, company, and phone number.)

Determine Awareness

Many customer-satisfaction surveys don't measure how well customers know your full product or service line. They simply stop after asking about customer-service issues and how well the product is performing. Your customers can't order products they don't know about, so a good place to find more business is by determining exactly how well informed they are.

> **F l a s h # 1 7**
>
> ---
>
> Product awareness, more information, and referral questions work best when you have a lot of customers you don't interact with frequently. More times than not, it's much easier to find leads from a snapshot survey of 100 customers than it is from a survey with only a dozen.

Make a list of all your products and services, placing them in similar categories until you have 10 to 20 items. Then, near the end of your survey ask, "Are you aware of any of the following products or services?" Depending on your company, industry, and how aggressively you've been marketing your products and services, you will likely find that many of your customers know about your main products or services, but only a handful of customers are familiar with your other products or services.

Unless everyone is familiar with everything (which is highly unlikely), you've found your first marketing opportunity. By examining your snapshot survey results to find the biggest gaps of customers who are not aware of a specific product or service, you can set your marketing priorities. If you have a product or service you think has great potential, but few people know about it, you can quickly fill in the gaps of your customers' knowledge and help increase leads by mailing them catalogs, brochures, press releases, or other literature.

The percentage of customers who will be aware of your full line of products or services will likely be 70 percent to 80 percent, if you've been doing a great job marketing. As many as 30 percent to 40 percent may not be familiar with a particular product or service, especially if it's one of your newer offerings or something you haven't been focusing on.

Offer More Product Information

Your customers may want more information about a product or service, but they may be too forgetful or too busy to ask for it. You can help remind them by asking if they would like to receive additional information about any of those products or services. Simply add a column of check boxes next to the products and services you just listed (to find out whether they were aware of the products or services).

In many surveys I've conducted, between 10 percent to 35 percent of customers want to know more about a specific product or service.

(Talk about blowing away response rates to a typical direct mail piece that may get only a 1 percent or 2 percent response!)

If you've guaranteed your customers confidentiality, make sure you include a place for them to put their names, or if you're conducting phone interviews, ask if it's okay if someone contacts them about it. Analyze each of your customers and offer to send information on a handful of products that you feel might be of particular interest to them. When customers conduct business at breakneck speed, it's difficult to anticipate their every need. By offering to send product information, you keep the lines of communication open, and open the door for new sales and leads.

Solicit Referrals

If you do a good job for your customers, they'll often give you the names of friends and associates who might be interested in your services. By asking for referrals on customer-satisfaction surveys, you allow your customers to do some of your prospecting for you. Even better, a referral can impart a sense of friendliness or familiarity to an otherwise cold call, increasing the odds that you'll get an appointment with a new prospect. Because a customer-satisfaction survey often marks the end of a sale, let the customer you served so well give you a lead that may bring you the next sale. Generally, 3 percent to 5 percent of your customers will give you a referral. I've seen this percent climb to as high as 10 in some surveys.

To reap the most rewards from your new survey questions, put the information to use. If your customer-satisfaction surveys don't guarantee confidentiality, you can evaluate each one, then contact prospects to discuss requests for more information or thank them for a referral.

Many surveys protect the customer's privacy to help ensure honest answers to survey questions. If you're obligated to keep survey responses confidential, tally the results of several customers' surveys and draw conclusions based on the totals. Prepare a brief report that summarizes your findings and fax or mail it to your customers with a letter explaining that in order to serve them better, you want to make sure they're aware of your entire product line and provide them with any information they need to order additional products or services.

You may want to set up an appointment to personally discuss the survey results with each of your customers. Remember, the purpose of the meeting is to discuss the survey results, so don't make your customers feel conned into an impromptu sales call unless they show genuine interest in a product. Let your customers do most of the talking and ask how you can do a better job selling, servicing, or keeping them informed of new products or product developments.

Customer-satisfaction surveys usually tell you how you need to adjust your performance to improve sales, but the right additional questions can turn them into a more direct selling tool. Once customers tell you what they know about your product line, which products they want to know more about, and who they can refer you to, you can often use this information to help you close a sale in a fraction of the time it would take you to find a new prospect and start from scratch. Consider your next customer survey not as an ending point for your previous sale, but as a starting point for your next one.

C *ase* **H** *istory*

Hospital Community Perception Survey

SITUATION:

In the past few years, hospitals and other health care organizations have jumped headfirst into marketing. To keep their patient base from eroding, they are starting to use a number of consumer marketing, physician relations, and other strategies to fend off competitors. To help them better understand how they are perceived in the communities in which they operate, I've conducted dozens of what I call *community-perception* snapshot surveys. These are much different than patient-satisfaction surveys (which are also very helpful to the institutions), because they are focused on people who live within their service territory. Some residents have been patients; others have not. Most will need hospitalization in the future, and it's good to find out how the hospitals are perceived.

QUESTIONS:

1. If you or someone in your immediate family needed to go to a hospital for health care, which hospital would you choose?

2. Thinking of all the hospitals in your area, which one do you consider to be the leader?

3. If you or a member of your family required a specialized nonemergency service, such as cancer treatment, how far would you be willing to travel to access that service?

4. Which hospital do you think you would choose for this kind of specialized service?

5. I'd like you to tell me how you would rate _____ hospital's service on a 1 to 5 scale, where 1 is "poor" and 5 is "excellent."
   - Overall reputation
   - Quality of medical staff
   - In-patient medical care
   - Outpatient services such as lab
   - Outpatient surgery
   - Emergency department
   - OB/maternity care
   - Diabetes education
   - Physical therapy
   - Acute in-patient rehabilitation
   - Radiation oncology
   - Medical oncology
   - Home health care
   - Hospice care
   - Wound care clinic
   - Cardiac care
   - Orthopedics
   - Radiology services (CAT scans, PET scans, MRIs)
   - Community outreach

6. Have you or a family member received treatment at any of these hospitals?

7. How would you rate the quality of care on a 1 to 5 scale, where 1 is "poor" and 5 is "excellent"?

8. In choosing a hospital, how important are the following factors on a 1 to 5 scale, where 1 is "not at all important" and 5 is "very important"?
   - My personal physician recommends the hospital.
   - The hospital accepts my insurance.
   - The hospital is affiliated with a large health system.
   - The hospital is easy to get to.
   - The hospital has a long history of being active in my community.
   - The hospital has a local board of directors.
   - The hospital offers free parking.
   - Friends or family members recommend the hospital.
   - The hospital is located in my community.
   - The hospital is financially strong.

- The hospital advertises on television and radio and in the newspaper.
- I know people who work at the hospital.

9. In the past six months, have you heard, seen, or read anything about the hospital?

10. If so, what did you hear, see, or read?

RESULTS:

What consumers think of each hospital varies and depends on how hard the hospital has worked to build its image in the community. Interestingly, the perception of a particular hospital is often stronger in its outer-service areas. The people who travel from further away to get to the hospital often think more highly of it than those who live next door.

SQUEEZING MORE JUICE OUT OF YOUR SATISFACTION QUESTIONS

In a customer-satisfaction survey, you have to learn how well you're doing, typically by asking customers questions that use a rating scale from "poor" to "excellent" or by reading them a series of statements and asking them how much they agree with each (strongly disagree, disagree, neither disagree nor agree, agree, strongly agree). These are typical rating statements you might use on a customer-satisfaction survey:

- Reaching the right person when I call
- Receiving quick responses to my questions, inquiries, or concerns
- Speaking with personnel who are courteous and helpful
- Having personnel with product and service knowledge

Flash # 1 8

The more specific you make your customer-satisfaction questions and attribute rating for your snapshot survey, the better insight you'll get. Knowing more about the subtleties of your customer-service performance is key and far more valuable than broad generalities about how well you're doing.

- Receiving suggestions, advice, and recommendations from person-nel about products and services
- Keeping me informed of progress and of potential roadblocks re-garding my orders or inquiries
- Receiving promotional material about new products or services
- Receiving periodic telephone calls to keep in touch
- Meeting face-to-face with representatives to discuss my problems or needs
- Having competitively priced products or services
- Having products and services I need delivered in a timely manner
- Having overall product quality

While there's nothing wrong with these statements, and they can be easily adapted to many customer situations, the question you have to ask yourself is if they are specific enough to measure the subtleties of your product and service performance. In other words, it's easy to figure out the big issues. If you don't call people back or you're constantly late with your deliveries, you can spot those problems a mile away. But it's a lot tougher to learn about the subtleties that can make or break a customer relationship. For that, you'll need more specific statements such as the following ones this supplier used to gather feedback from its customers:

Customer Service
- Has experienced, knowledgeable sales staff
- Has accurate and responsive sales and support staff
- Receive delivery as promised
- Has next-day delivery on stocked items
- Able to easily reach the person you are calling
- Provides value-added services and consultation not easily found with other suppliers
- Can customize products, services, and programs for customers
- Has state-of-the-art customer-support system that gives you imme-diate access to your account and projects
- Has a high ratio of support versus sales personnel to service your account

Product Development, Performance, and Other Issues
- Has large and varied product line
- Is financially stable

- Able to work with a supplier who knows the strengths, capabilities, and limitations of all the top manufacturers of the products and services we sell
- Offers custom design, consultation, and production
- Offers product bundling
- Provides technical assistance in the way of testing and regulatory guidance
- Ability to work with a supplier who will manage and monitor your product requirements, as well as set up and manage a customized and efficient inventory program that provides vital supplies but doesn't require you to store unneeded product
- Keeps you informed of new products, regulations, and other issues affecting your industry
- Has an experienced transportation department dedicated to finding the best carriers, routings, and freight rates
- Can significantly reduce the time and cost required to develop a new product
- Understands the complete product and can handle all your requirements, significantly reducing the number of vendors you need to work with
- Able to work with an objective consulting service, not tied to a single manufacturer or single material
- Access to a major independent supplier with niche patents and manufacturing techniques
- Has significant experience with government regulations and developments
- Is an expert regarding local recycling regulations and helps you comply with them

Web, Electronic Commerce, and Other Technology Issues
- Provides Web-based inventory management
- Able to order free samples online
- Offers an online catalog
- Able to make online purchases
- Provides account and order status
- Offers custom catalogs with only the product you buy or want

Obviously, there were a few more questions on this survey, but notice the depth and breadth of the questions that were asked. Instead of focusing on general customer-service categories, the supplier chose to hone in on those categories and find out what really matters to customers. Because the data the company received was more specific, it proved more useful.

Asking specifically targeted questions isn't so difficult as you might first think. You just have to break down your operational process and service to smaller, tangible units. If you're not sure what to ask in your snapshot survey, talk with a couple of trusted customers. Tell them what you're trying to do and ask them if they would walk you through what they think about when they buy your products and services. Keep asking them, "Why is that important?" and "What else did you pay attention to?" They'll help you quickly uncover the details that are worth asking about.

THEY MAY BE SATISFIED, BUT IS IT IMPORTANT TO THEM?

One way to make sure you are not wasting your precious time and resources on things your customers don't care about is to ask them a dual set of questions about each of the specific product and service performance areas. An example of this technique appears in Figure 4.2. First, ask them "how important" it is that you offer what you already are doing. When you rate several of these statements with a 1 to 5 scale, you can rank them from most to least important by their mean scores. Second, ask your customers "how satisfied" they are with your performance using exactly the same statements. Not only can you get a profile of how satisfied your customers are by ranking the highest to lowest mean scores, you can also compare the satisfaction scores with the importance scores to get even deeper insights.

Let's take a look at how you might ask the "importance" and "satisfaction" questions together on the same survey.

Obviously, your customers need to provide two answers to every question. Once you tally your results, you will likely have some statements that are higher and some that are lower, especially if you calculate the mean scores.

- One way to analyze your data is to look at how wide the gap is between the importance and the satisfaction scores. As a rule of thumb, I use a half point difference as something to pay close attention to, depending on how many customers you included in your survey.
- I pay even more attention to these gaps when the importance scores are higher than the satisfaction scores. For example, if you

FIGURE 4.2

Importance/satisfaction questions rating the same attributes

The questions in this section ask about quality and service at our location.

1. In the first column, please state how *important* the issue is in your decision to buy or not to buy a product or service.

2. In the second column, please state how *satisfied* you are with your experience in working with us.

	IMPORTANCE					SATISFACTION				
	Very Low	Low	Mod-erate	High	Very High	Very Low	Low	Mod-erate	High	Very High
Length of time it takes to provide a quote	☐	☐	☐	☐	☐	☐	☐	☐	☐	☐
Product quality	☐	☐	☐	☐	☐	☐	☐	☐	☐	☐
Price	☐	☐	☐	☐	☐	☐	☐	☐	☐	☐
Meeting agreed-to delivery deadlines	☐	☐	☐	☐	☐	☐	☐	☐	☐	☐
Speed and efficiency in which the supplier can fill your request	☐	☐	☐	☐	☐	☐	☐	☐	☐	☐
Level of service from inside sales	☐	☐	☐	☐	☐	☐	☐	☐	☐	☐
Level of service from outside sales	☐	☐	☐	☐	☐	☐	☐	☐	☐	☐
Availability of emergency service	☐	☐	☐	☐	☐	☐	☐	☐	☐	☐
Technical support	☐	☐	☐	☐	☐	☐	☐	☐	☐	☐

found that your customers said "product quality" was highly important to them (4.8 mean score), but their satisfaction for this same item was lower (4.3), you have a gap that needs to be closed. You should start by finding out why it's so important to them and what you need to do to improve their satisfaction.

- If your scores are close to a tenth of a point (4.3 and 4.2), take a closer look at everyone who answered these questions. You may find that you have a couple of customers who are very upset and have brought down your overall scores, but most are okay with what you're doing.

F *l a s h* **# I 9**

If you really want to know what your customers think, ask them how important something is to them before you ask how satisfied they are with your performance. This compare-and-contrast approach helps you to focus on what they care most about and to stop wasting time on things that aren't so important to them.

Another way to think about your results is to calculate the mean score of each question and plot it on a two-by-two matrix similar to the one in Figure 4.3, which goes from low to high on both the importance and satisfaction ratings. This matrix helps you think about where you should be setting priorities for improvement. Each of your attribute ratings will fall into one of four categories:

1. *Meeting expectations* (high importance, high satisfaction). If your customers recognize an area as important and express a high degree of satisfaction, then pat yourself on the back because you're meeting expectations.
2. *Opportunities for improvement* (high importance, low satisfaction). Conversely, if they say something is very important to them, but they are not so satisfied as they should be, then it's an opportunity for improvement. Focusing in this quadrant can help you quickly and dramatically improve your performance.
3. *Overkill* (low importance, high satisfaction). If customers don't think something is very important, but they are highly satisfied, I like to call this overkill. You're doing something great, but they really don't care about it. You might try eliminating these services or spending more time on the things they really care about.
4. *Irrelevant irritations* (low importance, low satisfaction). Finally, if they don't think something is important—and their satisfaction is also low—you are probably engaged in the fatal activity I call *irrelevant irritations* where you're agitating them over nonissues. The faster you knock it off, the better off you'll be.

If you calculate the mean score for each of your importance and satisfaction scores, you can easily plot them on the Importance/Satisfaction Matrix. Start with the importance score, then move to the satisfaction score. For example, if you used a 1 to 5 scale, where "5" was the high or

FIGURE 4.3
Importance/satisfaction matrix

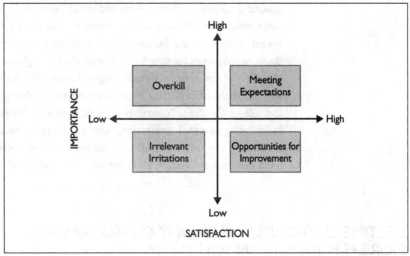

positive rating, you might have an importance score of 4.7, which should be somewhere on the right side of the importance line. If your satisfaction score is a 4.8, then you should also be near the top part of the satisfaction line. You'll end up in the "Meeting Expectations" quadrant.

Where you decide to cross your axis on this chart matters, because depending on the questions you ask, you might get scores that are pretty close together. So you're going to have to use the axis to divide smaller differences instead of using the entire scale from 1 to 5 and simply dividing everything at 2.5 (the halfway mark). For example, on a 1 to 5 scale, you might have mean scores that range from a low of a 3.5 to a high of 4.7. If this is the case, you will probably want to draw your axis somewhere in the middle, say around a 4.2. Any mean score about a 4.2 would go on the "high" side of either line, while all the others would go below your graph.

Case **H**istory

North Way Christian Community Church

Megachurches, or congregations with 3,000 or more members, are a growing phenomenon in the United States, while other traditional churches continue to struggle to retain and attract membership. North Way started with a handful of people and grew quickly by 10 percent to 15 percent when most of the churches around it continued their downward spiral. North Way wanted to serve even more people so it invited new members to attend a Christmas pageant, which presented an excellent opportunity to pass out a snapshot survey to find out what these people were looking for and what they thought of North Way.

One of the most important insights North Way learned from this research was that many of its current members thought the church was too big and growing too fast—a significant "customer-service" problem. The leadership worked hard to build strong personal connections with its members, reorganize its services, ease traffic flow, and undertake other solutions so current members and new visitors felt a personal connection and became comfortable with the organization.

LIFETIME CUSTOMER VALUE: WHY CUSTOMERS ARE MORE PRECIOUS THAN YOU THINK

When you think of marketing, are you primarily focused on finding new customers? If so, you're trying to meet people you do not know and trying to convert some of them into prospects and a few of them into customers.

While acquisition is an important component of marketing, this strategy is hard to sustain. An acquisition mentality is a huge problem for many organizations because it tricks managers into thinking that the faster they acquire, the faster they will grow. Everything is focused on finding the "next" customer—very little on exploiting the untapped value of the customers they already have. In time, they will just run out of prospects and wear themselves out.

The "lifetime customer value" philosophy says that marketing should be focused on all that a customer could represent to your organization: revenue, referrals, advice on new products, and help in defining your brand image. Instead of seeing the customer as worth only the next sale, you consider *all* that he or she might spend with you. The concept includes:

- The total amount of revenue the customer will spend over the life of your relationship
- The total number of referrals (and their worth) to your organization

1. Please tell us what is important to you in a church and your perception of North Way.

The Church . . .	IMPORTANCE TO ME IN A CHURCH					MY PERCEPTION OF NORTH WAY				
	Very Low	Low	Mod- erate	High	Very High	Strongly Disagree	Disagree	Neither Agree Nor Disagree	Agree	Strongly Agree
Is welcoming	☐	☐	☐	☐	☐	☐	☐	☐	☐	☐
Has caring members	☐	☐	☐	☐	☐	☐	☐	☐	☐	☐
Offers sound theological teaching, based on scripture	☐	☐	☐	☐	☐	☐	☐	☐	☐	☐
Offers uplifting sermons with practical applications	☐	☐	☐	☐	☐	☐	☐	☐	☐	☐
Provides opportunities for me to serve	☐	☐	☐	☐	☐	☐	☐	☐	☐	☐
Is in my denomination	☐	☐	☐	☐	☐	☐	☐	☐	☐	☐
Cares for people who are poor, sick, or hurting	☐	☐	☐	☐	☐	☐	☐	☐	☐	☐
Has (a) pastor(s) I like	☐	☐	☐	☐	☐	☐	☐	☐	☐	☐
Has a growing membership	☐	☐	☐	☐	☐	☐	☐	☐	☐	☐
Is financially healthy	☐	☐	☐	☐	☐	☐	☐	☐	☐	☐
Offers strong grade school programs	☐	☐	☐	☐	☐	☐	☐	☐	☐	☐
Offers strong middle/high school programs	☐	☐	☐	☐	☐	☐	☐	☐	☐	☐
Offers high-quality adult educational programs	☐	☐	☐	☐	☐	☐	☐	☐	☐	☐
Clearly communicates its purpose and mission	☐	☐	☐	☐	☐	☐	☐	☐	☐	☐
Has strong leadership	☐	☐	☐	☐	☐	☐	☐	☐	☐	☐
Has a lot of members	☐	☐	☐	☐	☐	☐	☐	☐	☐	☐
Has uplifting worship	☐	☐	☐	☐	☐	☐	☐	☐	☐	☐
Has contemporary music	☐	☐	☐	☐	☐	☐	☐	☐	☐	☐

2. What are three words that you would use to describe North Way?

3. From what you have personally experienced or heard from others, what are North Way's greatest *strengths*? (Please explain.)

4. What are North Way's greatest *challenges or weaknesses*? (Please explain.)

> ### *F l a s h # 2 0*
>
> Constantly chasing after the next customer instead of getting all you can out of the ones you already have is a formula for disaster and exhaustion. When you look at customers in terms of what they might mean to you over their lifetime, you begin to acknowledge—and respect—them for what they really mean to your business.

- Advice, recommendations, and other insights about new products and services
- Assistance with articulating and defining your organization's brand image
- Giving your business a fighting chance to succeed long-term and outlive your competition

This concept elevates marketing efforts and makes them significant, especially when they are designed to build and maintain relationships. Instead of making a $5,000 sale, you have the opportunity to make $50,000 over the next three to five years. Talk about dramatically improving your marketing return on investment (ROI)!

Lifetime customer value also keeps you focused on high-payoff activities—such as selling to your existing customers who are easier to close. In the long run, your profits will increase because you are investing fewer resources to bring in new business.

C *ase* H *istory*

World Affairs Council Membership Survey

SITUATION:

The World Affairs Council (WAC) is a nonprofit, nonpartisan organization that is dedicated to promoting greater understanding of international issues. Over the years, it has attracted a number of senior executives and influential business professionals as part of its membership base. To better understand what attracted members to their organization—and kept them as members for many years—the WAC conducted a mail survey.

QUESTIONS:

Listed below are a number of questions and a list of reasons for joining and maintaining membership in WAC. For each question, please mark all the statements that apply.

- Why did you first become a member of WAC?

- Why do you remain a member?

- Why would someone else join today?

	Why I First Joined WAC	Why I Remain a Member	Why Others Would Join Today
WAC provides a forum to learn expert opinion and insight about key issues facing us—our community, our nation, and the world.	☐	☐	☐
WAC offers important educational programs to secondary school students and teachers in our region.	☐	☐	☐
WAC is the premier organization for people with an interest in world affairs.	☐	☐	☐
WAC fosters understanding and tolerance among different ethnic and cultural groups.	☐	☐	☐
WAC membership dues are tax-deductible, charitable contributions.	☐	☐	☐
Your business or academic institution pays for membership.	☐	☐	☐
WAC members are important and influential people in the community.	☐	☐	☐
WAC provides a good place to network and to meet people who can help you in your professional life.	☐	☐	☐
You were encouraged by a friend/colleague.	☐	☐	☐
WAC programs are enjoyable social events.	☐	☐	☐
WAC is different from other organizations you belong to.	☐	☐	☐
WAC is similar to other organizations you belong to.	☐	☐	☐
Other: _____	☐	☐	☐

RESULTS:

The World Affairs Council used the results to develop a membership recruitment and marketing campaign. The organization discovered that the reason many members first joined were not the same as why they remained members, in some cases for decades.

WHAT I HAVE LEARNED FROM CUSTOMERS LIKE YOURS

In many businesses, if you do something long enough you will see just about everything. The marketing and research business is no different. If you run enough snapshot surveys on customer satisfaction, you will *hear* just about everything. You may get a few surprises every once in a while, but customers from one survey will often echo the same themes in another survey, even though they come from different size companies, different industries, and different operating perspectives.

So, what have I learned about customers like yours from conducting hundreds of satisfaction surveys over the years? Quite a lot. Here are some of the more predominant themes I've heard (of course, you'll actually have to conduct your own snapshot survey to know for sure):

- *Most of your customers will say positive things about your business.* If you're worried about what you might hear, don't be. There's a good reason they're buying from you. It's because they like you.
- *Not all your customers will love you.* Depending on how you've been treating them, some will be frustrated or angry with you, whether they are justified or not. Knowing how many are upset with you and what's driving them crazy is a lot better position to be in than carrying on in ignorant bliss. When you know how they feel, you can do something about the things that are frustrating your customers.
- *Just because your customers are angry with you doesn't mean they won't keep buying from you.* They'll let things fester for a while, before they decide to try someone else. If those new companies don't work out, and they can't find your products or services with anyone else, they'll be back.
- *Loyal customers may really only be loyal to a specific person within your organization.* They feel a bond and connection to this person, whether he or she is in sales, customer service, or some other de-

partment. When that employee leaves you, your customer may follow him or her.

- *A lot of your customers want you to know how they feel about your company.* Even if you guarantee them confidentiality in the survey, they'll tell you who they are. The more they invest with your firm, the more they want you to know how they feel about you.
- *Most of them want to deal with one person when they call–and the same person every time they call.* Their patience wears thin when they have to constantly explain the nuances of their business to someone different each time. Do them a favor and assign a specific account person to them.
- *Inconsistent performance drives customers more nuts than average quality.* If you do a great job on one project, an okay one on the next, then your best effort ever on the one after that, you'll drive your customers crazy. It would be better to be mediocre every time. At least they would know what to expect. When someone can't predict your performance, they express more dissatisfaction than when they can.
- *The fewer headaches your customers have from their interactions with you, the happier they will be.* If you take too long to answer their questions, screw up shipments, or can't seem to get all your billing on a single invoice, you're creating a migraine. When you make their life easier, they will make yours better by buying from you again and again.
- *In most industries, price is important, but it's not the most important factor in their decision to buy from you.* On a laundry list of alternatives, such as speed of processing order, shipping costs, quality, and others, price is usually in third to fifth place. It might be different for your company, but it's unlikely it will be first. Everyone wants a good price. But a good price with a big headache isn't worth the cost.
- *No one likes being a Ping-Pong ball in your phone system.* Just how many buttons do you want them to push to get to the right person? If you have the courage, why not have a real person answer the phone? This could become a key component of your brand image and a chance to differentiate yourself from the plethora of firms that are letting machines control the most important link to their customers.
- *Your company has multiple brands.* A brand is a collection of perceptions, hopefully positive. It's a promise about who you are and what you do. Strong brands give people confidence that

they are buying a quality product, so they don't have to waste a lot of time deciding whether to invest in you or someone else. Unless you've worked very, very hard at communicating one message to your market, there is a very high probability that your company has more than one brand. Those brands are typically a reflection of how your customers interact with you. If they are used to buying only one product or service, that's how they will see you (this is why it's so helpful to ask them if they are aware of your products and services and if they want more information about any of them).

- *Customers may buy from you for their reasons, not yours.* When I ask employees to rate the same questions customers are rating—only to give their answers as they think customers will respond—their perceptions are frequently different. The same is often the case for senior managers. Few can precisely predict why a customer buys. You have to ask them.

- *You think a lot harder about your company than your customers ever will.* They will have definite opinions about how well you're doing and how you might change things around to better serve them, but most of them will never be as emotionally connected to your firm as you are. It's your company, not theirs.

- *Most of them care less and less about perks.* They want to get their job done right so they can spend more time with their family and friends. Every once in a while, they might like to be wined and dined, but not like it was years ago.

- *When your customers are upset, the conflict will be less about what you did or didn't do and more about how you made them look or feel.* You shipped the wrong stuff. That's a problem, but when they have to go tell their boss they couldn't get a product out the door because of you, that's what's really bothering them.

- *Customers will be loyal to you, until they realize how easy it is to switch suppliers or put projects out to bid.* The easier it is to find someone else to supply the products or services that you offer, the harder you're going to have to work to keep your customers. Some industries, such as insurance, banking, and other financial services, use "inertia" as a key customer-retention strategy. If you have to pay off your loans, close all your accounts, and order new checks, that's a lot of aggravation to change suppliers. In other industries, however, once you've been through a change once or twice, it gets a lot easier. If your customers get used to switching, they'll switch more frequently.

- *There's a generational gap with communications technology.* Rarely have I interviewed a customer over 50 years old who wants to communicate with you solely through your Web site and e-mail. He or she wants to talk to a real person—one who's smart, experienced, and respectful of his or her current situation. Buyers who are about 30 or younger are a different story. They grew up with technology and want to use it to interact with your company.
- *Some of your customers are interested in how you market and manage your business, even more so than the products or services they are buying from you.* When you're a consultant, you quickly learn that a lot of your customers want to learn more about the consulting business. Many of them are thinking about it as a career option. Others are looking for someone to listen to them and talk in confidence about what's going on in their company, even though it has nothing to do with the products or services you sell. When you get connected with a customer on this level, you're offering something way more valuable than most competitors can supply. These are the types of customers you can build the strongest and best friendships with.

Customer feedback is a staple in managing any successful organization. With the right snapshot survey, you can find out where you stand and what it will take to keep your customers happy. When you realize the snapshot survey can also help you generate referrals, build loyalty, and develop lifelong partnerships, your job becomes even easier.

5

BUILDING A MARKETING PLAN THAT WORKS

Ensuring Your Messages and Tactics Resonate with Your Target Audience

Obstacles are those frightful things you see when you take your eyes off your goal.

Henry Ford

I'm not sure which is a greater disservice to your business: not having a marketing plan or using a plan that isn't based on feedback from your customers and prospects.

I guess I shouldn't be surprised at how many businesses don't have a formal or written marketing plan. Many organizations have built a solid customer base, continue to receive referrals, and engage in what I call "maintenance marketing" or repeating what has been bringing them success for years. Marketing to these organizations is like a morning routine: You know exactly what to do, even when you aren't thinking about it very much.

Running your business without a formal marketing plan can work as long as you want to stay about the same size and you don't have much pressure from competitors. When you decide that it's time to grow, however, you'll need a plan so that you don't waste a lot of time, energy, or resources on ideas that are not bringing in customers.

If you do have a written marketing plan, what is it based on? Are the strategies, messages, tactics, and other elements you selected based on solid information that your customers and prospects specifically told you were important to them—like how they prefer to receive information (direct sales, e-mail, Web, etc.) or which messages are most persua-

> **F l a s h   # 2 1**
>
> A marketing plan should really be a subset of a larger, more comprehensive business plan, which could include additional sections such as a general company description, products and services, operational plan, management and organization, structure, capitalization, financial plan, and other components. The marketing plan describes your marketing goals and action steps for how you plan to reach them. Using a snapshot survey helps you create a plan that's based on the reality of your customers, prospects, and other important target audiences.

sive to them and why? Or was it built on your best guesses, staff input, and ideas that you borrowed from other companies?

The snapshot survey is a big help for making sure your marketing activities resonate with your customers and prospects. You can use the snapshot survey in many ways to gather the insight you need to build your marketing plan, some of which are talked about in detail in other chapters of this book:

- *Defining your current situation.* You can use it to better understand your marketing situation. What are customers and prospects paying attention to? How do they see your company, products, and services compared to those of your competitors or other alternatives? How much do they know about your offerings? Answers to questions like these give you the broad-level perspectives for selecting your strategy and tactics.
- *Determining your marketing mix.* Where do your prospects currently get their information about your products and services? What do they watch, read, and listen to? Where do they hang out (trade shows, associations, shopping locations, etc.)? Asking about their media habits, as well as the various ways they make decisions about purchasing products or services like yours, helps you pick the right marketing tools. Questions like these help you decide whether you need to focus on developing an interactive Web site, printing new literature, attending specific trade shows, or all of the above. It also keeps you from wasting precious time and money on ideas that don't produce any results.
- *Testing your marketing messages.* What can you say to your prospects that is both persuasive and true? What do they want to know and

hear about your products and services? For example, do they want to know that you offer a money-back guarantee? What about free online training? Perhaps, the fact that your product is "made in the USA" matters to them. What about specific details about the way your products were made or how your services are delivered? Questions about your messages help you select the most potent ones so you can make them the lead ideas you want to communicate to prospects. But whatever you say, be sure you back it up with your actions. Everyone knows that talk is cheap, but your customers and prospects will avoid you like the plague if they get any hint that you're lying to them about what you or your product will do.

- *Setting your prices.* Rather than using trial and error to set your pricing or simply adding some percentage to your costs, you can ask customers and prospects about them through a snapshot survey. What do they think is a reasonable price? What combination of product features, services, delivery, payment options, and other decision factors do they want to see from you?

- *Assessing your brand image.* What perceptions do others hold of you and your key competitors? Knowing these insights helps you determine how you might change your marketing to reinforce or redefine your brand image through your specific messages or performance or in other ways.

- *Measuring marketing ROI.* How well is your marketing working? Which marketing tools or tactics are producing the best results? Which ones are dragging everything down? Questions that focus on the impact you're having on prospects and customers help you evaluate how well what you've been doing has been working so that you can make adjustments and move forward. Many companies formally measure their marketing ROI at least annually, if not at the end of a specific campaign. They take what they learn and apply it to the next campaign.

Figure 5.1 contains a questionnaire that I have adapted for many companies that gathers the basic marketing information most businesses need to prepare a good marketing plan. It's a set of overall survey questions that work very well to gather insights about many of the elements you might eventually include in your plan. Instead of being focused primarily on one single topic, such as determining pricing options for one of your products, these questions are broader in scope and can provide you with concrete insight about decision factors, buying habits, brand image, marketing mix, channels, messages, and other valuable data.

FIGURE 5.1
Typical questions to include in a snapshot survey for gathering feedback to use in a marketing plan

1. **In your opinion, who are the leading _____ manufacturers?** (DO NOT READ. MARK ALL THAT APPLY AND PROBE FOR "WHY?")

   Why?

   1 Company A
   2 Competitor B
   3 Competitor C

2. **When purchasing _____ , what are the most important things you have considered?** (PROBE. RECORD VERBATIM RESPONSE.)

3. **When buying _____ , is it important that you buy from an ISO-9000 certified manufacturer?** (MARK ONE.)

   1 Yes   3 DK/NR
   2 No

   (NOTE: IF RESPONDENT NOT FAMILIAR WITH ISO-9000, SAY: "AN ISO-9000 DESIGNATION IS AN INDEPENDENT CERTIFICATION PROGRAM THAT THE MANUFACTURER HAS COMPLETED TO ENSURE CERTAIN STANDARDS AND QUALITY LEVELS.")

4. **From whom do you typically learn about _____?** (READ. MARK ONE.)

   1 Manufacturer   3 Other: _____
   2 Distributor   4 DK/NR

5. **How do you typically find out about specific instrument products, supplies, and/or manufacturers?** (DO NOT READ. MARK ALL THAT APPLY.)

   1 Distributor catalogs
   2 Counter displays
   3 Distributor/dealer information/meetings
   4 Direct mail
   5 Direct sales calls from manufacturers
   6 Product news releases in trade journals
   7 Trade journal advertisements
   8 Trade shows and/or events
   9 Word of mouth (ASK FOR TYPICAL SOURCE: _____)
   10 Manufacturer literature/catalog
   11 Other: _____
   99 DK/NR

FIGURE 5.1 *(Continued)*

6a. Do you typically read trade or professional journals? (MARK ONE.)

    1 Yes   3 DK/NR (SKIP TO Q7a)

    2 No (SKIP TO Q7a)

6b. Which one(s)?

7a. Are you a member of a trade or professional association? (MARK ONE.)

    1 Yes   3 DK/NR (SKIP TO Q8)

    2 No (SKIP TO Q8)

7b. Which one(s)? (DO NOT READ. MARK ALL THAT APPLY.)

    1 Association #1   88 Other: _____

    2 Association #2   99 DK/NR

8. If a manufacturer of _____ was to offer the following product support services, how valuable do you think each service would be to your organization on a 1 to 10 scale, where 1 is "not at all valuable" and 10 is "very valuable"? (ROTATE. MARK ONE FOR EACH.)

	Not At All Valuable									Very Valuable	DK/NR
a. Off-site product training services to teach you and your staff how to apply and in which situations to use our products	1	2	3	4	5	6	7	8	9	10	☐
b. In-house application training services delivered at your organization	1	2	3	4	5	6	7	8	9	10	☐
ca. Educational and training materials, such as literature, videos, or other information, included with your product purchase . . . (IF "5" OR HIGHER, ASK:)	1	2	3	4	5	6	7	8	9	10	☐

cb. Which would you prefer?
    ☐ Literature
    ☐ Videos
    ☐ Other: _____

	Not At All Valuable									Very Valuable	DK/NR
d. Speakers and experts available to attend your company or association meetings	1	2	3	4	5	6	7	8	9	10	☐
e. Trade and professional article placements in the journals you read	1	2	3	4	5	6	7	8	9	10	☐

FIGURE 5.1 *(Continued)*

	Not At All Valuable		Very Valuable	DK/NR

f. Training and/or tools on how to present and sell _____ services to end users, consumers, and other audiences   1 2 3 4 5 6 7 8 9 10   ☐

g. How to make money with _____ products and services   1 2 3 4 5 6 7 8 9 10   ☐

9a. **Some manufacturers are considering developing a _____. If such a _____ were available, how likely would you be to purchase it?** (READ. MARK ONE.)

  1 Very likely   3 Not at all likely
  2 Somewhat likely   4 DK/NR (SKIP TO Q10a)

9b. **Why?** (PROBE. RECORD VERBATIM RESPONSE.)

10a. **I'm going to read you three statements that might be used to describe a company that manufactures _____. Tell me which one appeals to you by respond- ing that you really like this idea, like it somewhat, or don't care for the idea.**

  The first statement is . . . "I choose Company A because they're the experts. Not only do they make a good product, but they provide the training, educational infor- mation, and technical advice I need to do my job right. They really understand how to use the products and know what they're talking about."

  Would you say you . . . ? (READ. MARK ONE.)

  1 Really like this idea   3 Don't care for the idea
  2 Like the idea somewhat   4 DK/NR (SKIP TO Q11a)

10b. **Why?** (PROBE. RECORD VERBATIM RESPONSE.)

11a. **The second statement is . . . "I choose Company B because they're reliable. They have a good name and have been around for years. They make a good-quality product you can count on."**

  Would you say you . . . ? (READ. MARK ONE.)

  1 Really like this idea   3 Don't care for the idea
  2 Like the idea somewhat   4 DK/NR (SKIP TO Q12a)

11b. **Why?** (PROBE. RECORD VERBATIM RESPONSE.)

FIGURE 5.1 *(Continued)*

12a. The third statement is . . . "I choose Company C because they always respond to me. Whether I have a technical question or a replacement part or a product calibrated, they're always happy to service me. That's pretty impressive for a manufacturer."

Would you say you . . . ? (READ. MARK ONE.)

I Really like this idea	3 Don't care for the idea
2 Like the idea somewhat	4 DK/NR (SKIP TO Q13)

12b. Why? (PROBE. RECORD VERBATIM RESPONSE.)

13. How would you classify your company? (READ. MARK ONE.)

I Company Option #1	2 Company Option #2

14. What type of advertising or marketing do you do to promote your _____? (DO NOT READ. MARK ALL THAT APPLY.)

I Direct mail	4 Direct sales force
2 Yellow Pages advertising	5 Other: _____
3 Newspaper advertising	6 DK/NR

15. Would you consider participating in a co-op advertising program with a manufacturer of _____? (MARK ONE.)

I Yes	3 DK/NR
2 No	

These last few questions are to divide your responses into groups.

16. What brand of _____ do you currently use? (DO NOT READ. MARK ALL THAT APPLY.)

I Company A	3 Company C
2 Company B	

17. (IF DID NOT MENTION "COMPANY A" IN Q16, ASK:) Are you familiar with Company A? (MARK ONE.)

I Yes	3 DK/NR (SKIP TO Q18)
2 No (SKIP TO Q18)	

18. Have you ever purchased a Company A product? (MARK ONE.)

I Yes . . . **Why did you select Company A?** (PROBE. RECORD VERBATIM RESPONSE.)

2 No . . . **Why not?** (PROBE. RECORD VERBATIM RESPONSE.)

3 DK/NR

FIGURE 5.1 *(Continued)*

---

19. **During the next 12 months, is your organization planning to purchase _____?**
    (MARK ONE.)
    1 Yes   3 DK/NR
    2 No

TEN BUILDING BLOCKS OF A TYPICAL MARKETING PLAN

There are many ways to write a marketing plan and no two marketing plans should be exactly alike—even those created from canned software programs. In fact, the best plans are often simple, direct, and precise. While I like to divide the plans I write into ten specific categories (outline follows), you should use these categories as a guideline not as an exact outline of your marketing plan. Create additional categories and subsections that make sense. It's your plan. Make it fit your needs.

1. *Current situation.* I always start with a brief review of what's going on. I describe the environment in which a company is trying to market. It's best to be totally honest when comparing your products and services to those of your competitors. Figure 5.2 shows a diagram of a SWOT (strengths, weaknesses, opportunities, threats) analysis, which is a wonderful tool for helping you simplify and understand your current situation. Simply list everything you (and your colleagues) can think of in terms of your organization's, product's, or service's strengths, weaknesses, opportunities, and threats.

2. *Positioning.* You can't be all things to all people. If you try, you'll water down your image and confuse your customers and prospects. The real challenge is to select a unique position or market definition that attracts the people you want to sell to. If you're a "family-style restaurant," be true to that by serving great food at a great price. Serving expensive food in a family-style atmosphere will only confuse customers and water down your brand image.

3. *Marketing objectives.* Your objectives should be specific, quantifiable, and measurable. They should be something you can count. "To increase sales" is not a goal. It's an attitude statement. It's too

FIGURE 5.2

Categories for a SWOT analysis that can be used to organize and clarify marketing situations. Strengths and Weaknesses are typically focused on the inside of your organization, while Opportunities and Threats deal more with external influences.

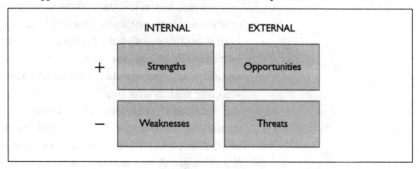

general. Make it more specific, such as "To increase sales from $50,000 to $80,000 per month by the end of this fiscal year." Limit the total number of objectives in your plan to a handful. It's better to do a few things well than a lot of things poorly.

4. *Marketing strategies.* Strategies are your overall approach to marketing. Tactics are the individual tools you will use to accomplish your marketing objectives (advertising, direct mail, trade shows, etc.). Selecting the right strategy is key. Without it, your tactics might become a jumbled mess of wasted resources. If you selected a public relations strategy, it might include increasing visibility in the local community using newspaper articles, having staff members join local groups, and other tactics. Another strategy might be to sell through a distribution network of established dealers (instead of building your own direct sales force). One of the more interesting marketing strategies I've seen is that of a tile and carpet store that spent no money on marketing. Instead, the company simply built its stores as close to national chain retailers as possible. It found that when people looked for tile, they frequently stopped at more than one store. So, the company's strategy was to get as physically close to its competitors as it could.

5. *Target audiences.* Target audiences are all the groups of people (customers, prospects, media, distributors, dealers, consumers, etc.) you're trying to reach through your marketing. Audiences can be classified in many ways: by geographic location (region, metro area, density, climate, etc.), demographics

(age, family size, family life cycle, gender, income, occupation, education, religion, race, generation, nationality, social class), psychographics (lifestyle, personality, urgency), and behavior (occasions, benefits, user status, usage rates, loyalty, status, readiness state, attitude toward your products or services). Target audiences should be focused (female consumers, 25 to 54 years old)—but not so focused that they are too small to sustain your operations (female consumers, 25 to 54 years old who live within one block of your store). Sometimes, identifying "primary" (the people you want to spend most of your marketing time and effort on) and "secondary" audiences is helpful in prioritizing your marketing messages and tactics.

6. *Key messages.* A key message is not a theme, tagline, or slogan. It may not even necessarily contain the words you will use when you start communicating and marketing. It's simply the main ideas you're trying to get across. For example, "Company A provides quality work, on schedule and within budget" could serve as one of several messages. You would find proof of this concept in its sales literature, on its Web site, through customer testimonials, and in other marketing tactics it is employing. Of course, not every marketing tactic would use all the key messages, but having a set of messages helps you decide what to say—and not say—once you start communicating. Most marketing plans have three to five key messages, with some of those messages designed for all audiences and others for specific audiences or for special situations.

7. *Tactics.* Tactics are the individual marketing tools, used in conjunction with each other, to accomplish your marketing objectives. I don't think anyone has ever written (or will be able to write) a book that includes all the marketing tactics ever used. Why should they? A lot of those tactics were failures. I always recommend that you stay with the basics with most of your tactics. The last thing you want is to spend all your marketing dollars on a single idea that doesn't produce the kinds of results you need. Instead, a marketing mix of advertising (print, broadcast, newspaper, posters, leaflets, point-of-purchase displays), sales promotion (coupons, rebates, trade-in allowances, fairs, samplings), public relations (press releases, seminars, community relations, trade articles), direct mail (catalogs, e-mail, telemarketing), and personal selling (sales presentations, samples, proposals, referral programs) is

often more productive, depending on whether your business sells to consumers or other businesses or is a professional service, nonprofit, or other type of firm (see the next section for more thoughts on which of these marketing tactics will work best for your type of business).

8. *Timing.* How long is it going to take to implement your plan (do all the things you say you're going to do)? Remember, some tactics may require a longer lead time. For example, trade media and magazine articles may be written and planned for publication two to six months prior to the date they are actually printed. Also, it may take several weeks for a brochure to be printed once it is written and designed.

9. *Budget.* Each tactic will cost money and effort. Few companies have an unlimited marketing budget. Therefore, you're going to have to set some priorities. Start with the tactics that are likely to produce the greatest results. If you could buy only one tactic, what would it be? If you can afford two, which two can you afford?

10. *Measuring marketing return on investment (ROI).* Marketing ROI should always be measured on two levels: programmatic (what did the overall program accomplish in terms of sales and meeting your stated objectives?) and tactical (what did each marketing tool produce?). The time to start thinking about how to measure your marketing ROI is not when you've finished marketing, but when you're building your plan. When you have a specific idea of what you're going after, it's a lot easier to find out if you got there. Chapter 10 is devoted to the principles and techniques of measuring marketing ROI using the snapshot survey.

SELECTING A MARKETING MIX THAT MAKES SENSE

The specific marketing mix or marketing tools and tactics—such as direct mail, attending networking events, or newspaper advertising—that will work for your company will vary and depend on which tactics you select, how you use them, and what you communicate through them.

One way to simplify your choice is to ask your customers and prospects: "How do you typically find out about the kinds of products or services that we sell?" You're likely to hear things like:

- Referrals from friends, colleagues, or family members
- Current customers wanting more work or to buy something else

F l a s h   # 2 2

The specific marketing tools (or tactics) that are likely to work best for your business will depend on who you sell to and what type of business you are. If you sell primarily to consumers, then advertising, direct mail, in-store displays, and similar techniques work great. These same tools will be dismal failures if you sell primarily to other businesses, where trade shows, personal selling, and similar tools work better. Finally, if you're selling consulting or professional services, you'll find that referrals, newsletters, and an information-rich Web site will serve you much better.

- Internet searching or checking out Web sites
- Walking or driving by (for retail establishments)
- Catalogs
- In-store displays
- Advertisements (radio, TV, newspaper, magazine)
- Direct mail
- Telemarketing
- Sales calls
- Trade shows
- Articles (newspaper, magazines, trade journals)

Of course, you can get much more specific with your questions and ask about which publications they typically read, which associations they belong to, which Web sites they visit, and so on. What you're looking for are the places where most of your customers and prospects "hang out." Once you know their habits, then it's much easier to select the individual tactics you need to reach them.

You may have found over the years by trial and error that some marketing tactics work great, while others are complete disasters. When I'm first learning about a customer's business and trying to decide which tactics might make the most sense for him or her and what we might ask about in a snapshot survey, I typically divide them into three broad categories: consumer, business-to-business, and consulting/professional service. The tactics in each type of marketing are very different and the results from numerous snapshot surveys continually back up these broad classifications.

Consumer (B2C)

Companies who sell their products primarily to consumers or individuals fall into this category and are often described as B2C, or business to consumer. Every time you go to a grocery store, the mall, or some other retail outlet, you're a consumer and the marketing tactics that will work to attract you to this store are very different than if you're a business or professional services customer. Companies marketing to consumers may use public relations–type tactics to support their marketing efforts (article placements and other earned media coverage), but most rely more heavily on advertising or marketing tactics that require them to purchase space to communicate their messages. Consumer marketing tactics often include:

- Advertising (all types)
- News releases to earn stories, product releases, and other articles in newspapers, magazines, and Web sites that consumers read
- Feature articles or the main stories in those publications
- Direct mail typically sent to your home through the printed pieces delivered by the post office or through newspaper advertisement sections delivered in your Sunday paper
- Telemarketing to existing customers (who are exempt from "do not call" lists)
- Billboards
- Promotions, coupons, door hangers, and the like
- Celebrity sponsorships or famous people who serve as spokespersons for particular companies
- In-store point-of-purchase advertising and events, designed to attract your attention while you are shopping
- Web sites, banner advertisements, portals, e-mail newsletters/specials, and other electronic advertising

Business-to-Business (B2B)

Businesses who sell primarily to other businesses (even though the buyers are often a single person) make up a very different type of purchaser than consumers and typically require a different combination of marketing tactics. Figure 5.3 shows the results from a recent survey I conducted of nearly 500 business-to-business marketing professionals and the percentage of companies who use the marketing tactics to sell

FIGURE 5.3

Marketing tactics business-to-business marketers use most frequently to sell their company's products and services

	Percentage Who Use Tool*
News releases	95%
Web site**	88
Sales literature/brochures/catalogs	85
Direct mail	77
Trade shows/events	76
Marketing research to determine marketing and/or communications strategies	73
Feature articles in local newspapers	71
Feature articles in business publications	70
Specialty advertising (gifts, giveaways)	69
Feature articles in consumer, print, and broadcast media	66
Trade magazine advertising	60
Marketing research used to evaluate marketing, communications, or advertising programs	60
Technical articles/case histories for the trade press	59
Company-sponsored conferences for customer education	50
Co-marketing partnerships (licensing deals, etc.)	46
Instruction videos/audiotapes	39
Marketing research used to generate publicity (proprietary promotional surveys, etc.)	38
Coupons/special offers	36
Promotional CDs	24

* Survey of 480 professional business-to-business marketers completed in 1999.
** 84 percent of these respondents indicated that their organizations were planning to increase the use of their Web sites in the future.

their products or services. From this chart you can see that many of them are using more of what I call a "public relations" method of selling their services and include tactics such as media relations (news releases, trade shows, article placements) supplemented with advertising tools. While some consumer companies may spend millions of dollars on their marketing budget, many business-to-business companies have more limited resources, so their marketing needs to be more focused.

Consulting and Professional Service

Completely different from consumer or business-to-business marketing is the way consulting and professional service firms market their services. In many cases, advertising, direct mail, ballroom-scale seminars, cold calls, sponsorships of cultural or sports events, and similar tactics are a complete waste of time, energy, and resources.

Not only have I learned this through snapshot surveys I've run for my customers, I once paid a telemarketer a salary for three months to make cold calls and set up appointments. The effort produced three leads, one proposal, and no sales. I think two of the prospects gave me an appointment just to get my telemarketer to stop calling them.

The tactics that work much better for consulting and professional service firms include:

- *Referrals from clients, partners, friends, and business associates.* I have a number of relationships with professionals who offer services different from mine who refer me to other clients. Some of those referrals are done as a courtesy, while others are paid a small referral fee on the total price of the project. I've found that it is often less expensive to pay a referral fee than to try to win the project using other marketing techniques.

- *Executive job changes.* Many of my best projects come from executives who were clients at one organization and who have recently moved to another. They frequently need the assistance of someone they trust to help them better understand their new situations as well as solve the new problems they face. When you can maintain a relationship with the company they just left and their new one, you're in a very advantageous position.

- *Small-scale seminars.* Delivered at public forums, industry meetings, and similar events, these seminars can be excellent places to meet potential clients. You certainly don't get a lead at every meeting, but sometimes you can get one or two. I recently presented at one of these events and got two follow-up sales from people I met there. I also received a nice gift and dinner for delivering the presentation.

- *Articles in trade publications.* Articles that you write in trade publications that your clients read can be effective marketing tools. Publishing them in journals that you and your competitors read are often a waste of time.

- *Propriety research or trend surveys.* Research or surveys that you commission about a topic that your clients and prospects might find interesting give you something specific to talk about. Over the years, I've conducted surveys like these on the ways companies use the Internet, how they measure marketing ROI, what they look for when they buy business books, and many other topics.

- *Books.* Books written from experience (like this one) are excellent calling cards. I've written a number of training manuals, booklets, articles, chapters, white papers, and other publications over the years. It's amazing the uses you can find for this material once it is developed. For example, I group more than a dozen articles I wrote on how to measure marketing return on investment together in one booklet and print about 1,000 copies a year. I give them to people who attend my presentations, include them in my marketing and sales literature, and ask my students to read them as part of the courses I teach. It's this type of merchandising of your ideas that helps build your expertise and credibility.

The three marketing mix categories—consumer, business-to-business, and consulting/professional service—are meant to be guidelines, not hard-and-fast rules of what you should or shouldn't do. Many more tactics also can work for one or more of these mix categories. That's why it's so important to find out from your customers and prospects which tactic will likely work in your situation, before you waste too much money.

HOW TO ASK ABOUT PRICE WITHOUT GIVING AWAY THE STORE

A key component to any marketing plan and overall effort is price. It's one of the four classic marketing "Ps," along with product, place, and promotion (some folks have added "position" as a fifth "P"). Product takes into account all of the product's key features and benefits and includes the reasons someone should buy it. Place is about how the product is distributed (retail store, mail order, Internet, and other channels). Promotion accounts for the marketing mix or combination of advertising, public relations, and other techniques that are used to sell the product. Price—you guessed it—is about how much it costs to buy the product or service and all the things that are included.

What is not so apparent, however, are all the things that should—or should not—be factored in the price of a product. The price could include everything from the list price, less discounts (quantity, seasonal, cash), less allowances (trade-ins, damaged goods), and other items. It

F l a s h # 2 3

Price is the only thing that brings in revenue. The rest of the marketing effort is a cost and requires expenditures to get the purchase. That's why it's crazy to drop your price at the first sign of customer pushback or stalling. All the marketing efforts to win the business are wasted if you can't generate a reasonable profit.

may also include the costs to make that product and deliver the service, such as salaries, wages, insurance, postage, telephone, travel, printing, advertising, and others. In fact, you have to be careful about how much cost you put into the "making of your product or service." Obviously, the more you say it costs you to produce, the more you have to charge.

Most companies set their prices using some "cost plus" formula. If the product cost them $100 to make, they simply add some percentage, such as 20 percent and set the price of the product at $120. The problem with this approach is that it ignores the true value that your product may have to your customers and prospects. What if they were willing to pay $200 or even $300? You'd be leaving an awful lot of profit on the table.

You can ask pricing-related questions in many ways in your snapshot surveys. Some of them include applying simple scales to questions, such as:

- At $12.95, how likely would you be to buy this product?" (very likely, somewhat likely, not at all likely)
- At $11.95, would you _____ buy this product?" (definitely, probably, may or may not, probably not, definitely not)
- If you went to the store and found only four brands of caulking compound at these prices, which one would you choose? (brand A, $1.78; Brand B, $2.10; Brand C, $2.18; Brand D, $1.69)

Questions like these can give you an initial hint of what someone might be willing to spend, but most customers and prospects will lowball their estimates. They will give you an answer that is really much lower than they might actually pay.

One way to get around this problem is by using a technique created in the 1970s by Dutch economist Peter H. van Westendorp, which asks four questions to determine the price of a product using a $1 to $20 scale (or some other range that is appropriate for what you are selling):

1. At what price on the scale would you consider this product a bargain?
2. At what price on the scale would you consider this product to be priced so cheaply that you would question its quality?
3. At what price on the scale would you consider this product to be priced expensively?
4. At what price on the scale would you consider this product to be priced so expensively that you would not buy it?

The answers to these questions help you determine a range in which you might try to price your product. Of course, you may want to test your price. If you set it and your product doesn't sell, lowering your price may be your only option, which is usually a better position than setting your price too low and trying to raise it. Once you set someone's expectations, it's very difficult to change them.

Other techniques might involve a type of trade-off research called conjoint analysis. Essentially, you take a project with a limited number of variables, such as a car that might have a two-door and four-door option, come in three different colors (tan, black, and midnight blue), and have three different price points ($20,000, $22,000, and $24,000). The options are each pitted against each other, asking the participant to select the one item that is most important to him or her. In the end, you get a series of statistical terms that show the relative value one option has over the other. Obviously, everyone would like the best product at the best price, but that's not always possible. So this type of research tells which items—and in which combination—are most attractive to most customers.

Finally, don't forget about some of the psychological aspects of setting your prices. For example, "odd price" theory suggests that if you set your price at $19.99 or $19.95 instead of $20.00, most people will round the number down to the nearest whole number ($19), which is a dollar—not a nickel or a penny less than $20.00. You'll also find that many buyers perceive differences in price based on a percentage of the total costs instead of an actual dollar figure. For example, if one product costs $1,000 and it's on sale for 40 percent off ($600), that will be much more attractive than a 2 percent discount on a $20,000 product reduced to $19,600. It's still $400, but it doesn't feel like it.

MAXIMIZING YOUR ELECTRONIC MARKETING

The snapshot survey can help you evaluate many of the specific marketing tools you might include in your plan. Two relatively new techniques—Web sites and e-mail newsletters—are becoming more and more important marketing tools for most businesses and have been the subject of many recent snapshot surveys. These are some of the more interesting insights, perspectives, and tips I've heard from both marketers and end users of these technologies that can be easily adapted for your site or newsletters (if you aren't doing them already). These types of findings are the useful data you want your snapshot survey to generate.

Ten Ways to Improve Your Web Site's Navigation

Following are some specific recommendations from Web site usability testing studies, in which participants viewed a number of different Web sites. They were observed by researchers to see what they did while visiting the sites, as well as asked about what content, functionality, and features they liked the best—and what drove them bananas.

1. *Use "natural" pictures to make your site more visually appealing.* Most respondents thought pictures were helpful in learning about an organization, or its products and services. They especially liked virtual tours and pictures of employees, buildings, and company-related visuals. They wanted to see photographs of people doing what they might be doing naturally if they were to visit the facility. Some liked viewing shots from a live-action camera, especially if it pointed to an interesting view.

F l a s h # 2 4

The more difficult you make it to navigate your Web site, the less your customers will want to use it to answer their questions and learn more about your company. The snapshot survey is a great tool for doing "usability" testing and finding out what customers pay attention to while they are on your site. If you can watch a few of them while they are navigating your site, it will tell you volumes about how well you've organized your materials and how intuitive they find your site's organization.

2. *Make the site easy to navigate and aesthetically pleasing.* Drop-down menus, fly-out menus, and any other navigation feature that made it easy to quickly locate the kinds of information they were most interested in viewing were preferred. In general, they did not like having to click multiple times to find what they wanted to see or click backwards to return to a previous page. Other specific insights regarding navigation and design included:

- *No side-to-side scrolling to read content.* Overwhelmingly, respondents did not like scrolling sideways to read text. Therefore, all content should fit within a specific frame and not require that a bar be clicked and held to move from left to right to read content.

- *Downward scrolling is okay.* However, respondents did not seem to read these pages as intensely as they read pages that presented all the information in one view, suggesting that the ultimate design might be to include information on a single page with an advancing or "next page" feature.

- *Resizing is not automatic.* About half the participants resized their screens (to make them larger on the computer screen); others did not know how or just viewed the pages based on the default that was on the screen prior to going online. This means that half the people will fill up their entire screen to look at it, while the rest will try to read the same information in a much smaller screen. Therefore, it's important to test your pages for readability on a reduced screen size and using smaller font sizes may not be appropriate.

- *Include site maps or ways to quickly learn what is on the site.* Many respondents viewed the site maps of the Web sites to quickly find the information they wanted to see. They want to find what they are looking for quickly and not waste time clicking an endless stream of buttons to find out what they need to know.

- *Do not use pop-up screens.* Many participants did not like Web sites that had information pop up in a commercial-style format. They preferred to view only what they physically clicked.

- *Using full margins is important to some.* Some Web sites center their information in the middle of the screen with approximately one inch of white or shaded space on both sides of the content. This was annoying to some participants and seen as a waste of space. They saw little benefit to artificially constricting the output to a smaller screen size and believed readability could be improved if resized to a full page.

- *PDF files received mixed reactions.* Some sites included PDF files that had to be viewed after they were loaded in an Acrobat Reader program. While viewing these files was acceptable by some participants, others saw them as a distraction and more difficult to use than simply including the information in another html file (what the rest of the Web site text looks like).

- *Many people still use dial-up access to the Internet.* Because of this, all pictures and graphics will have to be stored in the smallest files possible. Many people complained about the speed of their home computers when visiting sites that contained numerous graphics or large files. Some even complained about the length of time it took to load pages using high-speed connection, further emphasizing the desire of participants to view pages that load quickly.

- *Include searching capabilities that produce desired results.* Many participants wanted and liked the capability to search the sites to find specific information. However, they did not want to search the site only to find an error message or no information. They wanted to receive information close to what they were seeking. Therefore, search engines need to be intuitive.

- *Use readable typefaces and font sizes.* Some participants complained that some of the sites tested in these focus groups used font sizes that were hard to read or see.

- *Segment your Web site to reflect your audience.* Several participants recommended that sites should have easy-to-find sections relevant to different customers or preferences (e.g., undergraduates versus graduate students on a college Web site). They suggested that these sections be included in the home page.

- *Avoid constantly sending visitors back to the home page.* Many participants wanted to view information related to a specific section within that section. They did not want to travel back to the home page and dig down into another section to find related information.

- *Flash intros or sections are interesting to some, but others view them as distractions.* Several participants seemed turned off by the use of flash techniques during introductions or in other sections of the Web sites. They thought that these programs slowed down their computers and did not provide a tremendous benefit or important information.

- *Keep site layouts consistent with a unified look and feel.* Several participants commented that once they were inside a site, the design and structure of the site changed dramatically when they entered a new school or program. This was a distraction to others.
- *Make the links obvious within individual sections.* Links that were hard to see or difficult to find were seen as turnoffs by some participants. They recommended that links be easy to find so that viewers could spend time reading the information, not trying to navigate the site.
- *Include a way to contact the organization on the home page.* Participants did not want to click several levels down to find an address or telephone number, when a button could be easily incorporated on the home page.
- *Include a lot of information, but do not clutter the page.* Several participants commented that some of the sites evaluated in these snapshot surveys seemed cluttered. While they wanted to find information quickly, they did not want to wade through visually tiring or difficult-to-read pages.
- *Participants prefer an overall welcoming and calming Web site design.* Overwhelmingly, they liked Web sites that use subtle colors and shades, especially blue.
- *Avoid site navigation or menu bars near the bottom of the page.* Many participants overlooked or did not like the pages that had different locations for the sectional navigation bars. They preferred them to be located on the far left section of the site.

3. *Keep all information current and accurate.* A problem several participants found with some of the Web sites evaluated was out-of-date and noncurrent information. Old price listings, inaccurate employee contact information, and listings of other items that no longer are offered were a few of the examples participants gave of problems with keeping information current.

4. *Include detailed program content, but do not let it clog up introductory pages or confuse site navigation.* Many participants wanted to view detailed content about a specific school, program, major, or class, and were frustrated when it was not provided. At the same time, they preferred to see an outline of the available information and read only the sections that were most applicable

or interesting to them. In general, they did not want to read messages from the president or other company executives, but thought some people might. Introductory messages and welcomes should be very short (one or two sentences).

5. *Include the history, mission, values, objectives, job opportunities, and other institutional perspectives, because they resonate with some participants.* A number of participants said they viewed sections within the tested Web sites that talked about the institution's history and mission. Having a perspective on where the institution came from and where it was going was appealing.

6. *Because so many company Web sites look the same, build a unique, consistent design.* Generally, participants found that most of the sites evaluated included similar content and descriptions. Many thought that the organization of the sites was essentially the same.

7. *Use linked "bread crumbs" to identify which page is being viewed.* A bread crumb tells the reader where he or she is within your Web site. If this paragraph were a Web page, it might look something like: Building a Marketing Plan That Works → Squeezing More Juice Out of Your Electronic Communications → A Dozen Ways to Improve Your Web Sites and Navigation → Use linked bread crumbs to identify which page is being viewed. Once in a specific section, links along the top of the section page that indicate "where the viewer is" were seen as helpful. These links would go from general to specific and allow viewers to click back to previous sections without clicking the "back" key on their Internet browser.

8. *Use advance links that allow viewers to skip ahead within a specific section.* If a specific section has four or five pages, include linked titles or short phrases at the bottom (or top) of the page so that viewers can move forward and skip pages (if they desire). Pages that did not contain these links or simply listed "next" were not rated as favorably.

9. *Use drop-down menus on the home page.* These were widely viewed as better than sites that did not have them. Participants believed that they could quickly and easily find the sections they wanted to view in greater detail.

10. *Avoid using large pictures or graphics.* Pictures that took up almost one-half of the screen were viewed as a waste of space. They wanted smaller or narrower photos or graphics. They preferred pages that left room for reading.

Flash #25

E-mail newsletters are quickly becoming a mainstay for many businesses, especially professional service and consulting firms. They can be an effective and economical way to reach the customers and prospects who are interested in hearing from you. But make sure you give them information and ideas that are valuable and can't be easily found from other sources. You'll find that sending a newsletter on a consistent basis is a good way to "stir the pot," but don't expect customers to call about a specific topic you wrote about. If your newsletter sparks them to call you about a problem they need your help with, then it's worth the effort. It won't bother you that they aren't reading much of what you wrote, especially when you deposit their check.

25 Tips for E-mail Newsletters

A great way to market your products and services—as well as gently remind your contacts that you are still around—is the e-mail newsletter. It can be one element of your current marketing mix, especially if it's sent to people you've met or already know. In other words, it is a true marketing tool and not spam.

It is also a terrific tool for all the groups and associations you belong to, such as professional societies, neighborhood associations, churches, and other organizations. It is an efficient and cost-effective way to reach people who care about the organization.

For the past few years, I have been exploring assorted e-mail newsletter techniques, running various snapshot surveys on the topic and taking a hard look at what seems to be working best. Certainly many styles and approaches to e-mail newsletters are available, but most follow this core set of principles:

1. *Publish the newsletter in a ".txt" file, not an "html" version.* A number of browsers cannot effectively read html code. Your newsletter might be unreadable to them. The .txt files will also load faster for your readers who have dial-up service. A recent Nielsen survey found that almost two-thirds of current Internet users in the United States use dial-up, instead of faster connections, such as DSL or cable. So build your newsletters for dial-up. It's likely to be around for a long time.

2. *Limit each line in your newsletter to 65 characters.* Because everyone has their browsers set at different font styles and sizes, 65 characters seems to be readable on most formats—and it doesn't break the sentences apart on their screens when they receive your e-mail.

3. *Include a hard return at the end of every line* (like a typewriter). This helps reduce automatic wrapping that may look fine on your computer but not on theirs.

4. *Write your newsletter in a text editor, such as Microsoft Notes, then copy and paste it into an e-mail distribution program.* I've found the Notes program deletes most of the formatting commands that are in other programs. It helps you create a true .txt file. Remember, if you're going to use bullets or numbers, you have to physically space each item and line everything up.

5. *If you are just starting, place your e-mail addresses in a separate file* (e-mail software, Word, or Notes can all serve the same purpose). Include about 50 e-mails in each user group (some Internet providers will only let you mail less than 100 e-mails at one time). When you create the e-mail, paste the names in the "blind copy" section. This will keep everyone on your list from seeing who you sent your e-mails to. Microsoft Access also can be used to store your names and merge when sending your newsletter.

6. *Once your e-mail newsletter is up and running, either buy software or use a service to distribute it each month.* You can find a lot of information on both of these methods by doing a Google search on the Web. I use a mail-merge program one of my Carnegie Mellon University MBA students developed called "Mail List Pro 4.0" at *http://www.cgiparadise.com.* It costs about $100 (at the time of this printing). Most e-mail services seem to range between $50 and $100 per month, depending on how much you use them. Whichever method you choose, make sure it allows readers to automatically change their subscriptions or unsubscribe (which is required by law).

7. *Include a summary paragraph of the newsletter near the beginning.* Assume this is all most readers will read.

8. If you have multiple articles, content, or sections, include an "In this issue" section near the top that lists the titles of the articles or previews them.

9. *Develop a standardized system of breaking sections of your newsletter* (e.g., titles in ALL CAPS, inserting a series of **,* "~", or other symbols to break the sections and highlight specific details).

10. *Include listings of upcoming events, meetings, and other topics your readers might find interesting.*

11. *After your newsletter is published, include an html version with more graphics, layout, and other features on your Web site.* Long-term, you may want to repackage and update your newsletter articles into special reports, booklets, book chapters, or other documents.

12. *Provide a way for members to refer the site to their friends and colleagues.* I have a free program that gives you an html code you can paste into your Web site. Simply include a link to that section of your site in your newsletter. The site is *http://www.re-ferme.deadlock.com/basics.html.*

13. *Provide valuable content in your newsletter and don't make it one big commercial.* The only people I know who love advertising are in marketing—and many of them don't like to listen to commercials. Everyone else wants to find ways they can be more successful. Include this valuable information in your newsletters.

14. *Present case histories or examples of how you have helped your clients.* The goal should be to "show you in action."

15. *Set standard distribution dates and adhere to them.* I distribute mine on the last day of the month. Others may be set on a specific day of the week or month.

16. *Decide on a frequency for your newsletter.* For the first year, I started out by sending one every other month. I later increased it to once a month, which seemed to work better for me. Once a quarter seems too infrequent for most audiences. Every two weeks or even once a week will be a lot of work for you. You may find it difficult to maintain this pace.

17. *Number each edition* (number, volume, season, month, etc.).

18. *Include executive summaries and other valuable information.* As appropriate, direct readers to "more information" contained on your Web site.

19. *If you are writing in text, don't forget to include the "http://" in front of your Web site and the "mailto:" in front of your e-mail address.*

20. *If you're referencing a specific file in your Web site, pay attention to the capital letters and spacing.* For example, I have a file named "Marketing Tools.htm" on my site. To access it from a .txt e-mail newsletter, I need to type it this way: *http://www.corcom-inc.com/Marketing%20Tools.htm.* Notice the %20 for a space and the capital and lowercase letters were included as the file was named.

21. *If it makes sense for you, create categories you might update or use every month.* This technique gives your newsletter sections, much like a newspaper or magazine.

22. *Develop two or three issues in advance and stay at least that far ahead.* It can be very difficult to write a good newsletter when you're swamped a day or two before you send it out. Avoid the tendency to skip an issue and get off track. I've found that assigning the research and first drafts of each e-mail newsletter to a summer intern gives him or her an excellent experience and me a head start on writing each version.

23. *Invite others to contribute to your newsletter so you don't have to write everything.* Interviews and alternative formats can also work.

24. *Give the newsletter the same priority as your other projects,* and devote sufficient staff time to produce each issue.

25. *Include a copyright on each edition and state how others can or cannot use your materials in their newsletter or other materials.*

Producing an e-mail newsletter is like any other marketing activity. It will take time, energy, and resources. But the payoff can be substantial, and once you have your format established and your distribution system debugged, the newsletters become a lot easier to manage. I'll bet you'll even have fun writing them!

FINALIZING YOUR BLUEPRINT

Writing a marketing plan is like writing everything else that's important—the only way to get it right is to rewrite your plan, test the ideas, and make them a living document. Because it's really a listing of your marketing goals and how you plan to accomplish them, it should be a document that you refer to often and keep updated. Figure 5.4 includes 40 questions I like to use to help me apply the findings from snapshot surveys, secondary research, competitor assessments, and other data I try to immerse myself in to write my first draft of a plan. Then, I ask for feedback from some trusted advisors who know the market I'm going after. Together, these tactics create a viable, realistic plan, which is always better than making things up as you go—or basing all your important decisions on only one or two opinions that may be biased.

FIGURE 5.4

Forty questions for applying the findings from snapshot surveys to develop a workable marketing plan

Current Situation

1. What are you trying to accomplish?

2. What business are you in?

3. What are your products and services?

4. What are your target markets?

5. Who are your competitors?

6. What do you do better than your competitors do?

7. What do your competitors do better than you do?

Positioning

8. What is your Unique Selling Proposition (USP) that differentiates you from your competitors?

9. Are you high quality or low price? Are you number one in service or number one in sales?

10. What is your niche? What portion of the overall market (segment) do you serve?

11. What are the benefits of your products and services?

Marketing Objectives

12. What is the purpose of your marketing?

13. Is your goal to inform, persuade, or motivate?

14. Do you want more market share, increased sales, or a specific closing ratio?

15. How do you establish prices?

16. How does location affect your business?

17. What are your marketing goals for the next one to three years?

18. What are your sales and profit goals?

19. What might keep you from reaching these goals?

Marketing Strategies

20. How will you reach your marketing objectives?

21. What overall method or approach will you use?

FIGURE 5.4 *(Continued)*

Target Audiences

22. Who are your target audiences?

23. What size prospect or customer is best for your business?

24. Where are you likely to find prospects who are similar to your best customers?

Key Messages

25. What do you want to tell your target audience?

26. What is the main idea you would like your target audience to know about your company and its products and services?

27. If your customers could repeat one idea back to you, what would you want them to say?

Tactics

28. What combination of tactics will you use to accomplish your objectives?

29. Which tactics do your customers and prospects respond the best to?

30. What are your best low-cost, high-payoff tactics that you should keep using?

Timing

31. What is the timing for your program?

32. Which elements will you work on first?

33. Which elements are one-shot activities and which are ongoing?

Budget

34. How much money do you have to spend?

35. What percentage of your total revenue is your marketing budget?

36. How have you divided your marketing budget for different functions, including advertising, public relations (article placements, product announcements, etc.), and marketing communications (sales literature, direct mail, trade shows, etc.)?

37. What will it cost you if you don't market your company or don't market it adequately?

Measuring Marketing ROI

38. What did your marketing accomplish?

39. Which results can be tracked back to your marketing efforts?

40. Which marketing tactics generated the best results in terms of contacts, appointments, demonstrations, number of sales, and overall sales volume?

6

WHAT SHOULD WE CALL IT?

Picking the Right Name for Your Organization, Products, and Services

Names are not always what they seem.
The common Welsh name BZJXXLLWCP is pronounced Jackson.

Mark Twain

If you were trying to sell property in a run-down section of town, calling it a "ghetto" wouldn't generate many sales. This word has so much negative baggage that it would be virtually impossible to overcome the stigma and image associated with it. You would have better luck if you said your property was located in a "redevelopment zone" and gave examples of how buying property here is a chance to get a great deal and beat everyone else to the next big wave of development. The term *redevelopment zone* evokes a more neutral and perhaps even positive perspective—something you need desperately as you market and sell your products and services.

The problem is that it's rarely clear-cut which name is the best for your company, products, or services. Some differences are so slight it's hard to tell which one is best and will work well over the long haul. What makes sense to you today may not work for your customers and prospects tomorrow. The power of your name will likely change as competitors offer similar products (or you find out about ones they already have), you learn similar names used for products in other industries, and you expand into international markets with non-English-speaking customers, translations, or words that sound similar between languages but have dramatically different meanings.

The snapshot survey is a good tool for testing how customers and prospects are likely to react to the names you are considering, before you invest in expensive labeling, packaging, advertising, printing, and branding. A good name should be:

- Easy to say.
- Easy to understand when it's said aloud (e.g., over the phone).
- Easy to spell.
- Memorable.
- As short as possible, in both total number of words and length of syllables.
- Unique. You can trademark it, register it as a company name, and secure the Internet domain name.
- Marketable. It works in your literature and with your existing companies, products, or services.
- Able to outlast fads, market changes, and fickle buying behavior. You can change your logo and your graphic identity, but changing your name is more difficult, so it's important to pick the right one when you're starting out.
- Acceptable in other cultures and languages, especially if you plan to operate your company or sell your products and services internationally.

For many businesses and products, logos and taglines (short descriptive phrases about your company) are also an integral part of the naming package and should be considered as you are exploring possible names. Logos are a visual representation of the company and should evoke specific attitudes and feelings with your customers and prospects. Taglines work in a similar way. Both should be obvious and easy to understand with a quick glance. The problem is that too many logos are complicated and don't mean anything to your target audience. If you have to explain what your logo (or any parts of it) means, it isn't working and you should throw it out and start over. Just like with the names you are selecting, your logos and taglines should be simple and precise and not require extra effort to define them.

You'll also want to make sure that your logo and tagline works in different sizes and is clear when it's printed in black and white. Can it be effectively shrunk and still be visually clear? What does it look like when it's faxed? Using these simple tests can help you avoid big headaches later on.

If you're tough-minded on your names, logos, and taglines before you get too far into the process, then you can run a snapshot survey that'll give you the extra confidence you need to move forward. There's no benefit to being paralyzed because you're having trouble picking the right name or are constantly wondering if you have the right name. The snapshot survey clears up all these questions quickly and efficiently, so you don't regret your decisions in the months and years to come.

C a s e H i s t o r y

Vocelli Pizza or Pizza Outlet: How the Right Name Can Lead to Growth

In which delivery pizza store could you get better pizza: "Vocelli Pizza" or "Pizza Outlet"? Believe it or not, there's no difference in the product. Pizza Outlet, a franchise started by president and CEO Varol Ablak, grew nicely from one store located in Pittsburgh, Pennsylvania, to more than 75 stores, where it became a Pittsburgh tradition. It built a solid reputation as using high-quality ingredients to produce a great-tasting pizza.

The problem was that Varol wasn't convinced the name would work in the new markets he was considering entering, where there were already a number of well-established national and local brands. With the name Pizza Outlet, he was worried that people might think his pizza was made from cheap ingredients and was low priced; neither was true about the product. Years before, when he was first starting the business, Pizza Outlet was one of the few names available and it made sense for what he was trying to do at the time.

He asked me to take a look at the name Pizza Outlet and test it with consumers who regularly order delivery pizza in some of these new markets. I recommended a telephone survey of consumers living near his proposed store locations. This allowed us to not only test his name, but to learn more about specific competitors and what consumers thought of their pizzas.

The consumer feedback was negative. Many thought that the pizza sounded low class and they weren't even willing to try it—based on the name alone! The snapshot survey confirmed Varol's suspicion that he would have to change the name to have a fighting chance in these new markets. But this wasn't his only problem. He also had to decide if he should use two names or one, and change the names of the Pittsburgh stores as well, where he spent years and a fortune building up brand equity in the company name.

Of course, he decided to eventually change the name, redesign his overall look and marketing effort, and promote the change aggressively with franchises and consumers. He's also now opening up new stores faster than ever in Florida, Washington, D.C., Virginia, and other locations.

Interestingly, Vocelli gave Varol a new opportunity that was never possible with Pizza Outlet. Because the store now sounded more Italian, he could use this theme in his marketing efforts and, at the printing of this book, is focused on making the entire customer experience feel more Italian, such as using ads that feature a grandmother cooking a homemade pizza and having her son, dressed in a gondolier shirt, ferry the pizza across the canal to your house. When you order, you get good pizza and a little bit of Italy delivered to your doorstep.

THE POWER OF NAMING

The right name provides many benefits for your company and products. It's important to choose a name that:

- *Makes customer and prospect education easier.* When you have the right name, people get what you do and it makes sense to them right away. If your name has nothing to do with what you're offering them, consumers need to work harder to understand why you or your products might be relevant to them. A lot of successful companies have grown past their original business focus and entered new industries, making their names less relevant than when they initially started their organization.
- *Allows you to charge a premium for your products that you might not otherwise get.* Names that sound valuable usually command a premium. "Express" mail sounds more expensive than "Priority," which of course it is. While the service features are different (overnight versus two- to three-day delivery), there is also a corresponding difference between the names.

- *Helps you connect with your customers and prospects on an emotional level.* Is it hard for you to get excited about this product: Whole-grain oats (includes the oat bran), marshmallows (sugar, modified corn syrup, dextrose, gelatin, calcium carbonate, artificial flavor, yellows 5 and 6, red 40, blue 1), sugar, corn syrup, wheat starch, salt, calcium carbonate, color added, trisodium, phosphate, zinc and iron (mineral nutrients), vitamin C (sodium ascorbate). . . ? Is it easier for you to get excited about Lucky Charms, because they are "magically delicious"? When you look at the box, you see a leprechaun and a brightly colored rainbow leading to a pot of cereal (not gold). These visuals help complete the image.

- *Helps you organize your product and service offerings into families or similar category names so it's easy to figure out what goes with what.* These might include anything from a company name, product name, feature name, model number, and other identifiers. BMW names many of its vehicles using this strategy, with the three, five, and seven series cars. A 325i is a smaller car (and engine) than the 740i.

- *Can indicate the production date, model number, or other product information for service information and posterity.* Gretsch Guitars, for example, uses a numbering system that corresponds to the year the instruments were made, which is very helpful in dating them and determining their value.

- *Can be linked to other brands that have strong, positive connotations with your target market.* Gretsch Guitars named several of their models after the famous country-and-western guitar player Chet Atkins. It's a strategy that many manufacturers continue to use today, attempting to link the positive attributes of one musician with their instruments when they are presented to consumers.

- *Can help you build bonds more quickly by using names and words your prospect is familiar with.* Simply listening to the words your prospects use to describe their problems, then using those names to describe your product or service solutions, can give you a big advantage. When I write my proposals, I make sure I use as many of their words as I can. People typically want something they can easily understand and identify with. When I try to use too many of my words and terms, I generally end up confusing them and losing the business.

CHOOSING A NAME YOU CAN LIVE WITH

Picking a name for a company or product is a lot like naming a child. Many parents choose several names, narrow them down to a handful, think about them, ask others what they think, then end up with the one they think is best—then periodically wonder if they made the right decision. Many children end up with names of family members and loved ones, a similar strategy used to name products from the same family. When they get older in life, their friends and family give them nicknames, and when they get into and out of legal relationships, they change or modify their names again.

Steps for Selecting Names and Taglines

Figure 6.1 lists the key steps for creating and testing a name that works for your company, products, or services. Before you begin, it's important to set some overall criteria and parameters for your name. What attitude or feeling do you want your customers and prospects to have when they hear your name? Getting as clear as you can about what you'd like to accomplish makes the entire naming process easier.

Your next task is to create some names that you can test. Some companies like to create a handful of names, while others take a look at several dozen, using brainstorming, contests, and other techniques to generate the initial group that a team later reviews in detail. It's usually easier to pick the best of the alternatives than start with only one or two, then keep repeating this process as you find out your names are already taken by someone else or they don't work for some other reason.

Once you hone your choices down to a handful you like the best, it's time to do some preliminary database searching. Try a general Internet search using Google, Yahoo, or any other favorite search engine to see

FIGURE 6.1

Steps for creating a name that is unique, marketable, and effective for your target audience

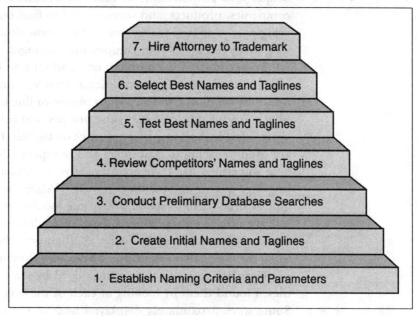

7. Hire Attorney to Trademark

6. Select Best Names and Taglines

5. Test Best Names and Taglines

4. Review Competitors' Names and Taglines

3. Conduct Preliminary Database Searches

2. Create Initial Names and Taglines

1. Establish Naming Criteria and Parameters

how the name is being used and by whom. These results will help you find the general ways your name might be used. Next, you'll want to see if you can get the site registered as a home page (I personally like www.GoDaddy.com, because it is reasonably priced. You will also want to contact your state government to find out if anyone is already using the name, which you will have to eventually register to get a checking account and operate. Finally, the U.S. Patent and Trademark Office (*http://www.uspto.gov*) has a good search engine that gives you several options for searching for specific terms and names. If you're planning to trademark one of your names or logos, the "™" is the designation for documents that have not yet been registered, but which you are planning to do. Once it's officially registered, the ™ should be changed to an "®," but not before. I learned the difference between these two designations while pitching a survey to a law firm. The firm asked me if my product name was registered, which I thought it was at the time. Apparently, it was not. It cost me the business because in the firm's field it cared more deeply about the appropriate designations at the time than I did. A good trademark attorney will keep you out of a similar situation.

After you finish your preliminary searching, you'll want to take a deeper look at what some of your competitors are saying about their companies, products, and services—not to find out if they are already using your proposed names, but to learn how closely what you're planning to say resembles your competitors' messages.

Sometimes your company or product name and logo are not enough to adequately communicate what you do and how you do it best. One solution is to add a short phrase or line to say in one sentence what you want your customers and prospects to remember. Many of my clients start by building these phrases or taglines based on things they are used to saying to customers and prospects. For example, I often hear something like, "We are innovative solutions providers" or "Cutting-edge quality and customer service." While these are a great start, I quickly urge them to spend some time looking at what their competitors are already saying, because they shouldn't spend a lot of energy just to sound like everyone else. After all, their goal should be to say something that helps them stand apart from who they are competing with.

Here are some of the taglines used by leading printing companies. I found them by looking at each of these companies' Web sites. Some were proximately displayed next to the company name and logo, while others were listed at the bottom of the page or in some other location, but they clearly were meant to be descriptors of what the companies did. Notice how the phrases can be grouped into the same type of categories and how several of them sound very similar to one another, perhaps one reason why this industry is facing such steep competition and price pressure.

- Solutions (provide printing and other solutions):
  - Balmar solutions in print. (Balmar)
  - Single source, multiple solutions. (Banta Corporation)
  - Many solutions, one company. (Ikon)
  - Innovative Ideas. Intelligent Solutions. (NCS Pearson, Inc.)
  - Integrated Print Solutions. We Prepare. We Produce. We Deliver. (RR Donnelley)
- Customer service (describe quality of service):
  - Exceeding customer expectations. (Pitney Bowes Government Solutions)
  - There's really only one hard and fast rule here: The work gets done. On time. Within budget. To the highest standards. (Digital Ink)

F *l a s h* **# 3 3**

Before you fall in love with your name, tagline, or logo, spend a few minutes checking out your competitors' Web sites and read what they are saying about themselves. You may be surprised to find out that they are already using what you thought was an ingenious burst of inspiration on your part.

- Total Focus on Customer Service and Technical Superiority. (Systems Integration Group)
- We make great impressions. (Phillips Brothers Printers)
- Document engineering to improve customer communications. (Prinova, Inc.)
- Company-related (descriptions that describe a specific company or an attribute of that company):
  - Publication, Catalog, and Book Printing Specialists. (Fry Communications, Inc.)
  - Printers for the packaging and pharmaceutical industry. (Lucas-Insertco Pharmaceutical Printing Company)
- Unique attributes (a specific attribute highlighted over all others);
  - Performance Driven. (D.B. Hess Company)
  - One Company. One Focus. (Quebecor World)
  - Uncover Hidden Opportunities. (Xerox Global Services)

Once you have a better understanding of what your competitors are saying about themselves and their products, you have the initial insight to help you develop a tagline that is unique to your company.

When you have a handful of names you think will work the best, it's time to get some feedback from customers, prospects, and other target audience members. The snapshot survey is an excellent tool for these kinds of tests, because you can simply list the names you've thought of and ask people what they think of each one. If you're planning to show logo designs or other visuals, you may want to conduct focus groups, intercept interviews, or e-mail surveys where people can visually see what you're talking about. I've used some mail surveys to test logos, but it works much better when you use color printing or mail or e-mail the logos and other artwork to the person you want to interview by phone so you can ask them a series of follow-up questions.

After you've tested your names, one should be the "winner"—in most cases, the name that is liked the best by most respondents. In the unlikely event that you have a tie, test the two winners a few more times and see if anyone likes one over the other.

Finally, after you've arrived at a name, and a tagline, and even a logo you think works well, consider having a trademark attorney file your paperwork and help you register everything. Nike wasn't worth much the first day it was used on a running shoe, but it is today.

Six Ways to Generate Names

You can use many strategies to create names for your company, products, and services. Let's take a look at six interesting approaches you might use to create the names you need:

1. Syllable rearranging. Microsoft is a terrific example of this type of name. "Micro" from microcomputer and "soft" from "software." This is the same strategy I used for my company name, CorCom, Inc. "Cor" was the first syllable of my last name (Corder) and "Com" the first syllable of "Communications." I didn't like the name Corder Communications, because it was limiting on both fronts. It sounded small and I wanted to be able to offer more than simply communications services. CorCom was a compromise from CordCom, which I used for a couple of years when I was first starting the business, which several people eventually told me was too hard to say. Everyone said they loved my name when the Internet was hot and they thought we were doing something with technology, something I would have never predicted when I first selected the name. It became a little rough when the tech bubble burst and any name that included "com" became a bit of a liability. Fortunately, I registered CorCom early on as a fictitious name in Pennsylvania and this protected my use of it over the years. There are a number of other Corcoms across the United States in several industries, something frustrating that many companies have to live with.

One of the best ways to use this technique is to list several names that are popular in your industry or that define features and benefits of your product. Then list the syllables of each of these words on index cards. Start rearranging the cards to form new words. Figure 6.2 shows an example of how this might be done with four words that could be used to describe the technology consulting industry (solution, consulting, technology, and innovation) and some of the new words that could be created.

FIGURE 6.2

Name creation using a syllable rearrangement strategy that simply takes parts of words and meshes them together to form new ones

Industry Words	Syllable	Possible Combinations
Solution	So-lu-tion	TechCon
Consulting	Con-sult-ing	ConTech
Technology	Tech-nol-ogy	ConSol
Innovation	In-no-va-tion	Consolution
		InnoTech
		Sovation
		SoCon

2. Proper names. J.C.Penney's, Sears, and thousands of other companies are named for their founders, which is still a good strategy for many firms. By adding descriptive phrases at the end, such as "and associates," "and company," or "enterprises," they can indicate that they are larger than one person, or by adding even strong words like "worldwide" or "international," they can project a global image. Oklahoma City's airport is called the Will Rogers World Airport, but for years they didn't have international flights. I like how they still wanted to project an image as a major airport and included "world" instead of "international."

3. Natural names. Sometimes, names just make sense for what they are or where they are located. Look in any major city telephone directory and you'll find a lot of different company names that begin with the city or local area names, because they make sense within the local community and sometimes work in the broader market after extensive publicity (New York Stock Exchange or San Diego Zoo).

4. Letters and numbers. Many technical products include some combination of words, letters, or numbers instead of entire words or phrases. There are pluses and minuses to this approach. On the plus side, it's typically easier to create a unique name than using entire words. The major problem with this approach is that the lettering or numbering system can become so complicated that it loses its meaning. For example, if you have an X-2500 model, you might expect that the X-3500 would be bigger or faster, but this isn't always the case.

To find out more about this technique, I ran my own snapshot survey with engineers, purchasing agents, trade editors, and other professionals on how they name large engines, such as those used for jets, gas turbines (for power plants), and others. Here's what some of the respondents had to say:

- "Most of the [gas-turbine engines] we make here are named AE and they slap some numbers on the end. Our most popular are probably the AE3007 and the AE2100. AE stands for Allison Engine. At the Rolls plant in Bristol, they name their engines similarly. Their most popular engine is the RB211. The RB stands for Rolls Bristol, and then they put a number at the end." (Aeronautical engineer, Allison Engines)
- "All of our products start with DR then a number. The DR clearly means Dresser-Rand. I am not sure what the numbers mean. Many companies use their name in front of the product code." (Engineer, Dresser-Rand Service Company)
- "Exxon uses different types of equipment for different jobs. We used a turbine on the last site I was on, but on this one we are using a pneumatic pump. I don't know where these things get their names. The one I am using right now is the Short AP-4. I actually know what that means. The pump is either long or short, AP means 'auto pump,' and 4 is the size. With the gas turbines, the names are different." (Environmental engineer, Exxon)
- "When we buy a power generation turbine, we care about who makes it and how much power it produces. GE and Westinghouse are all good names. We're not paying attention to the product name. I think the name depends upon the audience you're selling to. Products with numbers and letters are good for engineers and scientists. Ultimately, we sell to consumers. It might be interesting to explore whether a turbine name could be used in our marketing efforts. It could be a way we could stand out from competitors, especially given the changes occurring in our industry." (Supply chain/purchasing manager, Western Resources)
- "We don't put a lot of effort into our naming. By 'we,' I don't just mean the company I mean the industry in general. If you look at any other manufacturer, no one uses creative names." (Marketing professional, Allison Engines)

5. Animals, stars, and other inanimate objects. Many companies attempt to use the attributes from living or inanimate objects to name their products. The Mustang, a wild horse, makes sense for a sports car, because it's wild and fast. I doubt there will ever be a serious car named the "Turtle"—who wants to go that slow?

F *l a s h* **# 3 4**

Nothing beats running your names, taglines, and logos past a few current and prospective customers. They have experiences and insights that you don't—and will be able to help you pick something that makes sense to them, which is what you should be going for in the first place.

Solar systems and galaxies make good product names in some industries. For example, Caterpillar makes large-scale-engine product lines called Saturn®, Centaur®, Taurus®, Mars®, and Titan™. These go together because they are focused on objects or ideas found in outer space.

6. Simplified names. Sometimes a name just doesn't mean anything to your target audience, because they don't understand it or it uses technical language that has no meaning to them. This was the case with a community hospital who posted a sign called, "Ambulatory Surgery." After one of the hospital administrators found out that patients were asking if this is where they parked the ambulance before taking a patient into surgery, they changed it to something more direct: Same Day Surgery Center.

C a s e **H** *i s t o r y*

Testing New Names for a Technology Company

A leading producer of semiconductors wanted to rename its company, but wasn't sure which name would work best with its customers and prospects. So I put together a simple snapshot survey that was used to talk with 50 respondents.

The company provided a list of about a dozen names, such as Analog Devices, Fairchild, Infineon, International Rectifier, National Semiconductor, Maxim, Precision Monlithics, and Rockwell, which were presented in random order before asking these questions during telephone interviews:

1. Overall, what do you think of this name? (PROBE. RECORD VERBATIM RESPONSE.)

2. In general, would you say your opinion of this name is very positive (5), somewhat positive (4), neither positive nor negative (3), somewhat negative (2), or very negative (1)? (MARK ONE.)

3. Does this name sound like a company who would offer cutting-edge, high-technology products? (MARK ONE.)
   ☐ Yes
   ☐ No

4. If you were to personify this name, what famous person or type of person would this company be? (PROBE. RECORD VERBATIM RESPONSE.)

The results produced some very interesting insights, especially question 4 that asked respondents to personify the name. Customers and prospects thought that names didn't sound high-tech enough, while others sounded very close to existing companies.

REGIONAL MARKETING: NAMING AND LOGO TESTING FOR PITTSBURGH

If you haven't visited Pittsburgh recently, you may have an image—as most people do—of a dirty, rusty, run-down steel town. Visitors are often shocked at how much this city's landscape has changed, even in the past five years. We have new baseball and football stadiums, a new state-of-the-art convention center, not to mention several new hotels and office buildings. Even more important, perhaps, the steel mills have been torn down and new shopping centers, office parks, and residential communities have gone up in their place. It even seems like the sun comes out more than it used to.

A great honor in my life has been to participate in many of the positive changes that have occurred in Pittsburgh over the past several years by conducting research on many of the key projects that have helped reshape the city. These changes are very similar to what has occurred in other major cities and serve as a good example of how naming, taglines, and logos should be developed with a broader perspective than what might make sense for a single company or industry. When you market a region, it involves a number of complicated and connected entities that need to agree on doing a limited number of activities together that will benefit everyone. Consider these examples:

Building a Baseball-only Ballpark for the Pittsburgh Pirates

The Pittsburgh Pirates wanted a baseball-only ballpark so they didn't have to share a facility called Three Rivers Stadium with the Pittsburgh Steelers, the city's professional football team. To build this new facility, the Pirates would need taxpayer dollars.

I first worked on this project for community leaders who wanted to know how hard they should work to keep the Pirates from leaving Pittsburgh, something the Pirates said they would do if they didn't get a new ballpark. The research results convinced them to be the champions of this project and find a way to build the Pirates a new facility.

Following this, the Pirates repeated similar surveys conducted in other cities for major-league sports teams to see how Pittsburgh's residents compared to residents from those towns. In study after study, we found that the Pirates were less revered than the Steelers or Penguins (hockey). In other words, people liked the Steelers and the Penguins more than the Pirates and it was going to be a tough—next to impossible—sell to get them to build a new baseball stadium.

After struggling and thinking about how to sell this concept, I (along with the help of three of my colleagues) created something that was later called a "Regional Renaissance" strategy. Instead of building a baseball-only ballpark, I argued that it was important to fix up the entire city and build a new facility for the Steelers (Heinz Field) and a new convention center and revamp the arts district. I argued that the only way to do this was to "raise the water" so we could "float all boats."

Because all these facilities needed to be built, it was only natural that the Pirates' structure be built first. Interestingly, initial voter referendums that asked if the Commonwealth of Pennsylvania should use taxpayer money to fund the stadium were defeated, but the Pirates and other leaders pressed on to eventually build a new ballpark for the Pirates.

How the Pittsburgh Pirates Used Feedback from Young Fans to Build a Winning Logo and Uniforms

Professional sports teams change their logos and uniforms from time to time to generate new interest, signify a change in management, and reinvigorate their sales. In the mid-1990s, this is what the Pittsburgh Pirates decided to do, only with a slight twist. Instead of simply having management select one of the many logo alternatives provided

FIGURE 6.3

The Pittsburgh Pirates logo based on the individual elements most liked by young baseball fans who participated in focus groups to test the designs and new uniforms

by the major-league baseball association, they decided to ask elementary, middle school, and high school students what they liked and didn't like about the logos and uniforms they were considering. Sports-related clothing is an important part of most kids' wardrobes, even if they have to ask their parents to buy it for them.

I organized six focus groups over three nights, two each with elementary school, middle school, and high school students. The meetings were held in a conference room at the Pirates' offices. As an incentive and thank-you for participating, each participant was given four tickets to a game and received an autograph from the team's mascot, the Pittsburgh Parrot.

Figure 6.3 contains the current Pirates logo that was designed based on specific feedback from the students, all of which the Pirates followed to the letter. For example, the lettering was the favorite of several alternatives and they liked the "cross bats" behind his head and the eye patch. In the colored version, students liked the red polka-dot scarf instead of the white. An earring was okay, but the original scraggly beard was not. The students wanted to see the pirate's beard trimmed up a bit and they thought he should look a little meaner than in the first set of logos (so the redesign included a slight growling look on the Pirate's mouth). Other logos, such as a skull with an eye patch, were tested, but it scared the younger children. So it was offered as an alternative logo that could be purchased in some specialty shops.

The Pirates also tested several different color jerseys. My favorite part of these focus groups was watching the kids become very excited over the black jersey. It was obvious from their body language that they

> **F** *l a s h* **# 3 5**
>
> If you're going to test visuals like your logo or the typeface used in your tagline, you'll need to show them to your target audience. Remember, a lot more options are available than simply running a focus group. Try e-mailing them, posting them on your Web site, mailing them, or showing them in a face-to-face meeting. You won't need a lot of feedback. Typically, 10 to 20 responses are enough to find a "winner." Plus, you may be surprised at how honored some customers are to be asked for their suggestions on how you can grow your business.

liked them. In every group, however, after they were finished nonverbally telling me how much they liked what they saw, someone would raise his or her hand and say he or she didn't like the jersey. When I asked why, the child said because black is a dark color and in the sunlight, it will make the players hot. If the players are hot, they won't play well.

When the merchandise sales were tallied after the first year of sales of the new logo, the Pirates led all major-league baseball teams. Quite a testament to testing logo designs.

Naming PNC Park

PNC Bank, one of the nation's leading banks, wanted to be sure that spending $30 million dollars for the naming rights to a baseball stadium would sit well with its customers. The bank was convinced that the marketing benefit would be there, given the extensive exposure the bank would receive through television, print, radio, and promotions within the ballpark.

To help determine the potential reaction from its customers, I ran a snapshot survey that asked a number of questions about the awareness of the new facility. The five questions that pertained directly to naming the ballpark included:

1. Overall, would you say that you favor or oppose PNC Bank sponsoring and paying for part of the building of this new baseball-only ballpark? Why?
2. Why do you think PNC Bank purchased the naming rights of the new ballpark?

3. How much do you like the name of the new baseball facility—
PNC Park? Would you say you like the name a lot, somewhat, or
not at all? Why?

4. Does the financial support and naming of the new ballpark
change your opinion of PNC Bank?

5. (If Yes:) Would you say that your opinion of PNC Bank has improved, stayed about the same, or become worse? Why?

Overall, customers favored PNC Bank naming the ballpark and
thought it was a good business decision and a good way to support the
local community, a pleasant surprise given how much controversy sur-
rounded using tax dollars to build new facilities.

Naming Three Rivers Park

PNC Park and Heinz Field are located near each other along the
rivers in downtown Pittsburgh. This land, along with other riverfronts
of the Allegheny, Mongehela, and Ohio have been developed into attractive parks, walking and recreation areas, and a popular outdoor performance area in Point State Park. An organization called the Riverlife
Task Force, who did not own the land but was a consortium of interested parties, wanted to name the first 50 feet of shoreline and continue
to encourage development of an attractive place for residents and visitors to view the city. The idea was to name the area as a park and use it
to help promote Pittsburgh's transformed image.

Several names, such as Confluence Park, Golden Triangle Park,
and others were tested, but Three Rivers Park was liked by an over-
whelming number of consumers, because it made sense to them and
was near where the Three Rivers Stadium was located. The other
names just didn't stack up.

Fighting Pittsburgh's "Brain Drain"

Another regional problem, tangled up with the name and image of
Pittsburgh, is the fact that so many young people are born or study in
Pittsburgh, but don't choose it as a place to live. Instead, they move to
other cities where they can find jobs and what they think will be a better quality of life.

This is a particularly difficult problem for businesses trying to re-
cruit professional talent, such as technology firms. If there are no work-

ers—or not the right mix of talent—then there is no corporate growth. It's also a topic I've worked on through dozens of surveys for the Commonwealth of Pennsylvania, because affordable labor talent is a key decision factor for many businesses who are contemplating staying or moving to a specific region.

What I've always wondered was if Pittsburgh's image as a city was really what was driving students away. We are told the city does not offer the right nightclubs, nightlife, or other things for young people to do. We aren't focused on young people. The list goes on and on.

While these ideas may sound plausible, they are not based on any real data. They're simply theories that have been played up in the media and have grown in credibility over time. So, as part of a University of Pittsburgh class project, I had students survey nearly 600 undergraduates from various local schools to find out why they are leaving western Pennsylvania. It turns out they are exiting because of a lack of internships and jobs, not because they can't find anything to do. Here are some of the key findings from this study:

I. *In terms of quality-of-life issues, most students see a lot of positives in Pittsburgh.* Students were asked to rate ten quality-of-life issues. Here is the percentage who rated each item as "good" or "very good":
    - Sporting events (84%)
    - Entertainment (movies, shopping, etc.) (77%)
    - Restaurants (77%)
    - Cultural opportunities (museums, symphony, etc.) (75%)
    - Nightlife (social scene, bars, clubs, etc.) (61%)
    - Public transportation (56%)
    - Tourist attractions (48%)
    - Cost of living (44%)
    - Safety (36%)
    - Cleanliness of streets and neighborhoods (26%)

II. *Students are not optimistic about finding jobs in Pittsburgh.* While about one-third did not know enough about the local job market to comment, most thought it was inadequate. Using the same "good" or "very good" scale, here's the percentage rating each job attribute:
    - Number of available jobs (25%)
    - Quality of available jobs (19%)
    - Ease of finding good jobs (18%)
    - Opportunities for promotion and advancement (18%)
    - Starting salaries (16%)

III. *Those planning to stay in Pittsburgh rate it higher than do those who are planning to leave.* Not a big surprise here. Only 18 percent of those students surveyed are planning to remain in Pittsburgh. Almost half (47 percent) are planning to leave. However, 35 percent are undecided at the moment. This is the group we have to reach out to if we want to keep more young professionals in this region.

IV. *Native and nonnative Pittsburghers have roughly the same opinion of the city.* This is a surprise. When comparing the differences between students originally from Pittsburgh versus other regions, there's little difference.

What does all this mean? I think these findings go a long way in proving that college students aren't leaving Pittsburgh because of the city's image. Instead, they are looking for internships and jobs. Without employment opportunities, there is little chance that they will stay. The time seems right for building stronger bridges between our academic institutions, graduates, and local businesses. The more each group learns about the other, the greater the opportunities will be for all businesses in the region. This way, more graduates will stay in Pittsburgh.

There's no doubt that names are vitally important—so important that it's worth investing some time and energy into getting them right the first time. In the examples listed in this chapter and in dozens of others just like them, the snapshot survey pays big dividends when it's used to name products, services, locations, and ideas.

Part Three

ADVANCED APPLICATIONS

7

GETTING NEWS COVERAGE

How to Identify Trends, Insights, and Survey
Results That the Media Want to Publish

A *public-opinion poll is no substitute for thought.*

Warren Buffett

T here are only two ways to reach your customers and prospects through the media: either you pay for it (advertising) or you earn it (public relations). With advertising, you control the message. You decide what to say, where to say it, and how often to say it. Of course, there are limits to what you can say or show in your ads. The information must be truthful, and follow current Federal Communications Commission (FCC) regulations, as well as the guidelines of the publication. Some higher-end publications, for example, won't allow ads that appear to be low budget or are of questionable moral character.

This is a great marketing technique that makes sense for a lot of businesses, but it can be very expensive to sustain long-term, which is usually the length of time needed to raise the visibility of your company, products, and services.

Public relations—or articles and stories that you write, you are quoted in, or both—can also be excellent ways to promote your business. Earned media is often called "free advertising" although it really isn't, because it takes effort and money (especially if you're using a public relations agency or professional to help you). The great thing about public relations is that when your article appears, it is blanketed in the credibility of the publication. The better the publication, the higher

> **F** *l a s h* **# 3 6**
>
> Most companies don't have any news that's worth publishing. The media would rather see you buy the space, rather than use it to cover your story. That's why it's so difficult to get extensive, positive media coverage.

your story's credibility, and the better you look. The downside is that you can't control what a reporter or editor will actually write. It's their publication, after all. That's why it's referred to as "earned."

The reason most companies don't receive the positive earned media coverage they like is because they just don't offer any real news, nothing that an editor wants to print. The publisher would rather you purchase advertising space instead. When you do come up with news, most of it ends up in event calendars, in new product listings (which can be very helpful to some businesses), or in other sections of the publication that do not get read or listened to as heavily as the feature stories, which is where you really want your story to appear.

CREATING NEWS WITH THE SNAPSHOT SURVEY

One way you can dramatically improve your chances of getting a news story printed or reported about your company is to conduct a specific type of snapshot survey I like to call the publicity survey.

The secret to publicity surveys is that they are not about specific products, but about human behavior—how people act when they have a cold, what happens around the family dinner table today, how many safety experts actually understand government regulations. By providing the media with survey information their readers will find interesting, you will receive coverage more easily than by trying to pitch other stories. Publicity surveys can study consumers in general or focus on a specific industry or unique technical field that only readers of a specific trade publication would be interested in. The articles or stories are mostly about the survey results and what they mean but can easily include quotes and marketing messages related to your products or services. Instead of publishing an article that's all about you and your products, provide an interesting story about trends you discovered through survey results that include mentions of your products or services. It's a more subtle approach—and a lot of editors like it.

When I say generate media coverage, I'm talking about one consumer survey that produced 200 to 300 media placements (articles about the survey results appearing in different newspapers, magazines, radio shows, and TV programs), while a typical news story might receive only a handful of placements. With business-to-business publicity surveys, placements may be in two, three, or more trade journal articles and in several trade show presentations—something that just doesn't happen with other types of stories.

Since I first started using this publicity survey technique more than a decade ago and explored ways of improving it, the concept has grown in popularity. In fact, today so many of these surveys exist that it's difficult to pick up a newspaper or magazine and not find one or two stories that include survey results.

Following are just a few of the different kinds of public surveys I've conducted recently for a range of consumer and business-to-business clients:

- *Hamburger Lovers Survey.* Do you enjoy your hamburgers so much that it would be hard to live without them, because they are one of your favorite foods? This is what a leading fast food chain wanted to find out. How do people prepare them? What are their favorite toppings? What's the most popular cheese? What are the best side dishes for them? These and other questions were asked of a national sample of more than 300 consumers, which described dining, picnicking, and other hamburger-eating trends. The results from this survey appeared in hundreds of media outlets. Of course, the fast food chain serves hamburgers and was exceptionally qualified to sponsor a survey on this topic.
- *Heinz Boston Market Frozen Foods.* When Heinz launched Boston Market Frozen Foods—the same type of foods you could purchase at a Boston Market only distributed through grocery stores—a publicity survey that described how today's consumers use their kitchens and how more and more people are buying restaurant-quality appliances was used to articulate this trend. Kitchens have become the living rooms in many homes. Families hang out in them and use them differently today than they did in previous generations. Defining this trend helped Heinz generate publicity that supported the launch of this product line.
- *Coldtime Survey.* How many times do people blow their noses when they have a cold? How do they take care of themselves when they have a cold? Questions like these were used to pro-

mote a leading cold pill. The results helped generate news coverage about the product that it never would have received without a survey.

- *Grin-and-Bear-It Survey.* As part of the product launch for a whitening toothpaste brand, consumer and dentist surveys that asked about oral hygiene were undertaken. The campaign results helped drive media coverage for what is currently the number one whitening toothpaste. Who has whiter teeth: David Letterman or Jay Leno? Are people with whiter teeth better lovers than those who have yellow teeth? These questions may seem a bit silly, but they create an interesting story that editors of consumer publications want to publish.

- Quiz Show *Survey.* When director Robert Redford was making *Quiz Show,* a movie about a rigged 1950s game show, executives from one of the companies that sponsored the original show were worried that the production might damage their brand image. They feared that people might think negatively of today's product because it was a major sponsor of this rigged show years ago. Instead of fighting a legal battle, we encouraged them to "get on the media bandwagon" by running a consumer publicity survey that compared the oldtime shows with today's shows. Which shows had better prizes: Those from the 1950s or from today? Who's more attractive: Alex Trebek or Bob Barker? The results from these kinds of questions helped the company receive media coverage that coincided with the release of the movie and turn a potentially disastrous outcome into a positive one.

- *Fear 2000.* Leading up to the year 2000, it was easy to get media coverage about a computer problem called Y2K, which was a programming glitch that could inadvertently shut down computers, building elevators, and other electronic devices. The problem was that when the clocks turned to 2000, computer systems might mistake this information for 1900 and perhaps cause an economic disaster. Of course, none of this happened and a lot of IT consultants made a fortune as the millennium drew to a close. The problem seemed more acute with smaller companies, because larger firms had IT staffs or could hire consultants who could solve these programming problems. But what about the small business owners? What were they going to do? To find out, I ran a snapshot publicity survey of small company presidents to learn what they were planning to do if their

F *l a s h* **# 3 7**

A publicity survey—a type of snapshot survey that's designed to get your company "free advertising" and media coverage—should be focused on trends and interesting human behavior and ask questions such as, "What kind of cookies do most people leave out for Santa?" The answer is oatmeal, according to a national poll I ran for an online kitchen-supply Web site that asked about the different traditions consumers do during the holidays. Focusing on kitchen supplies is boring. Talking about how people act at the Thanksgiving table, on the night before Christmas, and on New Year's Day is news.

computers and other systems stopped working. Surprisingly, most said that they would be forced to buy new machines or upgrade their software. They were not planning to fix any Y2K problems, because most of them didn't know what to do and didn't want to take the time to learn. The results were publicized by a state governor who was quoted in numerous business publications. In addition to a news release, small business owners were offered a brochure on what the problem was and how to fix it, so that they could keep using their equipment.

- *The Most Dangerous Place on Earth: Your Home.* When Mine Safety Appliances (MSA), a company that has manufactured safety equipment for nearly a century, wanted to enter the consumer safety products market, it used a snapshot survey to find out how safe consumers perceived themselves to be when working around the house and yard. Questions like, "Do you wear a hard hat when you're trimming trees?" or "Have you had to go to the emergency room because of an injury you received while working at your home?" helped demonstrate that many consumers take unneeded safety risks in their own backyards; risks they would never take at work. The results were used to promote the launch of safety products MSA makes and sells via national home center retail outlets, such as The Home Depot and True Value stores. These products include respirators, hard hats, safety glasses, hearing protection, and other products. Prior to the launch of MSA Safety Works, many retailers did not have an organized approach to merchandising safety products, relying on consumers to find products scattered throughout a store.

With its successful launch and use of survey data, MSA had re-shaped this thinking and is today the fastest growing brand of safety products in North America. One additional technique MSA used was to release the survey results in the markets where retail partners were opening new stores. Instead of sending the news release to a broad distribution, this targeted approach yielded greater media results. The launch of MSA Safety Works was such a success that The Home Depot recognized MSA in its first year in business as its Partner of the Year in the highly competitive tools and hardware category.

C a s e   S t u d y

Chefs Cooking with Style

The American Iron and Steel Institute wanted to promote the positive attribute of canned food, because many consumers were purchasing foods that were fresh, frozen, or packed in plastic, glass, or other materials. Obviously, the more cans consumers buy, the more steel is needed to produce those cans. The campaign was needed because fewer consumers were buying canned food and many had negative impressions of the product.

How do you make canned food more appealing? I used a snapshot survey to interview chefs who were listed in *Gourmet* magazine's top restaurants to find out how many of them cooked using canned ingredients. To make the survey interesting, we asked the chefs to compare their cooking to fashion. The results were used to drive media coverage, which kicked off with a New York promotion at the former Fashion Café and included Ivana Trump and supermodel Carol Alt as spokespersons, along with chefs who had prepared their favorite dishes with some ingredients from canned food. These are the questions they were asked:

1. What is the most popular _____ your restaurant is serving now?
   Entrée
   Dessert
   Appetizer
   Salad
   Vegetable

2. Where does your inspiration for new menu items come from?

3. Some chefs are describing their cooking in terms of fashion, much like a clothing designer might. If you were going to describe your cooking style in terms of fashion, would you be most like _____?
Classic
Traditional
Hip (TRENDY, FUN)
Tres chic (TRENDY, SOPHISTICATED)
Haute couture (A DESIGNER ORIGINAL)
Avant-garde

4. If your most popular entrée was wearing clothes, how would it be dressed?
Polo—Ralph Lauren
Mizrahi
Tommy Hilfiger
Chanel
Calvin Klein
DKNY—Donna Karan
Armani
Versace

5. What is the most important element of a meal—to make it memorable?
The presentation
The method of preparation
The right combination of foods
Unique ingredients

6. Who is the most famous person you've ever cooked for?

7. In Europe, many chefs regularly use canned items as ingredients. Do any of the ingredients for your meals come from canned food?

8. Which canned ingredient or ingredients do you use the most?

9. Do you use imported canned goods?

10. What ingredient or food tastes best when it comes from a can?

11. What canned ingredient or food is easiest to cook with?

12. What is the most versatile food in cans?

13. Do you typically have canned food in your pantry at home? (IF YES:) What canned foods are in your pantry at home?

14. Do you agree or disagree that _____

   Canned food is as nutritious as its fresh counterparts.

   Canned food is as nutritious as its frozen counterparts.

   Today, more varieties of low-sodium canned food are available than were five years ago.

   The content of today's canned food is of higher quality than the canned food was five years ago.

   Steel food cans are completely recyclable.

   Chefs today are using more canned foods in recipes.

   The commercial canning process for fruits and vegetables does not require using preservatives.

15. Does your restaurant recycle steel cans?

WHERE YOU CAN PUBLISH YOUR FINDINGS

Over the years, the results of publicity surveys I've conducted have been published in many different types of consumer, business-to-business, trade, and other publications, including:

- *USA Today.* This newspaper typically publishes survey results as interesting graphics or charts in the bottom left-hand corner on the front page of each of its sections.
- *Most major and local newspapers.* Sometimes you can get a feature story by submitting your release to a daily news editor, but it's much better to be selective with where you try to get these articles placed. Your goal should be to get your news release in front of an editor of a specific section of the publication, for example, lifestyle or business. In the larger publications, these editors are usually more approachable and receptive than chief editors. And if you strike out with one, you can repackage your results and pitch it to another section within the same publication.
- *Magazines, including consumer, industry, and trade.* In these types of publications, you can sometimes get a feature placement, while other times you might be included as part of a trend article or sidebar. Most publications provide editorial calendars that list planned topics for future issues. By taking a quick look at these calendars, you can decide in which issue your publicity survey results might work best. I once published the results from one of

F l a s h # 3 8

More than 10,000 consumer and 5,000 trade media outlets (publications and radio/TV stations) exist in North America, plus thousands more internationally, all of which need constant news that their readers, listeners, and viewers will find interesting.

my surveys in *Training and Development Journal,* which published articles about recent survey results every quarter. The managing editor wasn't interested in my story, but the research editor was.

- *Online media.* A lot of people overlook the online media, but it is growing in readership and represents yet another outlet for your survey results. Many of the major publications provide online outlets, which are great places to start. Others are sponsored by reputable trade or industry organizations.
- *Books, such as chapters, sections, or sidebars.* I've had many surveys referenced in books, which can have a long shelf life depending on the industry and topic.
- *Special reports and white papers.* These are detailed, graphically designed summaries of your findings that are used as sales or trade show literature, proprietary reports, direct mail, and as other tools. These reports, although written by or for you, help position you and your firm as experts.
- *Brochures.* While these generally cover specific topics, some can refer to your survey findings and make good use of your data.
- *Conferences.* Presenting your survey results in front of your peers is valuable, but presenting them in front of one of your customer's peers is even more valuable. These are especially attractive if you've carried out an industry survey about a hot topic within the industry that the conference is focused on.

WHY PUBLICITY SURVEYS MUST BE SCIENTIFIC

Because all publications care about their reputations, they won't be interested in publishing survey results that aren't scientific—no matter how interesting these facts may be to their readers. It's great that your topic is whimsical and contains a lot of human interest, but you still need to treat it like a real survey.

> **F** *l a s h* **# 3 9**
> _____
>
> Just because a snapshot survey is designed for media consumption doesn't mean that it can be based on shoddy data. It should be every bit as scientific as any other survey, perhaps even more so.

What do I mean by scientific? The answer is different for each audience and each type of survey that you conduct.

Consumer Polls

In a consumer publicity survey, scientific means that you've chosen a random sample and completed between 300 and 1,000 total interviews. These types of polls usually appear in major newspapers and identify the sponsor of the research and the name of the firm that conducted the study. They also typically list the "margin of error" in the results. (For a more detailed explanation of margin of error, please refer to Chapter 2.)

Political polls are a good example of this type of research, where the paper or media outlet would say something like, "A total of 1,000 consumers were interviewed March 3 to 5. This poll has a margin of error of plus or minus three percentage points and was conducted for Candidate Smith by ABC Polling." Using a random survey, being up front about how it was conducted, and stating who actually conducted the research all help build the credibility of the research findings.

B2B Surveys

For a business-to-business publicity survey, scientific means that you took some precautions to get a representative sample. For example, if you're interviewing IT professionals, you would *not* be able to select them at random from the general population—at least not without spending a lot of time and money. In this case, you'll need to buy a list from a list house or obtain one from an association. A list you purchase could include names of individuals who subscribe to a particular magazine, possess an IT job title, or attended a recent technology trade show or conference. In a survey of these individuals, you may be able to get an editor to publish a story about your results with as few as 50 to 100 completed interviews or as many as several thousand. If you cover a hot topic, you'll need fewer interviews.

In a publicity survey for a leading manufacturer, I held 50 interviews with technical professionals and the results helped produce seven major trade stories (three were cover stories). But not one statistic from my survey made it in to any of the articles. Instead, my client used the survey results to convince the editors of these publications to write stories on new regulations that were coming out but that no one understood. Interestingly, part of this confusion was being driven by competitors of my customer who were telling buyers that the competitors products met recently changed government standards, when, in fact, they did not. The competitors were telling buyers that they didn't need to purchase products from my client—who was the only manufacturer at the time who met the stricter government standards. Of course, these statements were severely hurting my customer's sales.

I conducted a snapshot survey of 50 buyers to find out if they were aware of the new regulations and what they knew about them. As you might guess, most had never heard of the regulations and those who did were only vaguely familiar with them and understood what they meant to their organizations.

We shared the results with trade editors who elected to publish feature stories about the new regulations—and feature my client's products as examples of ones that were up to snuff. This is one of the few times I've been able to use a publicity survey to generate news coverage without actually publishing any results.

Proprietary Research

For proprietary research—or research you use to promote your own business and products somewhat more exclusively than releasing it to the media—the "scientific" nature of these surveys covers a broader range. For example, I've seen companies use the results from one focus group to talk about what consumers want when they are making investment purchases, while others complete much more rigorous investigations that they later sell to clients or that are promoted through trade associations.

Your sample size and methods will depend on what you want to do with the results. If you're just looking for something to include in your sales literature, 25 to 50 interviews may be enough. If you want to present the results at a conference or publish it as a special brochure or report, you may need 500 or more interviews. Spending a few minutes looking at what others within your industry are doing should give you a good clue about what you need to do to attract attention.

DRAMATIC, THOUGHT-PROVOKING INSIGHTS START WITH THE RIGHT QUESTIONS

Publicity surveys are usually very different from other marketing surveys, especially ones you plan to present to the consumer media. To write these questions, you need to start by putting yourself in a different frame of mind. These surveys are much less about information and much more about news, news that is different, interesting, and often funny. As you brainstorm the questions you want to ask in your publicity survey, you'll want to keep these five principles in mind:

1. **Ask questions that are interesting and humorous.** Figure 7.1 includes some of the questions I included in a publicity survey that I used to help launch a whitening toothpaste that are interesting and funny. However, don't direct your humor (or jabs) so strongly at any one person that he or she retaliates. Some years ago, Listerine ran a publicity survey that found one of the most unkissable people was Rosie O'Donnell, who was hosting a talk show at that time. Scope found out about it and asked Ketchum to develop an ad to capitalize on Listerine's blunder. The result was a picture of a bottle of Scope with a juicy, red lipstick kiss on it. Rosie made fun of Listerine for several days and helped sell a lot of Scope in the process.

FIGURE 7.1

Sample consumer publicity survey questions designed to discover interesting and humorous perceptions that will later be used to generate media coverage. The results from these questions helped launch a whitening toothpaste.

1. Do you think people who have whiter teeth . . . have a more romantic life, are more trustworthy, are more likely to make more money, are healthier?

2. If you were dating, would you go out with someone with yellow-stained teeth?

3. Are you embarrassed to smile when you're getting your picture taken because of your teeth?

4. Who do you think has whiter teeth? Oprah Winfrey or Rosie O'Donnell? Katie Couric or Matt Lauer? Bill Clinton or Hillary Clinton? Michelle Kwan or Tara Lipinski?

2. Limit your question categories so you get a "winner" for every question. After running several dozen publicity surveys, it dawned on me that you can generate much more news when you obtain survey results that show that most people think alike. Instead of asking questions with seven to ten categories, it's better to use three or four. If you were going to ask "How embarrassed are you to get your picture taken because of your teeth?" and then give a range of responses such as "extremely embarrassed," "very embarrassed," "somewhat embarrassed," and so on, you would generate a mess that even the best editor couldn't figure out.

When you offer too many answers to any one question, you're likely to end up with 15 percent to 20 percent of the respondents giving an answer. That's not news. If you simply ask the question as a "yes" or "no" response, you're likely to get 60 percent to 70 percent in one or the other categories—which is news and more enticing to an editor.

3. Ask several questions on the same topic to actually find an interesting trend. Figure 7.1 lists only some of the questions on the survey about tooth care. There were several others I included just in case some of the answers I received were lackluster. Of course, this doesn't mean that we're only going to select the questions that make my clients look the best and hide all the others (this would be biased). I've already said that when you run a publicity survey you need to be willing to release all the findings to all your questions. It's just that some of them may make better examples in your actual news release or article. By asking several questions, you give yourself more flexibility and don't end up with survey results you can't use.

4. If you're using a celebrity in your marketing, ask questions about him or her. Many consumer campaigns hire a well-known spokesperson to represent their company. These can range from famous actors, such as James Earl Jones, who played the voice of Darth Vader in *Star Wars* and represented Verizon, to more local celebrities, such as a college football coach or announcer who helps promote specific products in a market where they are well known and liked.

If you're running a survey about food, you might ask consumers which television personality they believe they cook most like: Jerry Seinfeld, Robin Williams, or Martha Stewart. If your findings match your spokesperson, that's even better.

5. Create "consumer personality" demographic questions.   In most surveys, you're going to want to ask a handful of demographic questions to examine your overall results in more detail. In your survey, do men think differently than women do? Do younger people have a different opinion than older folks? These comparisons help make your overall findings more interesting and sometimes make good sidebars or points in your story.

Another way to create very interesting publicity survey results is to create a demographic question about your topic that uses interesting labels or descriptions. Consider these actual examples that were used on recent publicity surveys. The text in parentheses was not asked of consumers, but was later used to describe how one group was different from the others (by examining how each group answered the rest of the questions on your survey):

- *Homemade Cooking Survey.* "As you know, there are many different ways to prepare and eat meals at home, ranging from formal home-cooked meals to microwave dinners. Which of these statements best describes the way your household or family eats at home?" (READ. MARK ONE.)
  - (SUZY HOMEMAKER:) Almost every meal at home is homemade, many of which are prepared from scratch.
  - (PREPARED-FOODS PAULA:) We cook for a hungry crew who is usually on the go. So, we do some meals from scratch, but most come from prepared foods or leftovers that don't take a long time to get ready.
  - (MICROWAVE MARY:) The microwave is our favorite kitchen appliance because we eat a lot of meals that can be prepared quickly.
  - (DRIVE-THROUGH DIANE:) We are so busy most nights that we don't have time to cook. So we usually get take-out food or order from delivery.
- *Health and Wellness Habits.* "If you were going to give yourself a grade on how well you take care of yourself—in terms of health, nutrition, eating, exercise, and lifestyle—would you give yourself an/a . . . ?" (READ. MARK ONE.)
  - "A," because you work hard taking care of yourself almost every day.
  - "B," because you work hard some of the time, but don't do as much as you should.
  - "C," because you do just enough to get by.

- "D," because you work at it only once in a while.
- "F," because you're not doing much of anything right now.
- *Lifestyle Habits Based on How Neatly Women Keep Their Homes.* "Which of the following best describes your home?" (READ. MARK ONE.)
    - (A SHOWPLACE:) Your home is a real showpiece decorated to the "T" with contemporary furnishings. It's a home worthy of photographing for *House Beautiful.*
    - (SHIPSHAPE:) Your home is an organized, well-run machine. Caring for your home and family is your full-time job. You run a tight ship.
    - (A REST STOP:) For you, home is a stopping place and transient location—a sign of a busy professional. You're hardly ever home and don't invest a lot of time into decorating or housekeeping.
    - (CHAOS CENTRAL:) Between work and caring for your family, your home is in a continuous state of chaos and you just get by with your household chores.
    - (DUST BALL:) You would describe your home as lived in and run on a tight budget. You're not interested in investing a lot of time or money to update your home with new furnishings or the most modern conveniences.

In the first and third example, none of the respondents heard any of the personality descriptions we eventually used to describe them (phrases in the parentheses). However, when we looked at how each group rated other questions in the survey, it also produced interesting

F *l a s h* **# 4 0**

The secret to getting the media to publish the results from your snapshot survey is to package these results in a way that makes sense to the media (news release or article) and fits the format of their publications. When you separate each publication into its basic content sections, such as feature stories, sidebars, monthly columns, quarterly columns, etc., it's easier to see the best place to pitch your story. The more you know about the publication and what it typically covers, the easier it is to pitch your story in a way that gets its staff excited about it.

differences we could use in our media materials. For example, with the survey about how neatly women keep their homes, we were about to create graphics of each personality type and talk about some of their behaviors. Those who said their house was a showplace were much more likely to say they spend a day at the spa, eat a rack of lamb, and use their credit cards frequently, which provided an interesting comparison to the other groups who were more focused on quick-fix meals, such as the moms who described their house as Chaos Central.

PACKAGING YOUR RESULTS IN A MEDIA KIT

Simply gathering interesting feedback about consumer or industry trends isn't enough to get your story published. You still need to write a news release or article and "pitch" it to an editor or reporter. If you're trying to get media coverage in a consumer publication, it's best to get some help from a public relations professional who has experience pitching media stories. This person should help you:

- Prepare a media list.
- Develop a media kit.

Prepare a Media List

A media list contains the names, mailing addresses, phone numbers, and e-mail addresses of the publications in which you want to publish your findings. For the larger papers and publications, this may include several editors or reporters—increasing the chances that one of them will be interested in what you have to say.

You can find these names using various approaches, such as simply targeting a publication that you've heard about or are familiar with, going to the newsstand to look over magazines and other publications, or reading books such as the *Writer's Market,* which list several publications. To find a more complete listing of publications, spend a few minutes at your local library using reference publications, such as Burrelle's *Media Director* or Bacon's *Directory.* Because of the vast number of media outlets, both of these publications provide multiple volumes for magazine, radio, and television, so make sure you refer to as many volumes as make sense for your situation. These publications offer both printed and electronic versions.

If you don't want to prepare your own specific media contact list, you can hire a wire service, such as PR Newswire. These companies do the distribution work for you.

Of course, your public relations professional may already have a list of some names to start with, so make sure you include those as well. Your PR person should bring both skill and contacts to your project.

Keep in mind that because you are dealing with contact information and people who are constantly changing jobs, you should expect 5 percent to 10 percent of your contact list to be inaccurate. Therefore, you need to verify it before sending out any materials. All you need to do is call the receptionist from each publication and say that you would like to verify its contact information. Mark any changes on a printout of your names, then accurately make the changes in your database. If your list is older than one month, you'll want to have it verified again before using it.

Every public relations professional has horror stories of inaccurate lists. While most editors and reporters are understanding, not all are. I learned this the hard way when distributing the results from one of my publicity surveys. A reporter who spelled his name as "Bryan" was sent a release where his name appeared as "Brian." He decided to write a negative, embarrassing editorial. This is an extreme case, but it shows why it's important to be as accurate as you can.

Develop a Media Kit

A media kit, which includes all the material that you're going to give to editors and reporters, can serve as a big part of the "package" of your survey. Simple media kits contain a news release printed on two or three sheets of paper. More elaborate ones might include custom-designed glossy folders and letterheads. The Grin-and-Bear-It Survey that was part of the Aquafresh Whitening® launch media kit was packaged in a box that looked like a bathroom medicine chest with a shiny, mirror-like cover. When you opened it, there were pictures of medications (all made by GlaxoSmithKline) and places to hold a tube of toothpaste and a toothbrush.

The basic components of your media kit should include:

- *News release.* This should be written as an actual newspaper story and not be too "salesy." Your goal is to make it so good that the editors or reporters who read it don't want to—or have to—rewrite it.

FIGURE 7.2

An interesting information graphic produced by the Canned Food Alliance, who conducted a survey of female consumers, 25 to 54 years old, to learn more about their shopping habits and how much they cook like their mothers

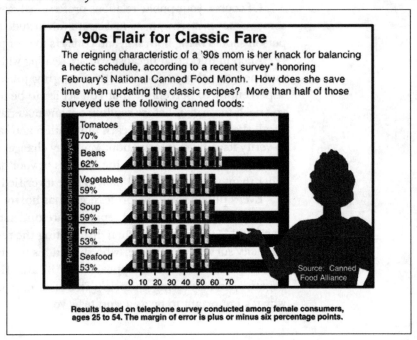

- *Interestingly designed information graphics.* These are bar charts, pie graphs, and other material that look like a graphic designer created them. Instead of a straight line graph, you might have the bars made from stacked cans, stick figures of people, or some other icon that makes sense for your topic. Figure 7.2 contains an example of one of these charts that was used to promote the results from a publicity survey sponsored by the Canned Food Alliance.
- *Photos.* These are very helpful communication aids, especially if you are showcasing products, recipes, or other visuals your target publication might be interested in printing. Make sure that you label each of the photographs and provide a description that they can be used exactly as written (caption).
- *Related documents.* Sometimes you'll want to include other items, such as product samples or backgrounders (information about a complicated story or product written to help educate the editor and not meant for publication).

Figure 7.3 contains the exact news release for the American Iron and Steel Industry's publicity survey called Chefs Cooking with Style (the questions in this survey are listed in the case history in this chapter). The survey, which was designed to help promote canned food (which, of course, is packaged in steel and not plastic, glass, or some other material), linked leading restaurant and food cooking styles with fashion. The survey found that many chefs like and used canned ingredients in their award-winning cooking.

This release appeared verbatim in numerous smaller and regional publications, because it sounds like a real news story and stayed away from hard-selling or blatant product promotion. The more you make your releases sound like news, the more likely they will be printed exactly as they are written. Some of the smaller and midsize papers will print your information, similar to the one in Figure 7.3, but expect the larger media outlets to use their own staff to redesign them.

TIPS FOR WORKING WITH THE TRADE MEDIA

Most trade editors are overworked and have a small staff of writers. They also have different needs than the consumer media. Instead of being limited to a geographical area, their publications are national or international in scope and highly focused on a technical topic. Therefore, it's important to read the types of articles they are publishing and determine if they are written by staff writers or industry professionals.

Over the years, I've had many of my own surveys printed in trade journals. I usually pick the best one and offer them an exclusive on the research findings, which means I won't give it to any of their competing journals, but might share it with another industry journal. This technique is usually very well received and goes a long way to build rapport with the editor.

Instead of writing a news release for these publications, it's better to write a feature story, not unlike the ones they are already publishing. If you don't have the time or desire to do this, you should be able to get a technical public relations professional to help you, especially if he or she has experience with your industry. Expect to pay between $500 and $2,000 for writing your article, depending on how long, complicated, and technical it is. Once in a while, you'll be able to find the same public relations professional who is good at working with both the consumer and trade media, but these are often different skill

FIGURE 7.3

News release for the American Iron and Steel Institute's survey, Chefs Cooking with Style, which appeared in dozens of newspapers verbatim (The more you write your releases like actual stories–and avoid blatant attempts to promote your product or position–the more receptive media outlets will be.)

TOP CHEFS USE TODAY'S HIGH-QUALITY CANNED FOODS

Cuisine, like fashion, always follows trends. Just as classic, tailored looks are showing up on fashion's runways, classic foods are what's fashionable at North America's hottest restaurants.

According to a recent survey conducted by the Steel Packaging Council among 161 chefs at top-rated restaurants in 20 cities ("America's Top Tables," *Gourmet* magazine, October, 1996), the majority of chefs are describing their cooking style as classic or traditional. When asked how chefs equate their cooking style with trends in the fashion industry, the most frequently mentioned look is the classic style of Giorgio Armani.

What foods are fashionable at top restaurants? Fish and seafood are big. "Signature" salads are hot, and chocolate everything is popular for dessert. While we all would like to cook with the same flair as America's top chefs, most of us are too busy to try. The simple solution? Incorporating the convenience of canned foods.

"The country's most fashionable dining-out menu items are easy to re-create at home with canned food," says Melanie Barnard, *Bon Appetit* columnist and cookbook author. To celebrate February, National Canned Food Month, the Steel Packaging Council has consolidated the findings of its survey to announce what's hot in canned food trends.

Nearly one-half of the most fashionable gourmet chefs surveyed say they use canned food for its convenience, nutrition, and versatility. "Almost every chef I know uses canned food," said Nick Malgieri, world-renowned pastry chef. "In many cases, you just can't do without it."

Tomato products lead chefs' lists of favorite canned items. Almost 70 percent use them for convenience, versatility, and taste. Other popular canned foods are soups, vegetables, and olive oil.

In addition to using canned items in their restaurants, the majority of chefs surveyed keep their home pantries stocked with canned food. From soups to vegetables to coffee, chefs are comfortable using canned products to create high-quality cuisine in their own kitchens.

More than 75 percent of chefs agree the content of today's canned food is of higher quality than canned food of five years ago. Surprising to some chefs, canned fruits and vegetables are as nutritious as their fresh and frozen counterparts, according to a nutritional analysis conducted by the University of Illinois.

According to Melanie Barnard, "Using canned foods to make a fashionable feast cuts down on preparation time without sacrificing quality, taste, or nutrition. I suggest using canned ingredients like fresh lump crabmeat for appetizers, water chestnuts or artichoke hearts for interesting salads, tropical fruits to make exotic salsas for seafood entrées, and decadent chocolate sauces to top off desserts. These

FIGURE 7.3 *(Continued)*

canned foods help to create a high-quality, high-style meal." With more than 1,500 canned foods available today—from artichokes to escargots to coconut milk—it is easier than ever to prepare fashionable cuisine.

The Steel Packaging Council, the Canned Food Information Council, and the Can Manufacturers Institute are partners in 1997 National Canned Food Month initiatives.

The American Iron and Steel Institute's (AISI) Steel Packaging Council is a consortium of North American steel companies engaged in the production of packaging steels. Its primary mission is to promote the versatility, convenience, and nutritional content of canned food, more than 90 percent of which is packaged in recyclable steel cans.

Established in 1984 by the National Food Processors Association, the Canned Food Information Council (CFIC) is a sponsor of National Canned Food Month and serves as a respected source for nutritional data, product information, recipes, and other industry-related information.

The Can Manufacturers Institute (CMI) is the trade association of the metal and composite can manufacturing industry and its suppliers in the United States. Members include almost 100 companies that account for more than 98 percent of the annual domestic production of 133 billion cans.

and mind-sets, so find the right person before you waste your money on doing something that won't work.

PITCHING YOUR STORY: HOW TO ENTICE AN EDITOR TO MAKE YOU FAMOUS

Don't expect to hit a home run every time you send out a release or an article. Strikeouts are the normal course of action—and expect to strike out a lot if you aren't planning on following up with every editor and reporter.

Media relations, or the process of pitching stories, is a lot like selling. You start with your list of prospects (media contacts you sent or are planning to send your materials to), attempt to talk with them, find out what they are looking for, and help them make a buying decision (publishing your story). If you've never handled media relations before, you'll quickly find out it's hard work. That's why it's important to take it seriously and get professional help from time to time.

Reporters and editors are people, just like you and me. The more you keep this in mind while you're pitching your story, the better. These are a few of the tips and thought processes that helped me the most:

- *There are millions of people in the world and tens of thousands of media outlets.* When one turns you down, get over it quickly and move on.

- *Each publication or station has sections or formats.* Your job is to figure out each one's format and work within it. In other words, don't try to pitch a business story to your local television station's evening news unless it has something very specific to do with its viewers. Most stations focus on crimes, fires, and other local problems, before moving to weather and sports. A few sign off with a brief human-interest story (sometimes the only positive news in the show). If you story doesn't fit in its format, the station can't and won't use your item.

- *Hearing "no" is not a personal rejection.* They are saying no to your ideas at this time. Try to make a friend. They may like your next story.

- *Realize they are busy people and may be under deadline.* Asking them "Are you under deadline?" before you start pitching is the only respectful thing to do. Find out when would be a better time to talk with them.

- *For consumer publicity surveys, focus on pitching news services.* If the Associated Press or Reuters picks up your story, so will dozens of their affiliates. Think of these sources as distributors of your story who are in turn selling it to their contacts.

- *Never lie.* Do what you promised. Send thank-you notes. These are basic manners that help more than you might first expect.

- *If a reporter calls, call him or her back as soon as you can.* When you get a reputation for being helpful, you'll get more calls and referrals from reporters who've talked with their friends.

- *Take a minute to look over the reporters other stories or articles before you call.* Most reporters cover a beat or similar topics. Explaining how your story fits in with what they are doing will help increase your chances of them taking your story.

- *Make sure you can answer these two questions for every person you call:* "Why do a story?" "Why do it now?"

- *Be realistic about your time frame.* Most newspapers who are interested in a publicity survey may not print anything for a couple of weeks. Magazines may be three or four months from their on-sale date. Trade journals could be two or three months away from using your story—even if they decided today to include it. Few outlets are instantaneous, so be patient.

8

ADDING POWER TO
YOUR PROPOSALS

How to Win More Business by Focusing Your Sales
Presentations on Your Prospects and Their Desires

If you would persuade, you must appeal to interest rather than intellect.
Benjamin Franklin

Differentiation and upselling are two diffi-
cult sales challenges that virtually every company faces. If a prospect
can't easily tell why it should work with you instead of one of your competitors, it's tough to win its business. When each competitor that's going after the same piece of business appears to the buyer to be "about
the same," the decision becomes very easy: Pick the firm with the lowest price.

At the same time, if you win only smaller projects and your customer doesn't see your firm as being able to solve bigger (and more lu-
crative) problems, this stunts your growth. You end up leaving money
on the table and lose out on work you should have won.

The snapshot survey can help you solve both of these problems. By
running a short snapshot survey as part of a major proposal or sales
presentation on a topic that is important to your prospect, you can easily stand out from the other firms you're competing against. When you
start talking more about what you learned about your prospect's current
situation based on your findings—and less about what you've done for
everyone else—you change the tenor of your sales meeting. The snapshot survey helps you give a big shove to your competitors so your prospect can get a good look at you.

F *l a s h* **# 4 0**

The snapshot survey is a versatile sales tool that can help you in two ways. First, when you find yourself short-listed as part of a competitive sales process and you're asked to present your proposal to a buyer's team, you can conduct a quick survey about your prospect's current situation and share the results during your presentation. Don't let your prospect know you're running a survey ahead of time. It's better to play this card in your presentation. Second, instead of trying to win a major project, sell a smaller diagnostic or needs-assessment study to help clarify and quantify your prospect's problem. Sell more like a doctor and base your recommendation on both experience and examinations. Let the snapshot survey find the numbers you need to convince your prospects to buy from you and buy more of what you're selling.

When you use the snapshot survey as part of a needs assessment or diagnostic tool that you sell as a first step in working with your customer, you can use the results from this study to help define your customer's problem and quantify the benefits of addressing it (or the cost of ignoring it). I like to call this sales technique "scientific selling," because it's the same process a doctor uses to consult with a patient. Instead of simply jumping into a solution, by using this step you can pinpoint what the real problem is when it's placed under a microscope. Scientific selling can make your entire selling process more sophisticated and professional.

Let's take a look at each of these tools in greater detail so that you can decide how these types of snapshot surveys might help you beat out more of your competitors and land bigger projects.

HOW TO WIN MORE SALES PROPOSALS

From the research I've conducted in multiple industries, I've found that competitors look and act so much alike that it's difficult for an outsider to tell one company from next. Their products are about the same. They use the same words and phrases to describe their customer service. Even their literature, Web sites, and proposals are similar. No wonder so many prospects or "buyers" are influenced by price. (It's the easiest and simplest way to differentiate one firm from the next.)

Many professional service firms, including marketing, advertising, and public relations, face this same differentiation problem. When going after a major account, as many as 10 to 12 firms may be invited to first submit their qualifications. Then, the 3 or 4 firms who are "short-listed" are expected to deliver a formal presentation, where members of a selection committee might have an hour to make up their minds about which firm has the best expertise and chemistry. This is particularly true when all the competing firms have established and respected brands or when none of them do. When the competitors are mixed (some known and some unknown firms competing for the same project), a firm with a strong brand name should be able to beat out smaller players, because it's always safer to buy from a known commodity. Smaller players, however, can usually exploit two weaknesses of larger firms: higher prices and bureaucratic operations.

From the agency's or "seller's" point of view, the buyer's inability to differentiate one competitor from another is also frustrating, especially when you're the one who loses the business to someone you think you're better than.

Walking a Mile in Your Buyer's Shoes

I've spent enough time as a seller, a coach, and a buyer to learn that buyers and sellers have different perspectives about the sales process. The more you understand what your buyers are thinking and feeling (about the selection process itself, not about your technical data, product features, or their specific circumstances), the easier it will be to differentiate yourself from your competitors.

Figure 8.1 highlights some of these different mind-sets and lists questions that I've gathered from both buyers and sellers. I've picked these up as I've sold my own services (and those of my former employers) from clients who've asked me to evaluate their sales process and while serving as a buyer on a number of selection committees asked to purchase products and services for government, nonprofit, and other organizations.

When my clients ask me to formally evaluate their sales processes, typically I take a good look at their proposals, sit in on a few of their sales presentations, and interview some of their customers (current and lost) and prospects. They give me complete access to their selling system and procedures. My clients do this so I can help them to the best of my ability. They value an outside perspective on what they should keep doing and how they can improve.

FIGURE 8.1

Key questions buyers and sellers ask themselves and each other about a group of competitors who are participating in a formal sales selection process, which typically includes a formal presentation to a committee responsible for selecting or recommending a winner

---

SELLERS VERSUS BUYERS:
WHAT EACH WONDERS ABOUT THE OTHER

Sellers

- What's it going to take to win this business?

- How are we being perceived compared to our competitors?

- (If selling to a committee:) Who's on my side? Who's against me? Who's the most important person I need to convince?

- How does our price compare to our competitors' prices?

- Are we leaving dollars on the table or losing business because of our price?

- Are we giving this our best shot?

- Is this a customer I really want to have or would it be best if we didn't win this particular project?

- Am I doing my best to present ideas clearly, answer questions, and overcome objections?

- Have I prepared enough not to squander this opportunity?

- If I win this project, can I make money at it?

- Are they going to try to beat me up on price?

Buyers

- Do I believe what these people are saying?

- Are they any good?

- How much headache and heartache will I have working with them?

- What does their proposal look like?

- Before this meeting, had I ever heard about them? If so, was what I heard positive?

- Have they worked with anybody in my industry on a similar project, especially someone I know (who I might be able to talk to)?

- Do they understand my problem?

- Am I dealing with the A team—the people who will actually be doing the work or is this just the sales staff?

- After looking at each competitor, which one(s) do I feel the best about?

- If this project goes badly, what will it cost me in terms of money, reputation, and relationships with my colleagues?

- How do I sell their proposal to my boss?

- If I move forward with this project, what will be my return on investment?

F *l a s h* **# 4 1**

One question all buyers have—whether they ask it or not—is if they are dealing with the A team, the actual folks who are going to do the work and be responsible for their account. A dramatic example of this point I learned while interviewing customers from a professional service firm who told me the partners were the A team and everyone else at this firm was on the B team, primarily because the firm's staff was younger and less experienced than the partners. When you understand this A-B team structure and many other mind-sets that most buyers experience, it becomes much easier to differentiate yourself from your competitors.

From the buying side, it's fascinating to see firsthand how different firms capitalize on (or squander) their selling opportunities. Frankly, by the second or third presentation, everything really does start to sound the same. I can sympathize with buyers who reduce their decisions to price.

These experiences have been very helpful to me in learning more about what the people I'm presenting to are actually thinking as they listen to each team. I've learned a great deal about what I should be doing—and not doing—to close more deals. You can do the same thing by looking more closely at what you're doing, what others firms outside your industry are doing, and how people sell to you.

One way you can help your company stand out from your competitors during a sales presentation is to conduct a brief snapshot survey regarding your prospect's current situation and use your findings as part of your presentation. This strategy transforms the meeting from "Let's talk about how great we are and what we've done for everyone else" to "Here's what we've learned about you and how we can help you reach your goals."

I've used the snapshot survey in this way dozens of times to find unique and interesting information that I've included as part of my sales presentation. It automatically makes me look different from my competitors. And it works like a charm.

The reason the snapshot survey is so effective in these sales presentations is because too many sellers are basically disrespectful toward their prospects. Most don't even realize what they are doing to communicate this negative attitude. They are certainly courteous, friendly, and professional. But when you listen closely to what they talk about in their proposals and presentations, it's usually about what they've done for everyone else and it's not truly focused on what the buyer needs and wants right now. They use case histories to describe the results they've obtained for other companies, or they spend a lot of time talking about the detailed steps they are going to take to complete the project.

When I suggest using a snapshot survey in your sales presentation, I'm not talking about doing something that simply regurgitates the facts and background information the prospect already provided you before the meeting. This is stuff they already know. Instead, I'm suggesting that you find a topic that's related to their current situation, but that is also more interesting and unique. Your goal should be to get them to say, "Wow. This is important information we didn't know. If this company is willing to give us this for free, imagine what they will do once we start paying them."

Keep in mind that I don't run a snapshot survey for every proposal I develop or presentation I deliver—only on special occasions. If I did, I'd go broke giving away my product. I suggest you save your snapshot surveys for your biggest, most important sales meetings—especially when you know you're going through a competitive selection process and you've already made it past the preliminary rounds. By this point in your sales process, you should have a good idea of what your prospect cares about and should be able to identify an audience to interview and some questions to ask. I wouldn't waste any time running a snapshot survey if I wasn't already short-listed and I knew enough about the client to come up with an interesting topic.

Shoot-out Results Using the Snapshot Survey

To illustrate how you can use the snapshot survey as part of your sales presentations, I've included the survey questions that were used in four sales presentations, all of which were shoot-outs and where I was one of the firms (or teamed up with a firm) who had been short-listed:

- *Zoo and aquarium.* One of the nation's leading zoos wanted to design and test new exhibit concepts that it might eventually build over the next five to ten years. To guide it through this process, the zoo asked a number of architectural firms to submit their qualifications with one catch: The zoo wanted the project to be research-based and include consumer feedback (something that many architectural firms are not accustomed to doing, but I am).

So one of the architectural firms asked me to partner with it on this proposal. I suggested we run a snapshot survey as part of our presentation and the firm liked the idea. I ran two quick surveys. In one survey, I asked 5 zoo directors what they thought the zoos of the future might be like and whether current trends, such as night tours and facility rentals (for weddings and banquets), would likely continue. I used their comments as specific quotes in the presentation. In a second snapshot survey, I asked 25 concierges from downtown hotels what they thought of the zoo and aquarium—and whether they recommended these attractions to their guests. During the presentation, we learned that the Audubon Institute had attempted to market through these individuals but was unsuccessful. Our results found out why: Companies who promoted other local tours paid the concierges a referral fee for every trip they booked, a much more attractive offer than sending someone to the zoo or aquarium. The results of these snapshot surveys were a significant component of our presentation. Instead of only talking about how great the architects were and reviewing what they had done for everyone else, the research results helped us talk about something more relevant to our prospect. We looked very different from the other teams. We won this project. As an added bonus, instead of simply asserting that we were research-based, we were already proving it by sharing the snapshot survey results.

F *lash* **# 4 2**

When you're selecting a topic for the snapshot survey you plan to include as part of your sales presentation, look for something that's going to make your prospect sit up and take notice. Avoid finding out more information about something it is already intimately familiar with. Instead, focus on hot trends, new concepts, what some of its customers are saying about its competitors, or other insights it will be interested in hearing. The results don't have to be the entire core of your presentation—and you don't need to do a lot of interviews. Instead, conduct a few interviews and use the verbatim quotes or statistics to spice up one or more sections of your presentation. This matter-of-fact approach shows you cared enough to fund your own study and you took some initiative that none of your competitors did.

SHOOT-OUT #1

Zoo and Aquarium Attraction Project

Questions used for telephone interviews with 25 concierges from local hotels to learn their opinions of the zoo and aquarium and how likely they would be to recommend these attractions to their guests.

1. What attractions or destinations do you recommend most frequently and why?

2. Have you recently visited any of these attractions?

3. (FOR EACH ATTRACTION VISITED IN Q2, ASK:) What is your overall impression of the _____?

4. (FOR EACH ATTRACTION VISITED IN Q2, ASK:) Why do you go there?

5. Which of these attractions do you recommend to your guests?

6. Who do you typically recommend these attractions to?

7. Why do you typically recommend it?

8. What do most of the guests have to say about their visit to these facilities?

9. Of all the attractions available to visitors, which statement best describes your thoughts about the _____ as a destination? (READ. MARK ONE.)
   • A top destination—I would recommend it to virtually everyone.
   • Interesting destination—I would recommend it to only those who asked about it or who had children they wanted to entertain.
   • Infrequent destination—I would rarely recommend it
   • DON'T KNOW—I really don't know enough about it to recommend it.

	Top destination	Interesting destination	Infrequent destination	Don't know
Zoo	1	2	3	4
Aquarium	1	2	3	4
IMAX Theatre	1	2	3	4
Nature Center	1	2	3	4
Cruise	1	2	3	4

10. What kinds of new animals, attractions, or other events could the Audubon Zoo build over the next few years that would make it a more attractive (or even more attractive) destination?

11. What could the zoo do to get you to recommend it to more of your guests?

- *Chemical manufacturer.* A manufacturer wanted to change marketing agencies and asked several firms to submit their qualifications. We were short-listed and asked to deliver a presentation and participate in an exercise to demonstrate our creative thinking. While looking through the firm's background information, I found a contact list of customers. It didn't take me long to ask 25 customers some questions about the manufacturer and how it prefers to receive marketing information. During the presentation, I reviewed the findings and said, "Based on what we've learned here, we recommend the following strategies and tactics." Engineers and scientists love making decisions based on data, especially when it's coming from someone they care about—their customers. It was no accident that basing our recommendations on data was exactly what we were doing during our presentation. Of course, I qualified these findings, saying that we would probably still need to talk with more customers and some prospects and ask them additional questions, but I got a lot of nods as I presented the findings. We were definitely in the right ballpark with our recommendations. Our new client told us that we blew away everyone else. Once again, the snapshot survey paid off.

SHOOT-OUT #2
Chemical Manufacturer

Questions asked customers as part of an agency pitch to win a marketing contract. Interviews were completed with 25 customers and based on a list the prospect included as part of the background materials for the project.

1. In your opinion, who are the leading producers of chemicals for compounding synthetic rubber and why?

2. In the next two or three years, what trends do you think are likely to dominate the synthetic rubber manufacturing field?

3. One trend is to brand specific synthetic rubber compounds. What do you see as the advantages of branding?

4. Other than lowering its price, what could a manufacturer of chemicals for compounding synthetic rubber do to make purchasing and delivering the products easier?

5. What could a manufacturer of chemicals for compounding synthetic rubber do to improve its technical product support?

6. How do you typically learn about new products used in compounding synthetic rubbers?

7. What kind of Web-based services could a manufacturer of chemicals for compounding synthetic rubber provide that would really make your job easier?

8. For your company, how important is it that you work with salespeople who have very strong technical skills when purchasing chemicals for compounding synthetic rubber and why?

9. Typically, when you have technical problems using a chemical for compounding synthetic rubber, how difficult is it for you to get in touch with the person at the manufacturer's facility who can help you?

10. What trade publications do you generally read?

11. Thinking of all the ways you could learn about industry trends, how useful do you find the following communications tools on a 1 to 10 scale, where 1 is "not at all useful" and 10 is "very useful"?
    - Trade shows
    - Articles in trade magazines
    - Advertisements in trade journals
    - Direct mail
    - In-person sales calls
    - Company-sponsored seminars
    - Web pages or electronic magazines
    - Word of mouth from friends or colleagues
    - Intranet services provided from within your company
    - College or university contacts/associations
    - Industry and professional associations

- *Trucking manufacturer.* To prepare for an advertising agency shoot-out, I completed ten telephone interviews with major trucking distributors who purchase and lease rigs from Mack Trucks, Freightliner, International, and other manufacturers. Similar to the other presentations, I used the results during the agency presentation to help highlight some of the perceptions buyers had of each brand. We didn't win this project, but we came close. Running the snapshot survey helped improve our chances and gained the respect of our prospect.

SHOOT-OUT #3
Trucking Manufacturer

Survey questions used to complete ten telephone interviews with trucking distributors. The advertising agency lost this shoot-out, but the survey results delivered as part of the advertising agency's presentation helped increase dialogue with the prospect and build credibility.

1. What percentage of your overall business is concentrated on _____ versus other lines?

2. What percentage of your overall business is vocational (e.g., dump trucks, garbage trucks, refuse, etc.) and what percentage is highway?

3. What is the most important factor or factors in your customer's purchase decision?

4. What does the manufacturer do to support your sales effort?

5. What could _____ do to improve its sales support to your organization?

6. What other truck brand or brands do you compete with most often?

7. Why do your prospects and/or customers choose these brands over _____?

8. What are the key challenges you face in running your dealership?

9. If you could give _____ some marketing and advertising advice, what would it be?

- *Victory Centre (MEC Pennsylvania Racing, "The Meadows").* Before building a new entertainment attraction that might include an outlet shopping mall, a Bass Pro Shop, hotels, indoor water park, athletic fields, and other attractions, MEC Pennsylvania Racing, who operates harness racing facilities and gaming attractions, wanted to test the viability of partnering with the developer, because the proposed shopping areas were across the street from the racetrack and proposed gaming center. This research was conducted before slot machines were legalized in Pennsylvania. The prospect wanted to know whether a wagering facility located near the proposed attraction would make sense to consumers. Would the same people who went shopping want to stop at the facility to wager? The prospect wanted proposals from three research firms to test the concepts in the planned attraction and learn whether consumers would go for the shopping and wagering concepts functioning together with similar architecture and joint marketing. To stand apart from my competitors, I had one research assistant spend two hours conducting intercept interviews at a local mall where he talked with 35 consumers. During the sales presentation, we spent most of our time reviewing the survey results and talking about what we still needed to learn from other consumers. I won this project. No one else did any research. By doing a little bit of work, we were more informed about the issue and it proved we wanted to win this project.

SHOOT-OUT #4
Consumer Preferences for Linking Outlet Mall Shopping and Gambling

Snapshot survey questions (including survey layout) used to complete 35 consumer mall intercept interviews that were presented during a sales presentation to focus the content of the meeting on the prospect's current interest and demonstrate that we cared about winning their business.

1. **During the past two years, have you visited an outlet mall?** (MARK ONE.)

   1 Yes . . . **Which one(s)?** (MARK ALL THAT APPLY.)

        1 Grove City   3 Other: _____

        2 Georgian Place (Somerset)   4 DK/NR

   How often do you visit outlet malls? (PROBE. RECORD VERBATIM RESPONSE.)

   When you go to an outlet mall, with whom do you typically go? (MARK ALL THAT APPLY.)

        1 By myself   6 Father

        2 Spouse   7 Female friend

        3 Son   8 Male friend

        4 Daughter   9 Other: _____

        5 Mother   99 DK/NR

   Why do you visit outlet malls? (PROBE. RECORD VERBATIM RESPONSE.)

   If a new outlet mall were built near Pittsburgh, what kinds of stores would you most like to see? (PROBE. RECORD VERBATIM RESPONSE.)

   2 No

   3 DK/NR

2. **During the past two years, have you visited a casino, racetrack, or offtrack betting facility to wager?** (MARK ONE.)

   1 Yes . . . How often do you wager? (PROBE. RECORD VERBATIM RESPONSE.)

   2 No

   3 DK/NR

3. **If slot machines are approved in Pennsylvania, how likely would you be to visit a wagering facility?** (READ. MARK ONE.)

1 Very likely   3 Not at all likely
2 Somewhat likely   4 DK/NR

4. **If a new outlet mall was built near an existing racetrack that had slot machines, how likely would _____?** (MARK ONE FOR EACH.)

	Very likely	Somewhat likely	Not at all likely	DK/NR
You—personally—be to visit the outlet mall?	1	2	3	4
You—personally—be to visit the race-track?	1	2	3	4
Someone you typically shop with at outlet malls be to visit the racetrack?	1	2	3	4
A family member or spouse who you typically do not take to outlet malls come to visit the racetrack?	1	2	3	4

5. **What would be your overall reaction to this idea of having an outlet mall and a racetrack that had slot machines in the same location?** (PROBE. RECORD VERBATIM RESPONSE.)

6. (DO NOT ASK, BUT RECORD:) **Gender?** (MARK ONE.)

1 Male
2 Female

These examples are typical of what's happened to me every time I've used the snapshot survey for this purpose. Asking as few as 5 people or as many as 100 what they thought about a particular topic that was of interest to my prospects has helped me greatly during the presentation. Just because you invest in a snapshot survey doesn't mean you'll win every proposal. I won three of these four examples and that seems about right for the other surveys I've run. However, conducting a snapshot survey always increases your chances and helps you stand out from your competitors—because it forces you to start talking about ideas and information that are relevant to your prospect. None of the firms I've ever pitched against have used this same technique. It's unlikely that any of your competitors have ever thought of this idea either.

SCIENTIFIC SELLING: USING THE SNAPSHOT SURVEY TO SELL BIGGER PROJECTS

While the snapshot survey is an excellent tool to use during your major competitive sales presentations (after some of your competitors have already been weeded out), it is even more effective if you use it as a first step in defining and clarifying your client's problem. The concept is to not sell a big project (at least not initially). Instead, your goal should be to sell a much smaller needs-assessment or diagnostic step so you can quantify your prospect's problem.

There's no point spending a lot of time and energy working for "free" as you develop your proposal and pitch to end up with nothing—which you inadvertently end up charging to some other client through higher fees to cover the "investment" you made in the business you just lost. I call this process "scientific selling," because you get paid for doing the investigative work, instead of working for several hours or days in the hopes of winning a project. Most clients value this type of detailed feedback about their business—and it almost always leads to bigger projects than the alternative—immediately making recommendations that are based on past experience, hunches, and opinion.

Why Physicians Are Great Salespeople

I've always admired the sales capabilities of physicians, even though most would deny they are sales professionals, much less admit that they are any good at it. They are mistaken.

Most physicians are extremely persuasive, because of their "expertise" and the "sales process" they use, which usually consists of three steps:

1. *Questions.* They start with questions, most of them pointed and precise. Within a few minutes, they have some initial ideas of what the problem may be.
2. *Diagnostics.* Next, they typically rely on some tests to help confirm their initial thinking. Some of these tests are simple physical exams they perform immediately while a patient is in the office; others require the assistance of equipment or other professionals (X rays, blood work, etc.).

F *l a s h* **# 4 4**

Rather than agreeing to write a proposal with detailed recommendations on spec, I like to first sell a snapshot survey. When the prospect says, "I think I have a problem," I reply, "That's why I recommend that you begin with our diagnostic step to find out exactly what's going on and what it's going to take to solve this problem." If the prospect agrees, I can usually define its problem more clearly and sell the company a bigger project.

3. *Treatment recommendations.* After the tests are completed, they make specific recommendations about what needs to be done, ranging from nothing to surgery.

I think physicians are effective sales professionals for the following important reasons:

- *They use a defined scientific process to help them understand and clarify the problem.* They ask questions, make observations, take readings—before they give their recommendation.
- *They get paid for their expertise and advice.* Even if you don't accept their recommendation, you still pay for their consultation and tests.
- *They base their recommendation on data, and rely less on hunches and guesswork, which naturally makes them more persuasive.* Surely, they rely on their experience, but when they couple it with printouts, readings, charts, and other measures, their recommendations are more convincing.
- *Most are highly respected by their customers (patients) and within society in general.*

Wouldn't it be nice if we could say the same things about you and your industry? The fact of the matter is that you can, once you find a way to incorporate more "science" into your sales process.

Transforming Your Sales Process

Figure 8.2 highlights the difference between a typical sales process and one that includes formal diagnostics or a "study," similar to physician consultations. In traditional selling, you ask questions and attempt

FIGURE 8.2

Scientific selling typically leads to larger projects, because a client's problem is better understood and more clearly quantified (size, opportunity cost, benefit, etc.) before the work of solving the problem begins.

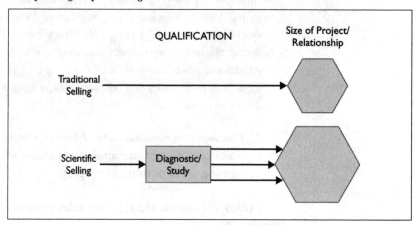

to qualify your prospect before making specific recommendations on which products or services it should buy. In scientific selling, you act more like a scientist, who uses a disciplined investigation process to define, qualify, and quantify your prospect's problem. The exciting part about scientific selling, as diagrammed in this model, is that your results often help you increase the size of your final sale.

You've probably already seen some examples of scientific selling in consumer purchases but were unaware of them:

- When a telephone carrier or other utility provider offers you a "free analysis" of your current bill, it is using scientific selling. Instead of saying how great its service is or trying to differentiate its services on a specific attribute (size of its network, customer service, etc.), it is using its analysis to provide value.
- Real estate agents use a similar approach when they offer to give you a marketplace valuation of your home and recommendations on how best to market the property. Instead of talking about all they can do for you, they start by giving away something valuable to you and get you thinking about how you might benefit by deciding to list your home.

The same technique works even better in professional services and other selling situations, such as in these needs-assessment instances:

- I worked with a leading property management company to develop a scientific selling system that was designed to help the company recuperate the time investment it took to win a new client. Instead of providing advice about how to manage the building, reviewing assorted contracts, using best practices to compare one building to the next, reviewing financial data, etc., I helped the company package the expertise into a "study" it could conduct and provide to its clients.
- For a banking software company, who was already using scientific selling to promote its assorted product lines, I was asked to help beef up this process by reviewing the Federal Deposit Insurance Corporation (FDIC) data of its clients to determine how well the banks that used my client's services performed compared to the industry average. Every quarter, the FDIC requires banking and savings institutions to file detailed reports about their earnings, profits, assets, ratios, and a laundry list of other numbers. Because searching these databases uncovered some interesting conclusions and insights that prospects would find highly valuable, this data was included in its literature and used as part of its ongoing sales efforts.
- An engineering firm I worked with decided to use a "scoping session" as its diagnostic tool. Instead of talking with a client, then going back to the office to write an elaborate proposal, the strategy was to sell a one-day planning meeting for a nominal fee. Key members of the engineering team, the client, and other representatives would spend the day talking about the project and reviewing initial ideas of what needed to be done. Not every prospect agreed to this step, but those who did said that it really helped clarify their thinking and gave them a chance to get to know the people they would eventually work with. From the engineering firm's perspective, this cut out the time to write the proposal and allowed it to get started working right away (and also get paid for writing the proposal).

It's usually much easier for a prospect to buy your diagnostics or needs assessment than your entire project, and the data you produce may help the prospect decide to move forward with information it can use to sell the idea to other decision makers.

F l a s h # 4 5

Some years ago, when my wife, Patti, and I bought our fixer-upper dream house, we were told we needed a new roof. We understood we had a problem, but we weren't motivated to do anything about it. One rainy spring morning, Patti started yelling to me to bring up some pots and pans from the kitchen to one of the bedrooms on the second floor, because there was water leaking through the ceiling. As I was running up the stairs, it dawned on me that the water was coming from the roof, through the attic, through the third floor to the second floor. I no longer had a problem. I had pain. I was emotionally ready to make a buying decision. I called the roofer that day. The snapshot survey can help you uncover and quantify your customer's pain, which makes buying your products and services a whole lot easier.

Quantifying Pain

Scientific selling works because it helps you quantify your prospect's problems or the challenges it is facing. I believe people are motivated by one of two basic forces: pleasure or pain. These are two big buckets that most of our problems, feelings, and ideas fit into. Deciding which bucket your products or services fits best in is critical.

In one bucket, pleasure, you find that people are motivated by things that feel good. Going out to dinner, watching television, taking a vacation—when someone makes one of these purchases, they do so because they are motivated by the enjoyment they expect to feel from having or using the product or service.

In the other bucket is pain, which is a deep-seated problem, concern, or desire. People are motivated to action so they can reduce or eliminate their pain. We file our taxes so we don't have to pay fines or go to jail. We buy new tires for our cars to keep our families and vehicles safe. We go to the gym so we can be healthier and lose weight. When someone makes one of these purchases, they are doing so to feel less pain.

The more pain your client is in—either caused by the factors of its current situation or that you uncovered through the questions you asked in your sales process and formal diagnostics study/needs assessment—the easier it is to sell it your products or services.

Following are some typical management pains that most business leaders experience from time to time as they are operating their businesses:

- Lower than anticipated profits (falling stock prices, missed sales projections, etc.)
- Rising costs (insurance, labor, materials, opportunity, etc.)
- Quality problems (product, service, employee, maintenance, etc.)
- Employee problems (low morale, lack of teamwork, turnover, reorganizations, safety, etc.)
- Lost customers and strained relationships
- Managing growth (finding enough talented employees, controlling space/rent costs, ensuring the organization has a unified focus, training and development, etc.)

Most businesses experience a number of marketing pains as well. The ones I've heard most frequently from my clients and I've found through assorted snapshot surveys are listed in Figure 8.3.

An effective diagnostic or needs-assessment tool should be focused on defining and quantifying what these pains are costing your prospect in terms of frustration, lost opportunities, money, time, and anything else that may be valuable to it. This is why the snapshot survey is such an excellent component of a diagnostic or needs-assessment study. When you ask questions that help put numbers to clients' pain, it makes them more willing to solve their problems. It clarifies just how much avoiding the pains costs and how good it might feel to get rid of them. When their pain is quantified, they are more emotionally ready to make a buying decision.

The Needs Assessment

One way I found I could use scientific selling to boost the total dollar value of a project was in the area of training and development. In addition to running marketing research studies, I hold a lot of professional development seminars and teach both undergraduate and graduate students.

I found that it was just as tough to sell a $2,500 one-day training program as it was to sell a several-month training engagement for $50,000, as long as I started with a needs assessment. That's right. The same amount of effort to sell both. The only difference was convincing my clients to begin with a needs assessment. This assumes that I was

FIGURE 8.3

Top 20 marketing "pains" or deep-seated problems, challenges, or concerns that marketing managers struggle with

---

FREQUENT MARKETING PAINS

1. Making products stand out in a crowd

2. Selling products that only a few people are aware of or understand

3. Determining the most effective way to increase your company's visibility

4. Educating prospects so selling is easier

5. Shortening a long sales cycle (the time when someone starts getting interested until he or she buys)

6. Not taking time to strategize the best approach

7. Basing key decisions on hunches and guesswork

8. Writing, developing, and designing effective sales materials

9. Understanding prospects' buying decision processes and learning who the real players are

10. Building customer confidence in regard to product quality

11. Spending a limited amount of money on the most effective marketing techniques

12. Effectively following up on sales leads

13. Establishing clear marketing objectives and developing a plan that works

14. Connecting marketing and sales

15. Evaluating and measuring results—and convincing management "it" worked

16. Abandoning effective slogans and brand materials because of "new" management

17. Not using "visual" words that tend to better persuade target markets

18. Always looking for the "silver bullet" tactic

19. When selling, not getting decisions about the next steps

20. Effectively measuring marketing ROI

---

calling on the right prospects and that they could afford a $50,000 investment. For smaller firms, I would develop off-the-shelf, noncustomized packages that I could use to quickly complete a needs assessment before beginning a training program.

One type of needs assessment I sold I called the "Organizational Assessment and Opportunity Analysis," or OAOA, which typically included the following components:

- *Senior management interviews.* I like to begin a project by talking to the organization's leaders and do these in face-to-face and one-on-one meetings, if possible. Nothing beats hearing first-hand what the leadership of a company is thinking. Sometimes we'd include similar interviews with managers and other employees to supplement the information.
- *Written surveys with managers and employees.* Next, I would usually put together a customized employee survey that asked questions about the management, communication, and other skills. Respondents were asked to rate "how important" they thought each skill or attribute was and "how satisfied" they were as an individual employee, within their work group and the organization as a whole. Figure 8.4 lists the attributes I used in a survey of managers. I charged $7,500 for the survey, which led to a $50,000 training program.
- *Summary report and presentation.* Once completed, the results would be summarized in a report and presented to senior management with recommendations. After running similar surveys, it became easier and easier to turn these reports around quickly.

In most needs assessments, I would find insightful and valuable information that helped my clients better understand their challenges. They would usually adopt our recommendations, which often included training.

Other times, the problems we identified didn't need training or any other services we offered to solve them. In these cases, we would recommend to our clients that they not work with us to fix whatever problems we uncovered. One time, for example, while conducting a needs assessment for a yacht club that included interviews with employees and focus groups with current customers, we found that the best use of the club's dollars would be to make some physical and structural improvements to its facility. Fixing broken kitchen equipment, repairing leaking bathrooms, and taking care of other problems would produce a much greater benefit than providing training, marketing, or any other assistance we could have offered. The client was certainly surprised that I recommended it not pay me any more money. It quickly realized what I was saying was the right thing to do, and I think the client respected me for it. I always want to do what's right for my clients. Sometimes that's having enough guts to not sell them anything.

FIGURE 8.4

Attributes used for a management training needs assessment to help quantify which skills managers needed the most help with in follow-up training programs

Goals

- Making correct staffing decisions
- Everyone working toward the same goals
- Communicating long-range goals
- Focusing on objectives
- Regularly participating in long-range planning
- Implementing the correct goal-setting program
- Having action plans to reach your goals
- Top management providing clear direction

Expectations

- Discussing how you can better meet customer needs
- Employees clearly understanding instructions
- Having orderly procedures for transmitting information between functions
- Determining how well your employees understand what is expected of them
- Establishing clear, individual accountabilities
- Having employees actively participate in establishing business unit goals
- Having specific job descriptions
- Establishing standards so that performance can be better managed

Management

- Giving recognition when a good job is done
- Quickly recognizing problems
- Quickly resolving problems
- Understanding motivation
- Understanding the individual strengths of your people
- Using different management styles with different people
- Your business unit's reputation
- Conducting formal performance appraisals
- Asking questions to help understand employee problems or situations before making decisions

FIGURE 8.4 *(Continued)*

Teamwork

- Having a sense of teamwork

- Raising the level of your employees' self-esteem

- Knowing how and when to effectively delegate

- Reviewing job performance on a regular basis

- Finding out your employees' perceptions about you as a manager

- Dissolving communication barriers

- Eliminating nonproductive, repetitive behavior

- Instilling pride in your staff of the work they complete

- Sharing perceptions of where the organization could be going

Personal Effectiveness

- Managing behavior rather than results

- Knowing that there is a viable opportunity for personal growth and advancement

- Making difficult decisions

- Handling emotional or upset people

- Organizing your time to accomplish priorities

- Determining where a change in policies and practices would have the greatest impact

- Meeting with your staff one-on-one on a regular basis

GETTING ON TRACK TO WIN MORE CUSTOMERS AND BIGGER PROJECTS

The snapshot survey will work for you either to differentiate you from your competitors during the big shoot-outs (by using it to gather feedback from an audience your prospect cares about on a topic it would like to learn more about) or to help you quantify your customer's pain by incorporating it into your selling process (as part of a diagnostic or needs-assessment tool). The best way to find out if it will work is to just try it. It's really that simple. Decide that you're going to do it—then go do it.

This is exactly how I learned to use the snapshot survey to overcome these two selling problems. I finally got so sick of losing projects to competitors I thought were less qualified than I was that I took the initiative to run a quick survey and present the results as part of my presentation. It worked, so I kept doing it.

The same situation happened with scientific selling. Once I found out I could win bigger projects if I sold them a needs assessment first, I kept doing it. In fact, you might make the case that this is what I do virtually every time I sell any kind of survey. I quantify my client's problems and opportunities so it makes its decision easier.

The first time you use the snapshot survey to help differentiate your products from your competitors' or as part of your scientific selling approach, it may not work out exactly as you hoped. You won't get it right the first time. But if you try it several times and keep tinkering with it until it feels right, the snapshot survey will help you get more sales results with less effort. The way I use the snapshot survey in my sales presentations and needs assessments is very different today than the first few times I tried it.

Keep after it. Using the snapshot survey in these situations will help you do better with the leads you already have and convert more prospects into customers—which, of course, is what every successful organization needs to do.

9

INTERNAL MARKETING

Using the Snapshot Survey to Gather Employee Feedback

The way a team plays as a whole determines its success.
You may have the greatest bunch of individual stars in the world,
but if they don't play together, the club won't be worth a dime.

Babe Ruth

Most people think marketing is only about communicating outside the company—trying to persuade prospects to become customers and customers to buy more products and services. Brochures, Web pages, printed advertisements, and direct mail are some of the many tools you might use to reach these outside audiences. For me, this definition is too narrowly focused and thwarts the true power of marketing.

I like to define marketing a bit broader: "Marketing is finding what the customers want. Developing it. Giving it to them when and where they want it—at prices they're willing to pay. And then telling them about it." I wish I could say that I thought this definition up all by myself. But I didn't. I stole it from my good friend, Dave Mastovich, who has spent his career as a professional marketer.

Marketing is about product development, pricing, distribution, positioning, and more, not just communications.

It's also about understanding and persuading your "target audiences," which in my view includes your employees. These are the people who interact with your customers, make your products, and possess the ability to make or break your company. Ignoring them is stupidity. The better informed they are about what you're trying to do as a company (and the more bought-in to your vision they are), the better work

> **F** *l a s h* **# 4 5**
>
> While marketing is usually thought of as an "external" activity, the same principles and techniques can be easily adapted to "internal" audiences, such as employees, managers, frontline supervisors, teams working from multiple locations, distributors, and others. And the snapshot survey can be equally useful within an organization. Whether it's assessing employees' current perceptions of their benefits package or finding out whether they think your organization has a glass ceiling, a well-designed survey can provide executives with important insights they would have trouble learning otherwise.

they will do for your customers. A colleague of mine was running an employee meeting recently with his company president when a worker admitted the staff did a better job making the company's products when they knew which customer it was for. When they didn't know who it was for or didn't like the customer, they cared less about quality and took more shortcuts.

TEN REASONS WHY YOU SHOULD ASK YOUR EMPLOYEES FOR FEEDBACK

I'm convinced that employees (outside of marketing and sales) are a central component of many successful marketing programs. Whether it's the receptionist who answers the telephone and tries to connect the caller with a live person who can help the caller (instead of always pushing calls to voice mail) or the shipping clerk (who gets the order together correctly and out the door on time), many of your employees can have a dramatic impact on marketing. These are the main reasons why I like to include employees as an audience in many of the surveys I conduct:

1. *To find out if your employees' perceptions match those of your customers.* Including employee feedback as part of an image and reputation audit helps me find out if and how much employees think like customers. Do they see the same strengths and challenges? In my snapshot surveys, I often find that employees are more critical about their company than are customers. Most customers are less emotionally attached to the companies they buy from than are the people who work there every day.

2. *To find out how well you're communicating.* Learning what employees think about communications from senior management helps the organization's leaders understand how well they're coming across and whether they need to spend more or less time communicating, not to mention what they should be talking about.

3. *To get good ideas for improving your business.* Asking employees what they think customers care about almost always uncovers ideas for improving service or creating new products. You'd be amazed at the great ideas employees have told me in focus groups and snapshot surveys.

4. *To see how they feel about their jobs.* Assessing employees' overall attitudes and perceptions to find out who's happy, who's not, and what can be done to improve the working environment. Losing employees you'd rather keep is a significant problem for many businesses, especially when the economy is good. If you're in a business where the majority of your assets (your employees and not your manufacturing equipment) go home every night, the problem can be even more critical. Over the past decade, businesses have started to understand the value of their knowledge base. I watched the president of a large technology firm get pushed out because he laid off the majority of his technical product development staff to save money (because he thought it would help his stock price). In doing so, the president jeopardized the future of the company and the board recognized it quickly and tried to hire many of these technical professionals back, but most found other jobs quickly and were disgusted by how they were treated. So, out the door the president went.

5. *To stop guessing about what they really think.* Once you ask them, you'll know whether something is a problem or not.

6. *To be respectful.* Most employees appreciate it when you ask them their opinion. You don't always have to do what they suggest and you don't have to do everything they recommend. But sincerely asking for their input communicates that you care.

7. *To find out what matters to customers.* The bigger your firm and the more customers you have, the less any one person knows about the "customer" as a collective whole. In addition to asking customers directly what they think of your company, employees can offer an interesting perspective, especially those who work with specific customers on a regular basis.

8. *To find out what to ask customers about.* Whenever I can, I like to check out the feedback I get from employees with customers. If

there's a hot issue, problem, or topic that employees say is important, why not include it on your next customer survey. If it's valid, you can do something about it. If it's only a perception, you can use the customer feedback to help change it.

9. *To participate in total quality programs.* A number of quality programs, such as that of Malcolm Baldrige, encourage customer and employee feedback. The requirements don't state exactly how to collect this data or which questions to ask, but these programs all recognize that employee feedback is important.

10. *To find out how well your managers are doing.* One of the—if not THE—best communications channels to represent your viewpoints to your employees is your frontline supervisor. I've delivered numerous communications training programs to frontline managers and supervisors from companies such as Dunlop Tires and FedEx to help them communicate and sell-in senior management's messages. I've also seen in most of the employee surveys I've run that it's the managers who employees go to to ask questions and get answers. Most managers have more credibility with their employees than does senior management, because they are known commodities. Keeping managers informed and then learning how well employees think they are passing along these top messages helps senior managers gauge the credibility of this communication channel (managers and supervisors) and determine what help they might need to be more effective.

F *l a s h* **# 4 6**

Given a forum, employees will talk. The challenge is finding the right forum and being totally certain that there will be no repercussions for expressing their true feelings.

SUCCESS STORIES: HOW SIX ORGANIZATIONS USED EMPLOYEE FEEDBACK

You can use the snapshot survey in many ways to gather employee feedback, ranging from simple surveys about benefits and human resources issues to more customized questionnaires that focus on specific topics relating to your overall marketing effort. I've included six examples in this section that I think demonstrate the different ways you might try using the snapshot survey in your business to help you address specific management and marketing challenges:

1. Increasing employee productivity and satisfaction by using more of their talents and abilities on the job
2. Developing a stronger marketing culture
3. Evaluating marketing tactics
4. Marketing specific ideas and programs to employees
5. Redesigning employee compensation packages
6. Communicating and simplifying employee benefits

1. Using More of Your Employees' Talents

Some years ago, I discovered that if I asked employees this simple question, "Are your talents and abilities being effectively utilized in your current position?" I could predict how satisfied they were with their jobs. The employees who said "yes," rated virtually every attitude statement on the rest of the survey more positively than did the employees who said "no." When you step back and think about it, it makes sense. People who feel like their talents are making a difference are happier. Many of the rest are frustrated because they want to be doing more and haven't taken the initiative, obtained permission from their supervisor (or whoever they believe is responsible), or don't believe they work in an environment where it's possible do more. It's like the old Zig Ziglar story about the Oklahoma City Indian chief who was given a brand-new Cadillac, but could never get it to go faster than ten miles per hour. He hitched it up to his team of horses and pulled it around town—not realizing that it had all those other horses under the hood.

One of the companies I used this question with was a leading telephone service provider, who discovered that many of the company's employees felt like they were bumping into a glass ceiling. Thousands of its employees perceived a "lack of opportunities" within the organization. They were working very hard at their jobs, but there were only a few places they could be promoted or advanced in their careers.

To combat this problem, the organization's training department wanted to put together a program that would help them enrich their jobs by taking on new and different job responsibilities and, therefore, using more of each employees' talents and abilities.

To determine if the training was having any positive impact, a simple attitude survey was prepared and is contained in Figure 9.1. Surveys were distributed to all employees by division before the training program began. Then the training was provided to all members of each division. Six months after the training program, the survey was conducted again to find out what impact the program had, if any. Overall, the survey showed that employees were feeling much better about their jobs and more agreed that their talents were being used following the training than before. In fact, the initial findings were so dramatic that management agreed to fund the entire training program and budgeted more than $1million for its implementation, a substantial win for the training department.

On the survey itself, when ratings on the 1 to 5 scale in question number one were compared to the employees who answered "yes" to question three (their talents and abilities were being effectively utilized in their current position), employees with the highest attitude scores were the same employees who felt they were using more of their talents and abilities. This conclusion was not limited to this company. In fact, it's been true on virtually every employee survey I've conducted and it's likely true in your organization as well.

Here's the beautiful part about this finding when you think about it from the other direction: If you want more satisfied employees, find a way to use a maximum amount of their talents and abilities. That's right! If you find more work for them to do (using skills they aren't currently using now), they'll do more work. Your productivity will go up. You'll reach more of your goals. Your organization will operate more efficiently.

How do you get your employees to use more of their talents and abilities? If you're not going to offer a training program as the company in this example did, I recommend a second approach. During your performance appraisals with your staff or in a specific meeting, say, "One of the things we learned in our past employee survey is that some people think we are doing a good job of using their talents and abilities, but others do not. So, we're asking everyone to spend some time thinking about how they might use more of their talents and abilities. How could we be using more of your talents and abilities?" Of course, this can't be a forced conversation that you use to trick your staff into working harder. They'll see right through that. It has to be genuine. You have to want to listen to and accept some of their recommendations. When it is, you'll get their cooperation, buy-in, and support—and you'll find it's a lot easier to manage them, because their satisfaction is on the rise.

FIGURE 9.1

Survey used to measure the impact of a training program designed to help employees use more of their talents and abilities in their current job

CAREER DEVELOPMENT SURVEY

Please take a few minutes to complete and return this survey in the envelope provided. Your feedback will help us better understand the current career development opportunities within your business unit. **Your responses are completely confidential.** Only group summaries will be presented in the final results. Please **do not** write your name on this form.

1. **How would you describe your career development opportunities at Big Company?** (Circle one response for each statement.)

	Strongly Disagree	Disagree	Partly Agree/ Partly Disagree	Agree	Strongly Agree
a. I have identified my skills, interests, values, and needs for career development.	1	2	3	4	5
b. I understand career options available to me at Big Company.	1	2	3	4	5
c. I have written personal career goals.	1	2	3	4	5
d. I have developed an action plan to reach my goals.	1	2	3	4	5
e. I work with my manager to design challenging and rewarding assignments.	1	2	3	4	5
f. I understand my department's strategic direction and challenges.	1	2	3	4	5
g. I have recently identified the skills that will be needed to meet business challenges.	1	2	3	4	5
h. I speak openly with my manager about my career opportunities.	1	2	3	4	5
i. I receive feedback from my manager about skills I need to develop.	1	2	3	4	5
j. I work in an environment that supports my career and professional growth.	1	2	3	4	5

2. **Have you changed positions within the past year?** (Check one.)

   ☐ Yes   ☐ No (Skip to question 3.)

FIGURE 9.1 *(Continued)*

If "Yes," the move was: (Check one.)

☐ Voluntary—lateral within current business unit

☐ Voluntary—lateral to different business unit

☐ Promotion

☐ Involuntary due to reorganization

☐ Other (Please specify): _____

3. **Are your talents and abilities being effectively utilized in your current assignment?** (Check one.)

☐ Yes   ☐ No

4. **In which of the following career development activities are you most interested?** (Check all that apply.)

☐ Rotational assignments (*within* my business unit)

☐ Rotational assignments (*outside* my business unit)

☐ Informal mentorship

☐ Learn about opportunities in other departments

☐ Job shadowing/internship

☐ Other (Please specify): _____

5. **Have you attended either the Career Development Workshop for Employees or the Career Development Workshop for Managers delivered by the University of Excellence?** (Check one.)

☐ Career Development Workshop for Employees

☐ Career Development Workshop for Managers

☐ Have not attended either program

6. **Length of service with Big Company?** (Check one.)

☐ Up to 5 years   ☐ 21 to 30 years

☐ 6 to 10 years   ☐ More than 30 years

☐ 11 to 20 years

7. **What is your position classification?** (Check one.)

☐ Nonexempt   ☐ Supervisor, manager, director

☐ Exempt without direct reports   ☐ AVP and above

8. **Age?** (Check one.)

☐ Under 30   ☐ 50 to 54

☐ 30 to 39   ☐ 55 and over

☐ 40 to 49

FIGURE 9.1 *(Continued)*

---

9. **Gender?** (Check one.)

   ☐ Female   ☐ Male

10. **Race?** (Check one.)

   ☐ White   ☐ Asian/Pacific Islander

   ☐ Black   ☐ Native American

   ☐ Hispanic   ☐ Other

11. **Education?** (Check one.)

   ☐ High school/GED   ☐ **Undergraduate degree**

   ☐ Some college   ☐ **Advanced degree**

---

2. Developing a Stronger Marketing Culture

Do any of these situations sound familiar?

- You're a marketing professional who battles with the "marketing nonbelievers," individuals of all types who sometimes say they support marketing efforts, but deep down inside they really don't understand the function that well—much less believe in its value. These individuals may be spread throughout your organization from senior managers (sometimes even presidents and CEOs) all the way down to the front lines.

- You're a business owner or senior manager who's interested in building a marketing culture and you've wrestled with the best approach for getting your staff and colleagues to adopt simple marketing principles and ways of thinking. It can be very, very difficult to get the right people to think in new, outwardly focused ways.

- You're a consultant, advertising or marketing firm account executive, or leader of a professional service practice or agency who's undoubtedly seen up and down cycles in the volume of your business. When you reflect on why some periods are better than others, it's easy to see a pattern. When things are good and you're busy, there's less time for marketing. After time—because your marketing activity decreased—your business drops. So you refocus on marketing and before long business picks up.

F *l a s h* **# 4 7**

If you think of employees as a target audience you're trying to market to, the snapshot survey can be used in virtually every way that it's used with any other audience. The same principles and techniques apply. The more focused you are in your topic and questions, the more clear-cut your results usually will be. There's no reason why the snapshot survey can't shed light on and guide your most important internal decisions.

- You're a nonprofit professional, executive director, or board member who's looking for ways to develop new funding streams for your agency that rely less on traditional foundation support. Many agencies are beginning to question their long-term viability if they can't find new funding streams, many of which are directly connected to marketing efforts.

If these scenarios sound familiar, then you've already struggled with building and implementing a stronger marketing culture—a culture where marketing isn't an afterthought or a part-time activity. A culture where marketing is front and center, making valuable, strategic contributions every single day.

An employee snapshot survey can help you better understand what challenges and obstacles you're likely to face as you attempt to build this new culture inside your company. Figure 9.2 contains the questions asked by Green Manufacturing (the fictitious company I've referred to in several previous examples and chapters) of their employees as part of a combination of snapshot surveys they ran to better understand their brand image and develop a new marketing strategy. This survey asks some typical questions about employee satisfaction, but it also includes several questions on marketing, even going so far as to find out what employees think are the most persuasive reasons a customer or prospect should choose Green Manufacturing or one of its competitors. If you look closely, you'll notice that many of the questions on this survey were also asked customers. Thus, the results from the employee feedback could be compared with what everyone else was saying, a valuable point of view for senior management.

FIGURE 9.2

Employee survey used to assess the marketing culture of a manufacturing organization. The results were compared to similar questions asked customers, prospects, distributors, and suppliers.

EMPLOYEE SATISFACTION AND MARKETING AWARENESS SURVEY

Part 1: Employee Perspectives (What do you—as an *employee*—think of Green Manufacturing?)

1. **How much do you agree with these statements about *Green Manufacturing?* (Check one for each statement.)**

	Strongly Agree	Agree	Partly Agree/ Partly Disagree	Disagree	Strongly Disagree	Not Applicable
Green Manufacturing is an excellent place to work.	☐	☐	☐	☐	☐	☐
Green Manufacturing is innovative.	☐	☐	☐	☐	☐	☐
Green Manufacturing has high standards.	☐	☐	☐	☐	☐	☐
Green Manufacturing is headed in the right direction.	☐	☐	☐	☐	☐	☐
I feel good about the future of Green Manufacturing.	☐	☐	☐	☐	☐	☐
Green Manufacturing provides value to our customers they can't easily find elsewhere.	☐	☐	☐	☐	☐	☐
Green Manufacturing has a positive impact in the communities where it operates.	☐	☐	☐	☐	☐	☐

Comments and suggestions: _____

_____

2. **What do you think are Green Manufacturing's greatest *strengths?* (Please explain.)**

3. **What are our greatest *weaknesses?* (Please explain.)**

4. **To continue to be a successful company over the next three to five years, what will Green Manufacturing need to do in terms of *marketing?* (Please explain.)**

FIGURE 9.2 *(Continued)*

5. How much do you agree with these statements about *your job?* (Check one for each statement.)

	Strongly Agree	Agree	Partly Agree/ Partly Disagree	Disagree	Strongly Disagree	Not Applicable
Green Manufacturing offers excellent opportunities to acquire new skills and knowledge.	☐	☐	☐	☐	☐	☐
Working at Green Manufacturing is a rewarding experience.	☐	☐	☐	☐	☐	☐
Green Manufacturing values its employees.	☐	☐	☐	☐	☐	☐
My ideas and suggestions have been used to make changes in the company.	☐	☐	☐	☐	☐	☐
I receive enough feedback from my supervisor about how well I'm performing my job.	☐	☐	☐	☐	☐	☐
When I perform my job well, it has a direct impact on customer satisfaction.	☐	☐	☐	☐	☐	☐
My talents and abilities are being used effectively in my current position.	☐	☐	☐	☐	☐	☐
Green Manufacturing is well regarded by its employees.	☐	☐	☐	☐	☐	☐
I'm proud to say that I work for Green Manufacturing.	☐	☐	☐	☐	☐	☐
There is a direct connection between the work I do and the success of Green Manufacturing.	☐	☐	☐	☐	☐	☐

Comments and suggestions: _____

_____

6. Overall, what do you like *best* about working at Green Manufacturing? (Please explain.)

7. What do you like *least?* (Please explain.)

8. What marketing or sales training would help you do your job more effectively? (Please explain.)

FIGURE 9.2 *(Continued)*

9. **How much do you agree with these statements about *Green Manufacturing owners and management?*** (Check one for each statement.)

	Strongly Agree	Agree	Partly Agree/ Partly Disagree	Disagree	Strongly Disagree	Not Applicable
Management:						
I feel comfortable talking with management about my ideas, suggestions, job, and other topics that are important to me.	☐	☐	☐	☐	☐	☐
Management cares about me as an individual.	☐	☐	☐	☐	☐	☐
Management has created a positive work environment at Green Manufacturing.	☐	☐	☐	☐	☐	☐
Management trusts me to do my job and avoids micromanagement.	☐	☐	☐	☐	☐	☐
Senior Management:						
I feel comfortable talking with senior management about my ideas, suggestions, job, and other topics that are important to me.	☐	☐	☐	☐	☐	☐
Senior management cares about me as an individual.	☐	☐	☐	☐	☐	☐
Senior management has created a positive work environment at Green Manufacturing.	☐	☐	☐	☐	☐	☐
Senior management trusts me to do my job and avoids micromanagement.	☐	☐	☐	☐	☐	☐
Divisional or Department Managers:						
I feel comfortable talking with divisional or product managers about my ideas, suggestions, job, and other topics that are important to me.	☐	☐	☐	☐	☐	☐
Divisional or product managers care about me as an individual.	☐	☐	☐	☐	☐	☐
Divisional or product managers have created a positive work environment at Green Manufacturing.	☐	☐	☐	☐	☐	☐
Divisional or product managers trust me to do my job and avoid micromanagement.	☐	☐	☐	☐	☐	☐

Comments and suggestions: _____

_____

FIGURE 9.2 *(Continued)*

Part 2: Customer Perspectives (What do you think our customers think of Green Manufacturing?)

10. **Put yourself in our customers' shoes. If you were a customer, how important do you think the following items would be in your decision to select a specific supplier like Green Manufacturing? For each statement, fill in a response from 1 to 10 where 1 is "not at all important" and 10 is "very important." (Mark one for each statement; if you're not sure or don't know, leave it blank.)**

1–10 Rating

Customer Service:

The supplier...

Has experienced, knowledgeable sales staff who have experience in your industry's packaging.   _____

Has accurate and responsive sales and support staff.   _____

Makes deliveries as promised.   _____

Offers next-day delivery on stocked items.   _____

Is there when you call and/or quickly returns your calls.   _____

Can customize products, services, or programs for you.   _____

Has a state-of-the-art computer system that fills orders and requests quickly.   _____

Has enough sales and support people to service your account.   _____

Product Development, Performance, and Value-added Services:

The supplier...

Has a wide selection of products to meet your needs.   _____

Is financially stable.   _____

Knows the strengths, capabilities, and limitations of all the top manufacturers of rigid packaging.   _____

Offers custom design and mold advice and production.   _____

Offers product bundling (chance to buy several different products as one unit).   _____

Will manage and monitor your packaging, as well as set up and manage an inventory program.   _____

Keeps you informed of new products, regulations, and other issues affecting your industry.   _____

Has an experienced transportation department dedicated to finding the best carriers, routings, and freight rates.   _____

Can significantly reduce the time and cost required to develop a new product for your situation.   _____

Understands the complete situation and can handle all your needs, reducing the need to work with a lot of other vendors.   _____

FIGURE 9.2 *(Continued)*

	1–10 Rating
Provides objective consulting, not tied to a single manufacturer or single material.	_____
Has access to a major independent supplier with specific patents and manufacturing techniques.	_____
Has significant experience with dangerous-goods regulations and packaging development.	_____
Is an expert regarding local recycling regulations and helps you comply with them.	_____

Web, Electronic Commerce, and Customer Self-service:

The supplier...

Has a Web site you can use to check inventory.	_____
Lets you order free samples online.	_____
Has an online catalog.	_____
Has online purchasing capabilities.	_____
Provides account and order status on the Web.	_____
Offers custom catalogs with only the products you buy or want.	_____

11. **For each of these attributes, how do you think our customers would rate Green Manufacturing on a 1 to 10 scale, where 1 is "poor" and 10 is "excellent"?** (Mark 1 to 10 for each statement; if not sure or don't know, leave it blank.)

	1–10 Rating
Accountable—does what is promised, when it's promised	_____
Creativity—offers innovative products, services, and solutions	_____
Growth—establishes relationships that help all stakeholders (customers, prospects, suppliers, etc.) grow and prosper	_____
Integrity—ethical in dealings, you can rely on it, shows integrity	_____
Respect—demonstrates concern and understands customers' situations	_____
Satisfaction—works hard at keeping its stakeholders (customers, prospects, suppliers, etc.) satisfied	_____

Additional Statements:

Industry leader—number 1, lots of people use and like the company, favorite of many people	_____
Technology oriented—introduces new and improved products and services	_____
Offers value—provides services and ideas that can't be easily found in other places	_____

FIGURE 9.2 *(Continued)*

12. **Overall, what do you think is the most *persuasive* reason(s) a *customer* or *prospect* should choose Green Manufacturing (or one of our business units) over one of our competitors?** (Please explain.)

   a. Business unit 1

   b. Business unit 2

   c. Business unit 3

   d. Business unit 4

   e. Business unit 5

Comments and suggestions: _____

_____

_____

3. Evaluating a Marketing Tactic

Besides asking employees questions about your overall marketing efforts and culture, you can use the snapshot survey to find out what they think about a specific tactic. This is what a leading motor oil company did as the company was evaluating an interactive driving display that would be customized to feature the company's motor oil and race teams. The attraction was housed in a semitrailer and would be pulled around to state fairs and other community events for publicity purposes. To find out what employees thought, the company brought a working model to the company's headquarters and asked employees to go through the exhibit during their lunch hour. When they exited the display, they were asked to fill out the survey questions contained in Figure 9.3, which asked them to rate their overall experience and state how well they thought such a tactic might represent the company. Employees said they didn't think it worked for the company, so the company didn't move forward with the idea at that time.

4. Marketing Specific Ideas and Programs to Employees

Just as external marketing campaigns can focus on educating a specific audience about an idea, product, or service, so can internal campaigns. Many firms are focused on ethics right now, because of the

FIGURE 9.3

Questions used by a leading motor oil company to evaluate an interactive display that would travel to different events and be used to promote the company's products.

1. How would you rate the exhibit? (1 to 10, from didn't like at all to liked it very much)

2. If we customized the exhibit to feature our own race team and put it on tour, do you think it would project a positive image of our company?

3. After going through a customized exhibit, how do you think a rider would view us? (1 to 5, strongly disagree to strongly agree)
   - As a company that is clearly focused on the future
   - As a company with a high-tech, intelligent motor oil
   - As a company whose products they would like to try

4. How much would you pay to ride the exhibit?

5. How long have you been with our company?

6. Gender?

countless scandals and ongoing law enforcement scrutiny. Some firms have gone so far as to hire an ethics director, whose job is to ensure that the company is behaving ethically in all its dealing with customers, employees, and other audiences. For these programs to work, employees must understand what the initiatives are designed to do and what their role in the process should be.

General Dynamics Armament and Technical Products division understands the value of ethics and designed a communications program to promote its beliefs and principles to employees. Similar to other examples in this chapter, it wanted to gather employee feedback and learn more about what employees were thinking and whether the messages of the program were getting through to the people who needed to hear them.

Figure 9.4 contains the questions that General Dynamics developed to gauge employee feedback. It asked employees to rate each using a general attitude scale and then asked only one demographic question (whether employees were hourly or salaried). Because the organization has multiple divisions, the surveys, which were distributed internally, were printed on different colored paper so that the results could be examined by location. At the time, the division had more than 2,500 employees, so getting a good read on how well the communications was reaching everyone would have been impossible without the help of a survey like this one.

FIGURE 9.4

Attitude statements used by General Dynamics Armament and Technical Products division to rate the effectiveness of an internal ethics educational marketing program. The campaign was designed to inform employees about the company's ethics policies and practices.

Basic Beliefs

- We do what we say we'll do.
- We are our customers' trusted partner.
- We treat people fairly and with dignity.
- We reward exceptional performance and do not tolerate mediocrity.
- We develop our people and value their ideas.
- We enhance shareholder value.
- We insist upon ethical behavior.
- We give back to the communities in which we work.
- We are proud to do our part to keep America strong.

Ethics Awareness

- I know who the Director of Ethics is at ATP.
- I know who the Local Ethics Officer (LEO) is for my facility.
- My immediate supervisor/manager requires me to follow our policies and procedures.
- Coworkers in my area are accurate in recording quality data, manufacturing data, engineering data, time charges, etc.
- Coworkers in my area are timely in recording quality data, manufacturing data, engineering data, time charges, etc.
- If I knew a violation of our standards occurred, I would report it to the Ethics Department or the Ethics Hotline.

---

5. Redesigning Employee Compensation Packages

Employee compensation, usually the single largest expense for most organizations, is a concern for many executives who want to ensure that they are rewarding the right employees and positioning their organizations for long-term success. One of the more interesting pay challenges is within universities, who have traditionally given raises based on the length of time someone has been in his or her position and using some cost-of-living formula. In recent years, the thinking is shifting to a "pay-for-performance" concept, where employees are compensated on how well they are doing and the value of their contribu-

FIGURE 9.5

Questions used to gather feedback about a significant employee compensation change to "pay-for-performance" (raises based on merit, not tenure and cost of living) by first talking with representatives from peer universities who had already made the switch

1. Does your university offer pay-for-performance compensation to any of its employees?

2. Which type of employees participate in the pay-for-performance system? (Faculty, maintenance, housekeeping, administrative, support, professional)

3. In the future, are more jobs or departments at your university slated to fall under pay-for-performance salary guidelines?

4. How long has the pay-for-performance system been in place at your university?

5. Can you tell me a little bit about why your university decided to adopt a pay-for-performance system?

6. Overall, how effective would you say your pay-for-performance system has been in achieving the program goals and why?

7. What was your role in selecting a pay-for-performance system and adapting it to the needs of your university?

8. What do you call your pay-for-performance system when talking to your faculty or staff?

9a. What methods did you use to communicate the pay-for-performance system to your employees?

9b. Overall, what were the most effective methods of communicating information about the pay-for-performance system to your employees?

9c. What were the least effective methods?

10. What were the primary benefits of a pay-for-performance system you communicated to your employees?

11. How long was it from when the pay-for-performance system was first announced to when employees first began getting evaluations under the system?

12a. When the system was first announced, was there much difference in how various departments or groups of employees reacted to the pay-for-performance system?

12b. Which departments or groups of employees seem to appreciate the pay-for-performance system the most and why?

12c. Who seems to have been most resistant to the change and why?

13. What are some of the typical complaints you hear about your university's pay-for-performance system?

14. What, if any, were the unforeseen obstacles to implementing a pay-for-performance system at your university?

FIGURE 9.5 *(Continued)*

15. Looking back on how the pay-for-performance system was communicated and implemented at your university, what do you think could have been changed to make its introduction smoother?

16. What advice would you give to a university that was planning to implement a pay-for-performance system for its employees?

17. What other persons at your university could we speak with to learn more about how your university has implemented a pay-for-performance system?

18. What other universities do you know who are considering or have adopted a pay-for-performance system?

19. Earlier, you mentioned that you used a variety of tools to announce the program to your employees. We're helping another university plan for announcing a similar program. Could we see any of the brochures, letters, or documents you found effective in communicating the program to employees?

tions, not on how long they've been around. Any change like this ruffles feathers.

One of the leading universities I worked with wanted to shift to a pay-for-performance system and thought that it would make sense to conduct two snapshot surveys. One was focused on employees and their perceptions of pay-for-performance. The other was concentrated on peer universities who had already shifted to this new form of compensation. Instead of having my client discover all the pitfalls on its own by trial and error, I suggested that my client visit with these other universities and find out what worked—and didn't work—for them. By spending a few minutes "picking their brains," my thought was that we could save a lot of heartache and consternation as the new compensation package became a reality. See the survey used in Figure 9.5.

F *l a s h* **# 4 4**

While employee surveys are frequently about satisfaction and benefit, they can easily be focused on selecting an internal marketing strategy, choosing tactics, and evaluating the impact of your efforts.

6. Communicating and Simplifying Employee Benefits

One purpose of benefits packages is to help attract and retain quality employees. Although basic health care coverage is becoming scarce in many companies (and employees are asked to work for wages alone), bigger firms still offer this benefit. Sometimes they offer many more services. With some of the largest firms, the benefits packages actually become so complex that it's very difficult to communicate to employees exactly what they are entitled to and to help them understand all that the company is offering (which when tallied up is usually substantially more than their salaries). During orientation, they are usually handed a thick packet of information, which many employees never get around to reading, much less understanding.

A number of companies are missing a golden opportunity to brand their organization to employees through their benefits package. This was the same problem that one of my clients, a very large regional bank, believed it faced with respect to its benefits package. The bank was convinced that most employees had no idea how extensive their benefits package was and, if they did, they had trouble figuring out how to use it.

My client suspected that these branding problems contributed to a secondary problem. The human resources department was viewed as the "police" who were always around when there was a problem but never there to help. They believed that if they did a better job branding the benefits and providing more useful communication, it would eventually help them improve their internal image, not to mention help the employees be more productive in their work.

Figure 9.6 lists the focus group questions we used to ask employees about the bank's benefits and how they might be better organized. Groups were conducted with managers, tellers, and professional staff to see if my client's initial thinking was accurate or if there were any slight variations in opinion between the groups. Part of the groups involved testing some creative and graphic concepts initially on how the dozens of benefits might be organized into three or four key categories, much like a Web site that has a limited set of navigation buttons on its home page. The results were used to help the bank better brand and promote its benefits. Its plan was to measure the impact of these changes by tracking changes in ratings on questions it was already running on other employee surveys.

FIGURE 9.6

Focus group questions asked employees of a large regional bank to determine how to improve the organization and communication of an extensive benefits package that, the company suspected, most employees were unaware of or didn't know how to access.

Perceptions of Human Resources (HR)

1. When you think of HR as a function or department, what comes to mind and why?

2. What do you think is HR's primary role or function? How well do you think they are meeting this(these) role(s) and/or function(s)?

3. As far as you know, what kind of services and/or programs does HR provide?

4. In what ways does HR do a good job of supporting you as an individual employee to help you be productive and effective? What about supporting your team or work group?

5. What improvements could they make to help you and/or your team be more effective?

6. If you could say in one sentence what HR's mission should be, what would you suggest?

7. Can you think of anything that has surprised you and/or your coworkers about HR? Have you had any pleasantly surprising circumstances where HR helped you address a situation? If so, please tell us about it.

8. I need you to stretch with me on this next question. If HR were a person, would it be a man or a woman? How old would it be? What kind of car would it drive?

Human Resources' Communications

1. What kinds of information do you typically look for when you need to know something related to benefits or other services and programs offered by HR? What do you (or your employees) need to know the most about and why?

2. How do you typically find out about your benefits and related human resources information?
   - Where do you typically look for information?
   - Who do you talk with?
   - How reliable are these sources of information?

3. What kind of communications do you receive from HR? (PROBE FOR:)
   - E-mail alerts
   - Web site
   - Welcome packet
   - Printed newsletter
   - *Insight* magazine
   - Seminars
   - Training and development

FIGURE 9.6 *(Continued)*

4. How do you typically use these different communications?
   - Do you read them?
   - What do you do once you've looked at them?
   - Do you ever refer to them again?
   - To what extent do they help you do your job?

5. Within the past few weeks, have you visited Regional Bank's employee Web site?
   - Were you aware that the site has been restructured?
   - Did you find what you were looking for?
   - From what you remember, did the information seem well organized?

6. Which HR communications *stand out* and are most effective and/or user-friendly? Why?

7. Which HR communications *do not stand out* and are not very effective or user-friendly? Why?

8. Which channel (or type of communications) is most effective for you? Why?

9. Overall, would you say that the amount of communications from HR is too much, about right, or not enough? Why?

Organizing Information

1. In general, how organized and intuitive are the materials you receive from HR?
   - Do they seem like they are presented in categories or "buckets" that make sense or are they more of a laundry list of programs and services? Why?
   - How might the way in which the materials are organized and communicated be improved?

2. One idea we are exploring is organizing all the benefits and program materials into three or four broad categories. The categories might eventually have icons or colors to show that they go together. They would be consistently presented to employees on the Web site, through e-mail, and in printed documents. (SHOW CATEGORIES AND OPTIONS)
   - Do these seem like good categories? Why or why not?
   - What benefits, services, or programs would you put in each category?
   - If all you saw were these categories, do you think it would be easy to figure out where a specific benefit was located? Why or why not?

3. Typically, when a new person is hired, he or she is given a packet that contains a lot of information. Another idea to simplify the information besides better organizing into categories or buckets is to give it to the employee over several weeks. Overall, do you think HR information should be presented all at once to an employee or over a several-week period? Why?

FIGURE 9.6 *(Continued)*

---

4. To what extent could better, simpler communications of HR materials improve:
   - How well you performed your job?
   - How well your department or team operated?
   - How you feel about working at Regional Bank (e.g., motivated, excited, etc.)?
   - The enrollment process?
   - Help you find the information you need?
   - Learn all the benefits you are eligible for?

A DOZEN TIPS FOR GATHERING EMPLOYEE FEEDBACK YOU CAN USE

Employee surveys can be very different from other types of research. Please consider these 12 recommendations before you start asking for feedback. You can have the best intentions but fall flat on your face because you ignored some of the typical problems and challenges associated with gathering employee feedback.

1. *Ask for solutions to problems.* If the only thing your employee feedback does is give everyone a chance to vent, it's a failure. Every company has problems. Simply letting employees sound off about those problems—and never asking them how the company might solve them or what it could do differently that would make things better—is not the answer. Instead, keep the general tone of your questions and focus on looking for solutions. If you manage these expectations with employees, they'll come around.

2. *Don't ask for their names.* This also means not including so many demographic variables that employees think that you can figure out who they are. I've had a lot of employees say they tell lies while filling out the demographic questions (such as saying they work in a different location than they actually do). The more sensitive the topic or the more strained the relationships are within your company, the greater this problem will be. Survey numbering doesn't work either, because a lot of employees will simply rip off their numbers. If you need to include a demographic question, keep it simple and broad.

3. *Expect about half or a little more to complete their survey.* If you're running a mail or e-mail survey, you should expect about 50 percent to 60 percent of your employees to return their forms. If you do

F *l a s h* **# 4 5**

Don't let your snapshot survey degenerate into only a gripe session that explores in excruciating detail the problems the employees see in your company. Instead, also ask employees for their ideas on how you can make things better. Employees are smart. They know how to fix a lot of problems. All you have to do is start by asking for their help.

better than this, great. If not, it may be because of the topic, they don't perceive your survey is actually anonymous and confidential, or some other problem. Sending a reminder e-mail or postcard (for mail surveys) helps increase the response rates. (It typically gets you another 50 percent from what you've already collected.)

4. *Make sure your employees have access to your survey and collection method.* If you're planning to run an e-mail survey, does everyone have an e-mail address? Do they check it on a regular basis? If you're running a mail survey, does everyone speak English or do you need to have it translated for some employees?

5. *Include a postage-paid return envelope.* If you're mailing a printed survey to employees, distributing it through meetings, or sending it through interoffice mail, make sure you don't ask them to pay for the postage to get it back to you. They'll think you're cheap and some of them won't return it.

6. *It's okay to send it to their home, if it's right for your organization.* You'll know. Some of my clients have sent surveys home, while others have said that it will cause problems with employees (asking them to do company business on their time).

7. *Make your questions "readable."* If you have a mix of employee educational levels and backgrounds, pay extra attention to how you word your questions. Your questions should be clear and precise. They should also be written with short words and even shorter sentences. You'll get better feedback and won't inadvertently frustrate your employees.

8. *If you're not planning to share the results, don't conduct the survey.* Manager presentations, newsletter summaries, internal Web site stories, or a CEO road show are all good tools for sharing the results of your survey. But don't show up to simply say, this is what we learned from you. Make sure you take it to the next step and clearly describe what you're going to do next.

9. *If you're not planning to follow at least some of your employees' sugges-tions, don't bother asking the employees for them.* I recently ran a focus group for a restaurant chain that included meetings with wait staff and managers. I found out in the focus groups that senior management had held similar meetings a couple of months be-fore but never did anything with the results. The participants in the meeting told me point-blank: "If we're not going to see any-thing come out of this meeting, then why are we wasting our time talking with you?" Don't waste your employees' time. It will only make it more difficult the next time you try something.

10. *Consider using an outside party to gather your feedback.* Because of the delicate nature of employee feedback, many of my clients have told me that they don't want to be involved in gathering the feedback, asking the questions, or observing in any way. They realize that their mere presence is enough to bias the re-search and shut everyone down.

11. *Turn off your recorder.* Whenever I'm running employee focus groups, I use my tape recorder as a prop. As I start the groups, I physically turn it off and tell everyone in the group that I would rather hear what they have to say—and what they are say-ing is confidential. Usually, a tape recorder helps me be more accurate in my findings and works great with other audiences. Turning it off is akin to loosening my tie. It's a purposeful change in demeanor designed to get them to relax and trust me.

12. *Protect the confidentiality of their responses.* Sometimes the num-ber of responses I receive to particular demographic questions are very low. It would be easy for my clients to guess who the five or six people are who marked this response. In these cases, I simply recode their answers into one of the other categories or I don't present any comparison data for that question. This way, there's no chance that a small group could be highlighted so directly in the findings.

Once you understand how to modify your snapshot surveys to make them work for employee research, you'll be able to more easily find out what your people are thinking. When you combine their perceptions with those of your customers and prospects, you reduce your blind spots even further. You put yourself in a position to find out what's re-ally going on both inside and outside your company.

10

MEASURING MARKETING ROI

How to Prove *and* Improve *Your*

Marketing Effectiveness

Half the money I spend on advertising is wasted,
and the trouble is I don't know which half.

Viscount Leverhulme

Everyone in business understands the concept of "return on investment," or ROI. To stay in business, you need to earn more than you spend, and the higher the ratio of revenue over investment, the more successful the business. ROI numbers give you a clear, definitive yardstick for success.

The same principle applies to marketing: Either every dollar you spend on marketing should bring in the maximum amount of revenue, or you should spend that dollar somewhere else. Marketing ROI lets you *prove* that your marketing is—or is not—working. As a marketer, chief executive, or business owner, you need to do more than simply *say* that your marketing is effective. You have to back up your words with credible evidence that your marketing efforts are actually connected to some beneficial results for your organization. Then you can stop guessing about which marketing tactic is working the best, or working at all.

The snapshot survey is a powerful tool for gathering useful information about ROI at several stages of the marketing process: measuring awareness of a new product, for instance, or testing a new pricing schedule. But it may not be the right method for gauging results at other stages. This chapter explores the whole process of measuring marketing ROI, showing when to use the snapshot survey and when to use other tools so that you can create a thorough, balanced picture of your efforts and outcomes. Then, and only then, will you be able to show that your marketing is working.

HOW DID YOU FIND OUT ABOUT US?

Marketing ROI can begin by simply asking the question, "How did you find out about us?" as one of my clients discovered. CopyCat, the fictitious name I'll use to tell this true story, was a small, family-owned distributor of copiers and fax machines produced by a major copier manufacturer. It faced stiff price competition from a slew of larger distributors who were backed by even bigger manufacturers with better-known brands. In CopyCat's market, customers *expected* quality and service. They were ready to run to a competitor if they could save a few pennies. Because that market was so tight and the company was small, it was critical that CopyCat *got* something for every dollar it spent on marketing.

To start the process of measuring its ROI, CopyCat had its receptionist ask each prospective customer who called four questions:

1. "What's your name and company?"
2. "Are you a current customer?"
3. "How did you find out about us?"
4. "Are you interested in a copier or a fax machine?"

Over one year, the receptionist spoke to 756 prospects. She wrote their answers on a simple paper form that she kept at her desk. The process was simple and unobtrusive. CopyCat started on its own, without consulting outside marketing experts, and kept up this effort for a year. (When we looked back, it was clear that the first 50 or 100 contacts would have revealed the same patterns in a shorter time; that's the value of a snapshot survey. Having a whole year's data, however, made CopyCat more confident about its results, knowing that they didn't reflect seasonal variations.)

CopyCat's goal for its survey was to determine how fruitful its marketing was. Specifically, the company owners wanted to answer these questions:

- What percentage of our leads resulted in sales?
- How many leads did each of our marketing tools produce?

- Which marketing tools produced the best leads—the ones that we most often converted into sales?
- Which marketing tools provided the most and the least value (cost per lead or cost per sale)?

By asking questions in "real time" when the prospects called—not calling back several weeks or months later—the company was able to gather better, more accurate data.

THREE STEPS FOR DETERMINING YOUR MARKETING ROI

To answer these questions, CopyCat had to take three steps: It first had to determine who bought what, then summarize the lead and sales data it had collected, and finally examine the costs of generating each type of lead. By completing these three steps, CopyCat could answer fundamental questions about its marketing ROI.

1. Determine Who Bought What

The distributorship's sales manager went through the 756 leads and marked which contacts actually became customers for a new copier, a new fax machine, or both. This took several days of pulling customer records, updating the tracking form, and verifying each lead one at a time—not a quick task, but an essential one.

2. Tally the Results

This step is where CopyCat asked for my help. The firm had gathered all this data but didn't know what to do with it. I took the stacks of records, entered them into a computer spreadsheet, crunched the numbers, and began looking for trends and insights.

To keep things simple, I made each line of data represent one contact or prospect. Each column represented one tracking variable—for example, whether the contact was a customer or prospect, the source of the lead ("How did you find out about us?"), whether the contact made a purchase, and, if so, what type of purchase. Figure 10.1 shows the leads, sales, and closing ratios for each of CopyCat's marketing tools (left-hand column).

FIGURE 10.1

Results from a yearlong tracking form that asked prospects, "How did you find out about us?"

MARKETING TOOLS (BASE)	LEADS (756)		SALES (125)		CLOSING RATIO** (756)
	#	%	#	%	%
Sales rep lead	199	26%	28	22%	14%
Current customer	169	22	55	44	33
Manufacturer lead	135	18	2	2	1
Yellow Pages	58	8	9	7	15
Donnelley Directory	53	7	5	4	9
Referral	52	7	11	9	21
Cold call	28	4	7	6	25
Trade show	10	1	1	1	10
Brochure	2	*	0	0	0
Other	50	7	7	6	14
Total	756		125		17

* % indicates a percentage of less than 1.
** Sales divided by leads.

What does this data tell us about how well CopyCat's marketing was working? Here are at least three important conclusions:

1. The most leads came from sales reps (199), who were responsible for their own prospecting activities. Leads from current customers (169) were close behind, however.
2. While many manufacturer leads (135) were generated by advertising the copy machine manufacturers paid for, these leads were relatively unproductive for the effort they required: only 2 were converted into sales.
3. Almost 1 in 5 contacts (17 percent) bought something. However, current customers were the most likely group to make a purchase (33 percent). The worst lead sources came from brochures (0 percent) and the copy manufacturer's leads (1 percent).

3. Determine the Cost to Make Each Sale

CopyCat had spent $60,000, a very significant portion of its marketing budget, on advertising in two business-to-business directories:

the *Yellow Pages* and the *Donnelley Directory*. But the company could trace only 15 percent of its leads to these sources—and only 14 sales. Compounded by the price of its products and overhead, the firm had spent several thousand dollars to sell each copier and fax machine through this channel. They were actually losing money with this tactic.

For many businesses, directories displaying their ads are worth their weight in gold. But in this case, the money CopyCat spent on directory ad space wasn't producing the results it needed to justify that expenditure. Maybe there was something wrong with the ad copy or layout. Maybe it was placed in the wrong part of the books. Competitors may have had some edge in this channel. The point is that the "big ads" the firm had invested in weren't working.

Even more eye-opening was the honest look at where the company was getting its best leads—from its existing customers. Yet CopyCat had no newsletter or formal, ongoing communication with those customers. In other words, it was generating these leads without spending anything on marketing. But in a competitive market, that windfall wouldn't necessarily keep coming. In a nutshell, the firm was basically ignoring its customers from a communications standpoint, and thus ignoring its best source of growth. CopyCat wasn't capitalizing on the resources it currently had.

After CopyCat's management evaluated each of the company's marketing tactics, they decided to spend more marketing dollars on a customer newsletter and to buy smaller directory advertising space. Instead of investing more money in something that wasn't working, they decided to focus marketing resources on the tools that were providing the best leads. CopyCat's survey results had made it possible to *prove* what worked and *improve* the company's marketing.

F *l a s h* **# 4 6**

Measuring marketing ROI is like athletic training. Frequent, steady, disciplined workouts lead to fitness. Haphazard workouts, however frenzied, create only sore muscles. For marketing ROI to be effective, it must be consistent and ongoing, not sporadic and only when you feel you suddenly have to.

SEVEN LEVELS OF MARKETING ROI MEASUREMENT

Measuring and improving marketing ROI is a process. It's not a one-shot deal. It's an ongoing effort, an integral part of well-oiled marketing campaigns.

Before tackling the specific steps of the process, it's important to understand what you can and cannot measure. You can't measure all facets of your marketing. If you tried, you would spend all your time and money collecting and analyzing data and do nothing to market your products, services, or ideas. Instead, you want to focus on the most important and easily measured data, and to collect it efficiently. Figure 10.2 lists the seven primary areas or levels your marketing ROI measurement can focus on.

The best place to start is with an account of what you're doing. List all your marketing activity—all the techniques you're using to send a message to the marketplace. I call this "measuring your output," and simply doing this from time to time helps remind you how hard you're working (or not working). For instance, you and your colleagues might produce brochures, make cold calls, visit trade shows, and design advertising. Each of these forms of "output activities" has a cost that you can quantify. The total cost of each effort is an investment and serves as your denominator when it comes to calculating marketing ROI.

Next you need to find a way to measure the "outcome," or results, from your activities. Possibilities include:

- *Placements.* How successful are your media efforts?
- *Awareness.* Did anyone see your communications?
- *Attitude.* Did your activities change people's opinion about anything?
- *Incoming contacts.* Did your messages motivate anyone to do anything, like call an 800 number or respond to an e-mail offer?
- *Sales.* Did you get any new customers as a direct result of your marketing efforts?
- *Lifetime customer value.* What is the value of a new customer over the lifetime of its business with your organization?

To illustrate these stages, let's say that you wanted to conduct a direct mail campaign to companies, trying to get some of those prospects to call an 800 number and request more information. You and your marketing department might write and print a brochure, among other

FIGURE 10.2

Seven levels of marketing ROI measurement

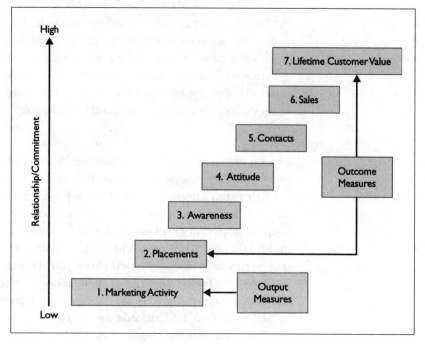

output activities. Those brochures would go to a list of prospects; the number of firms that see the material is a measure of "placements." Through telephone follow-up with each of the prospects, you could learn how many of them remember seeing the brochure ("awareness") and if the people who saw the brochure were influenced by it in any way ("attitude"). Then you could track what percentage of those prospects actually called the 800 number ("contacts") and if any of them became a new customer ("sales"). Looking at past customers, you could estimate the value of that new customer to your business over the life of your relationship ("lifetime customer value").

In this example, the goal of your marketing effort is to get enough people to call the 800 number so that your sales staff can convert at least some of these prospects into paying customers—enough new business to pay for the brochure and more. If you tracked marketing ROI at each step, you could develop a very good picture of how well your marketing material worked once it left your office. For instance, you might find that your brochure isn't getting noticed by the right people (not enough awareness), that people call but don't end up buying (good contacts, not

> **F l a s h # 4 7**
>
> There is no magic formula, wand, or even bullet for measuring marketing ROI. It's best to group your measurements into different categories or levels based on what type of relationship you have with your prospects and customers. This way, you can better track what happens once a communication leaves your office and whether those marketing efforts produced any results (inquiries, traffic, sales, repeat business, etc.).

enough sales), or that the brochure works so well that you don't need to carry out more expensive activities that produce a smaller return.

Sales aren't necessarily the best way to measure the result of a campaign. If you're trying to build awareness of a law firm's expertise or a hospital's specialty service, marketing is more about establishing and building a positive image. Thus, when someone needs your services, they would have already "heard about you" (which is a much better position to have them in instead of them asking, "Who are you?"). In these situations, marketing ROI assessments are heavily focused on placements, awareness, and attitude measures.

Let's take a deeper look at each of these measurement levels and explore ways to use the snapshot survey and related tools to better understand your marketing effectiveness.

I. Marketing Activity

No doubt, output activity is the most basic type of marketing measurement. This is where you try to measure what you are doing or have already done. At this stage, you have little concern for what other people—even your customers—are thinking or doing. In this type of measurement, an organization counts the number of items that its marketing staff wrote, developed, designed, or completed in order to accomplish its objectives. It might also include the number of phone calls, meetings with reporters, advertising expenditures, and other activities you completed. This form of evaluation focuses primarily on your efforts to communicate—not on the impact of that effort on any target audience. (A brief listing of some of these tactics appears in Figure 10.3, grouped into advertising, sales promotion, public relations, direct marketing, and personal selling categories.) All can be assessed on an output level.

FIGURE 10.3

Types of marketing tools that can be assessed on a marketing activity (output level)

Advertising	Sales Promotion	Public Relations	Direct Marketing	Personal Selling
• Print/broadcast ads	• Contests, sweepstakes, lotteries	• Press kits	• Catalogs	• Sales presentations
• Outer packaging	• Premiums and gifts	• Speeches	• Mailings	• Sales meetings
• Packaging inserts	• Sampling	• Seminars	• Telemarketing	• Incentive programs
• Brochures	• Fairs	• Annual reports	• Electronic shopping	• Samples
• Booklets	• Trade shows	• Charitable donations	• TV shopping	• Sales proposals
• Posters	• Exhibits	• Sponsorships	• Fax mail	• Referral programs
• Leaflets	• Demonstrations	• Publications	• E-mail	
• Directories	• Coupons	• Community relations	• Voice mail	
• Reprints of ads	• Rebates	• Lobbying		
• Billboards	• Low-interest financing	• Identity media		
• Display signs	• Entertainment	• Company magazine		
• Point-of-purchase displays	• Trade-in allowances	• Events		
• Audiovisuals	• Tie-ins	• Media relations		
• Symbols				
• Logos				
• Videotapes				

2. Placements

So you've produced a spiffy catalog, a timely press release, or an invitation to customers to visit your showroom. Once you put something like that "out there," what happened? Just because you sent out a news release doesn't mean anyone printed it. And your advertisement may look very classy, but how many people have the opportunity to see it? To find out, you need to determine your marketing ROI on the placements level.

This assessment step covers the territory between you and your prospects (if you haven't already reached them directly). It looks at what other people did to help you send your messages, such as the media and the mail carrier. With mailings, you can usually assume that anything that doesn't come back to your mailroom got through to *somebody*. Whether that person was part of your target audience, and whether he or she actually read your material, are questions for the next stage of marketing ROI.

For press releases and advertisements, the assessment of placement is more difficult. One very simple measurement is to track the total amount of coverage your organization received from all sources of news: newspapers, radio and television stations, and online outlets. Thus, you can count the number of clippings you've received about your product, or the number of ads you ran, but that treats a story on the back page of your local shopper's newspaper as equal to a feature in *The Wall Street Journal*.

Impressions.   A more sophisticated form of assessment used by many companies is called *impressions,* generally defined as the number of potential readers, listeners, or viewers who could have seen your message. This involves multiplying the number of stories or ads that ran by the number of people who could have read, heard, or seen each. Radio and television stations report their audience numbers to advertisers, and often these figures are published as well. For articles in print, more than one person usually reads the same copy. Therefore, it's typical to multiply newspaper and magazine circulation numbers by 2.5 to determine how many people might have been exposed to an article.

Impressions = circulation × potential readership (typically 2.5)

Thus, if one of your press releases appears in your local paper, you would determine that publication's total readership number (for example, 72,436) and multiply by 2.5 to quickly figure out how many people might have had a chance to read your article (181,090).

A keyword in that last sentence, however, is *might*. Tracking print coverage and calculating impressions doesn't determine how many of your audience actually saw, understood, or were influenced by what was printed. It's great that as many as 181,090 people could have read your article, but what does it really mean? Don't forget, readers might skip pages. Similar problems hold true for radio listeners and television viewers. Impression measurement gives only limited insights and shouldn't be your sole form of measurement.

Ad dollar value.   Another way to measure the value of news release placements is to use the *ad dollar value* formula. With this technique, marketers measure the length of each article in column inches and multiply that total by the ad rates for the same space. (You can easily find advertising rates by contacting each publication.) The idea is that your news release has earned you "free advertising." An article that is 12 inches long might be worth $500 of advertising space. Again, this tool can't measure the coverage's actual impact on your intended readers, listeners, or viewers; it just calculates the value of the information that was made available to your target audience if you had had to purchase the same space.

Content analysis. Still another technique is to analyze the content of the news coverage you received. Did the reporter or editor change your release in any way? If so, did the paper or broadcaster still transmit the gist of what you were trying to say, or were important elements deleted? Those important elements are called *key messages,* or the central idea of your communications. They are the core ideas you must communicate. By reading or listening to each of the news stories, you can decide if your key messages actually got through. Looking at the key messages and several other variables (the image of each paper or broadcaster, total circulation or audience, the section of the paper or media program where the article appeared, and so on), you can better determine the potential value of the placements.

3. Awareness

It's fairly easy to confirm that the communications your firm developed were actually sent and made available to your target audience. The remaining marketing ROI assessment steps determine how members of your target audience received, accepted, and acted on these messages. These types of measurement go beyond tracking the effort to communicate and begin to determine the impact of the communication. They measure *outcomes* not output. For those measurements, the snapshot survey is one of the most efficient tools.

Before people become prospects for your organization, they are what I call "suspects." No, they haven't committed a crime, but they aren't yet solid leads who have expressed some need or desire for your business. Good marketing can turn some of these suspects into prospects.

The most basic form of outcome measurement is to assess changes in awareness levels. Does anyone remember seeing your ad, story, brochure, or other communication? If not, there's little hope that you can influence people's opinions and perceptions. You've got to find a way to get their attention. Marketing ROI measurements on the awareness level help document the number of people who know something about your product, service, or idea through what they heard, read, or saw.

To find out awareness levels, you often have to talk directly with the people you are trying to reach. You can't assume they saw the ads you bought or read the news stories. Even if customers come into your store the day after your ad ran, that does not prove that your placements were successful—those people may have come because of some other reason, and to have good marketing ROI you have to know that reason. You have to ask questions to get useful answers.

Assessing awareness levels can be accomplished in many different ways. For example, you could document *changes* in what consumers know about a product, service, or idea. Measure how many people are aware of your product or service before you run your marketing program, and then find out how many are aware of it afterward. That data lets you see if you've made an improvement or "moved the needle."

A high-tech company used a snapshot survey in this way to assess the value of creating and sponsoring an industry conference. It asked 50 prospective customers before and after the event to answer these questions:

- Have you ever heard of the conference?
- From what you have heard, seen, or read, what is the focus of the conference?
- Did you attend the conference? If yes, what is your perception of it?
- What other conferences do you attend within your industry?
- What is the most effective method to inform you about conferences (e.g., direct mail, e-mail, faxes, etc.)?

The baseline and follow-up survey results showed substantial increase in the awareness of the conference, as well as a better understanding of its focus—both of which could be directly attributed to the marketing efforts to promote the event. This simple snapshot survey helped demonstrate the value of the conference.

Depending on your target market (current and potential customers), you could use telephone polls, written surveys, face-to-face conversations, group discussions, and other snapshot surveys to find out what people are thinking before and after you communicate. For example, a readership study is a good way to determine the awareness of your print or electronic newsletters. By sending a survey to readers, you can ask a number of questions about the publication, its content, format, or layout, as well as other topics. What articles or stories do readers remember? What was most useful or meaningful to them? If they can't

> **F l a s h # 4 8**
>
> One reason marketing budgets and staff often end up on the chopping block is because marketers don't quantify the value of their activities in financial terms. In a tight budget year, marketing costs look like expenses with no clear connection to income. Marketing ROI measurements can change that.

remember much of anything, you might want to think about improving your article topics or writing style.

Within studies of total quality measures and customer satisfaction, managers can also gather useful data on awareness. For instance, you might ask how many of your existing customers are aware of the full line of products or services you offer. Several dozen surveys my colleagues and I have completed for a variety of companies and industries indicate that the percentage of customers who are aware of a firm's full line of products and services ranges between 30 percent and 100 percent. This level of awareness typically depends on the number of customers a firm has; companies with several hundred or even several thousand typically can't communicate with each of those customers as often as someone who has only 25. Awareness levels also depend on the types of products or services sold; companies that offer many products or services have a lot more to communicate. Similarly, companies who have products that have been on the market for several years or even decades are typically better known than are newcomers. Certainly, the frequency and overall quality of communications influence awareness levels.

If your firm ends up on the low end of this scale, with more than half of your customers unaware of the full range of what you offer, then you have a fine opportunity. Your existing customers may be your best prospects for other goods or services. You already know how to contact them, and you've already built a relationship. Making this type of sale is relatively easy and inexpensive, with a great ROI.

4. Attitude

Once people are aware that you're trying to communicate with them, the next step is to determine if what you said shifted, reinforced, or changed their attitudes in any way. Remember that attitude changes come before customers contact you. You can't measure those changes by sitting in your office—you have to find potential customers and ask them questions, as in a snapshot survey.

As an example, I surveyed firefighters for a company that makes protective gear. First we cut 40 different advertisements out of firefighting magazines that, as in trade magazines for other professions, displayed plenty of creative (sometimes bizarre) ways to catch readers' attention. Then we took our stack of clippings down to the local fire department and asked a couple dozen firefighters to evaluate them. To my surprise, out of all the advertising, our snapshot survey respondents rated one of the ugliest, low-budget ads substantially higher than many of the glossy, clever ads. When I asked why, the firefighters told me that this one ad showed how the product worked in a real situation, helping them evaluate it before they made a purchase. Because they had a limited budget, it was extremely important that they bought equipment they would actually use. The results of this snapshot survey had an obvious value for my client, the equipment maker. The company learned that it didn't have to spend extra money on eye-catching ads; it could produce a higher marketing ROI by simply showing its customers how its equipment worked. Flashy ads may have entertainment value, but the bottom line for advertising is whether it makes people feel like actually *buying* the product.

The broader your marketing is, the more difficult it is to determine which parts are most effective. Let's say you're selling toothpaste. Your brand is displayed in several dozen stores around your town. You run a campaign to get more people to buy more of your product, combining ads in several media, discount coupons, free samples, and promotion through dentists. How do you know your marketing is working? Certainly you could track new sales orders to specific stores. This is a terrific technique, as long as you have historical data (previous months' sales) against which you can compare. But which forms of marketing have been effective? Which have the highest ROI?

In this case, it's highly unlikely that you could hire people to stand in stores, identify individual customers who considered purchasing your brand, and talk to them about all the ads or other communications they saw. Even a snapshot survey would be inefficient in this situation. It would be better to test your ads and offers with a segment of potential consumers in an auditorium, in focus groups, or through product insert surveys. With the help of a questionnaire, you could learn how many consumers were "likely" to try your product after hearing the ad. Notice the measurement is about someone's "state of mind," their feelings. It's not always about whether they actually make a purchase.

All of us have a thought and feeling about a product, service, or idea before we physically act on that thought by entering a store, placing a call, clicking a button, or agreeing to see a sales rep. Before people decide to purchase a product, they have an attitude about that product that influences their decision. The more important the purchase, generally, the greater the role attitudes will play in deciding whether to make the purchase. Most consumers, for example, have stronger feelings about the brand and make of their automobile than they do about the brand of filing folders purchased at a local office supply store.

As with determining marketing ROI on an awareness level, many options are available to assess changes in attitudes. One option is to explore how well your target audience comprehends what you're talking about. This is especially useful if you're working on social and political issues. It's important to know if members of your community are aware of an issue and if they understand how that issue might affect them. The minds of people closest to the issue—which includes you—might be crystal clear, but the general public typically has less interest. Potential supporters (and opponents) may be only casually aware of the topic and be familiar with few or no details. An attitude assessment can help you determine if you are talking in the right language and with the right messages to your target audience. If they know practically nothing about your topic, and you want to focus your communications on the minutiae, nothing but trouble lies ahead.

Other marketing ROI assessments on the attitude level might include:

- Opinion change, or the percentage of people who would consider using a product, service, or organization after learning new information
- Brand acceptance, or the reasons behind consumers' willingness to try a product or service
- Baseline and follow-up assessments that document changes in opinion after a marketing program is implemented. Many attitude analyses require repeated measurements to be successful. For example, a study designed to determine if a marketing campaign changes a company's image over time would require—at a minimum—both a baseline assessment before the campaign and a follow-up assessment afterwards. More sophisticated programs use multiple and ongoing assessments.
- Tracking studies, which are ongoing assessments to determine the long-term impact of programs over several months or years.

F l a s h # 4 9

If you don't have written marketing goals, you're just messing around and making it virtually impossible to measure marketing ROI.

The way that consumers think about milk, beef, automobiles, and many other products today is very different from their attitudes in years past. Tracking studies help show the evolution of our thinking over time.

The National Aviary, which is located in Pittsburgh, Pennsylvania, used an attitude snapshot survey to evaluate the impact of adding a bird theater to its attraction. Once a day, birds would perform in an entertaining show that told visitors more about the animals. Management wanted to know if the visitors who saw the show had a better overall experience than the visitors who did not. Figure 10.4 shows the survey they used. Volunteers asked visitors as they were leaving to take just a minute to complete the form.

The National Aviary ran surveys at multiple times to measure *changes* in visitors' opinions. The organization found out that virtually every visitor who saw the bird show said that he or she really liked the visit. The ratings of these visitors for the whole visit were much higher than the scores from visitors who did not see the show. This snapshot survey helped management better understand the value of the bird theater and the impact it was having on its customers.

5. Contacts

Contact evaluation studies are a more advanced form of outcome measurement than awareness or attitude assessments. They measure success at marketing's primary purpose: to help create bottom-line results, such as:

- Generating more sales leads
- Suggesting where to find potential new members, volunteers, donors, or customers
- Increasing store traffic
- Boosting telephone inquiries about new products or services

FIGURE 10.4

The National Aviary's Wow! Index, which tracked how "wowed" visitors were who saw a show at the newly designed Bird Theater

1. **How did we do today?** (Check one for each.)

	Excellent	Very Good	Good	Fair	Poor	Not Applicable
Overall experience	☐	☐	☐	☐	☐	☐
Ease of finding/seeing birds	☐	☐	☐	☐	☐	☐
Being near the birds	☐	☐	☐	☐	☐	☐
Information about bird habitats and conservation	☐	☐	☐	☐	☐	☐
Watching birds act naturally (flying, swimming, etc.)	☐	☐	☐	☐	☐	☐
Variety of bird species	☐	☐	☐	☐	☐	☐
Staff friendliness	☐	☐	☐	☐	☐	☐
Staff knowledge and explanation of birds	☐	☐	☐	☐	☐	☐
Did you attend any performances today?	☐	☐	☐	☐	☐	☐
Owl Encounter . . . How was the performance?	☐	☐	☐	☐	☐	☐
Penguin Premiere . . . How was the performance?	☐	☐	☐	☐	☐	☐

2. **Is this your first visit?** (Check one.)

   ☐ Yes

   ☐ No . . . **If no, how long has it been since your last visit?** (Check one.)

   ☐ < 6 months   ☐ 6 months to 1 year   ☐ 2 years   ☐ 3 to 4 years
   ☐ 5+ years

3. **Are you here today _____?** (Check one.)

   ☐ By yourself   ☐ As part of a school group
   ☐ With family/friends   ☐ As part of a tour group

4. Are you a member? (Check one.)

   ☐ Yes

   ☐ No . . . **If no, are you planning to become a member?** (Check one.)

   ☐ Yes   ☐ No   ☐ Not sure

FIGURE 10.4 *(Continued)*

5. **As a result of your visit today, are you more likely to do any of these activities?** (Check all that apply.)

☐ Visit other animal attractions (zoos, aviaries, aquariums)
☐ Build a bird house/sanctuary
☐ Make a donation to a bird/animal conservation group
☐ Recycle
☐ Take an ecotourism vacation to wild and scenic rain forests, mountains, and other locations
☐ Feed birds in my yard
☐ Nothing

6. **Have you visited any of these animal attractions?** (Check all that apply.)

☐ Akron Zoological Park   ☐ Erie Zoo
☐ Cleveland Metroparks Zoo   ☐ Oglebay Park Zoo and Aquarium
☐ Columbus Zoo and Aquarium   ☐ SeaWorld
☐ Disney's Animal Kingdom   ☐ ZOOAMERICA (Hershey, Pennsylvania)

7. **How do we compare to other attractions that feature birds?** (Check one.)

☐ More impressive/exciting   ☐ Less impressive/exciting
☐ About the same   ☐ Not sure

8. **Would you recommend visiting us to a friend or family member?** (Check one.)

☐ Yes   ☐ Depends on family member
☐ No

9. **How long do you think it will be until your next visit?** (Check one.)

☐ Less than 6 months   ☐ 3 to 4 years
☐ 6 months to 1 year   ☐ 5 years or more
☐ 2 years   ☐ Not sure

10. **Where do you live?** (Check one.)

☐ Metro area   ☐ 100+ miles from area
☐ Less than 100 miles from area

11. **What is your age?** (Check one.)

☐ Younger than 10   ☐ 35 to 49
☐ 10 to 17   ☐ 50 to 64
☐ 18 to 24   ☐ 65+
☐ 25 to 34

FIGURE 10.4 *(Continued)*

12. **Are you a** _____**?** (Check one.)
☐ Male (boy)
☐ Female (girl)

Comments and suggestions: _____

_____

_____

_____

It's often easier to measure this type of behavior because it takes place right in front of you—in your store, on your phone line, in your mailbox. Depending on your type of business and the marketing tools you're using, you could track the number of contacts generated at a trade show or through an article placement, the number of "bingo cards" (postcard responses) that came in after magazine advertisements, the number of prospects generated by a direct-mail campaign, or the number of new association membership applications recruited during an annual drive. You might track call-ins or requests for information (as CopyCat did by asking, "How did you find out about us?"). You might even be able to sort contacts by product, territory, or some other significant categories. You could also use the contacts generated during these measurements to conduct a snapshot survey that digs for more information.

Often, however, companies are so busy with these potential customers and so pleased to have them that they don't take the time to assess what brought those people in and how they can bring in more. So if you're interested in learning more about why potential customers come to you (and who isn't?), it's wise to set up a system to collect that information in advance.

When someone contacts you, their status begins to change from what I previously called "suspects" into real sales prospects. And by measuring their behavior, you can learn more about what it will take to turn these people into your customers. All prospects start out as "contacts." At first, you really don't know if they're serious about buying your product or service. In fact, you don't even know if they need or have enough money to pay for what you offer. Some of these contacts will eventually turn into "appointments" in which you can talk about their needs or problems. A smaller number will ask for a proposal or demonstration. Even fewer will make an initial purchase and become customers. The purpose of marketing, therefore, is to provide enough leads that the firm's sales staff can close a portion of them and build a profitable customer base.

6. Sales

The process of further qualifying prospects and converting them into new customers follows something I call the "sales cookbook." As with kitchen cookbooks that help you create delicious meals, this approach gives you a recipe for mixing the right ingredients in the correct order: from contact to appointment to demonstration to sale (or through other primary steps in your sales process).

The sales cookbook can help you determine how much marketing activity your firm needs to reach your sales objectives. How? By tracking the "closing ratio" between each step. Let's say that all your marketing activity combined generates 500 contacts annually. Furthermore, let's say that your closing ratio is 20 percent between each step in the sales process. In other words, 1 out of every 5 people will go from contact to appointment, from appointment to demonstration, and so on. The numbers in your sales cookbook would look like this:

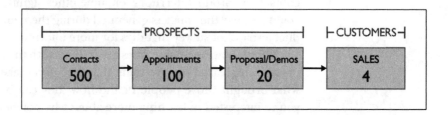

Using this formula, we can see that if the organization's goal is to make 25 sales a year, its marketing must generate 3,125 contacts. If your marketing can't do that or your company can't afford that much marketing expense, you had better find a way to improve your selling process.

The dramatic effects of improving closing ratios.   Under this model, a slight improvement in closing ratios can produce a dramatic improvement in sales. If the number of prospects moving from one step to the next increases from 20 percent to 25 percent—that's only 1 more person in every 20—the number of total sales will double. By moving 1 in 4 people to the next step instead of 1 in 5, the total number of new customers will double:

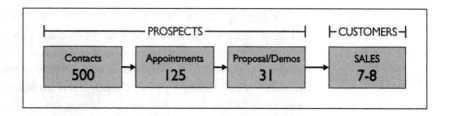

With this sort of closing ratio, if the company's goal is still 25 sales annually, it needs only 1,563 contacts—half as many leads as it would need with a 20 percent closing ratio.

The implications of this formula to marketing are very important for three reasons:

1. Your marketing must generate enough contacts to sustain and meet your sales goals. Therefore, the more efficiently your marketing produces contacts who can be converted into sales, the more success you will have.
2. If you have a strong sales staff, your marketing effort will be more efficient.
3. By understanding the numbers in your firm's sales cookbook, you can determine how much activity it will take at each stage to achieve the results you need. Instead of focusing on sales volume, you can then manage your staff's sales behavior—ensuring that the firm is doing efficient marketing to bring in leads and that the salespeople are converting those contacts into sales. Manage the day-to-day activity, and good results will follow.

How could CopyCat have used the sales cookbook formula to increase its total number of sales? Remember that the firm's owners started with 756 total leads and had 125 total sales, for an overall closing ratio of 17 percent. Could it close all its prospects with the same closing ratio that it was using to sell existing customers (33 percent)? The result would be phenomenal: 249 total sales, practically doubling its business. That may seem like a stretch, but if the firm changes its marketing to produce better leads—by aggressively focusing on the existing customer base and scrapping the unproductive marketing tools—its staff would convert more of those leads into sales. Even if CopyCat's overall closing ratio never rose to 33 percent, it could still expect dramatic growth without having to significantly change its selling processes.

Adjusting prices.   Another benefit of the sales cookbook model is to help companies make adjustments to their pricing. For example, a company may calculate that it needs to win one out of every two prospects it pursues. If the company is currently winning more than 50 percent, it can raise its prices slightly, thus increasing revenue without probably falling below the target closing ratio. If, on the other hand, the same company starts consistently losing more than 50 percent of its bids, a slight decrease in price may be in order. With all things being equal, knowing how well your company is tracking between each step of the cookbook model allows you and your fellow managers to make informed decisions about what *is* and *is not* working. Talk about a powerful ROI tool!

Adjusting the tracking.   While the sales cookbook evaluation approach can be extremely valuable, it is often difficult to implement because many organizations don't have the proper internal tracking mechanisms in place. For example, if a marketing, advertising, and public relations program generated 500 leads, but there was no way to identify, classify, or report the results of those leads to a manager who could analyze them properly, the true results of the program will never be known. If your company sells through a distributor network, but has trouble getting reports about what happened to the leads you provided, your tracking system won't work.

CopyCat did figure out how to accurately track leads. But it required work. The firm made one person, the receptionist, responsible for asking everyone who called in the "How did you find out about us?" question. And it invested the time of a manager and a consultant in analyzing the results. Because of this effort, the distributorship was able to use the formula to see what was working and what wasn't. Without it, CopyCat would have had little way of determining its marketing ROI.

Studies to evaluate the recipes in a firm's sales cookbook work best when they are coordinated with existing internal tracking systems. If you don't have an effective tracking system, building one should be your first priority.

7. Lifetime Customer Value

When people think about marketing, they almost always focus on finding new customers. That means meeting people they do not know and converting some of them into prospects and a few of them into customers. While acquisition is an important component of marketing, this strategy is hard to sustain. An acquisition mentality is a huge problem for many organizations because it tricks managers into thinking that the faster they acquire, the faster they will grow. Everything is focused on finding the "next" customer—very little on exploiting the untapped value of the customers they already have. In time, they will just run out of prospects and wear themselves out.

The "lifetime customer value" philosophy says that marketing should be focused on all that a customer could represent to your organization: revenue, referrals, advice on new products, help in defining your brand image, etc. Instead of seeing the customer as worth only the next sale, you consider all that he or she might spend with you. The simplest way to estimate the lifetime customer value is to follow the following four steps:

1. Determine how much a customer is likely to spend with you over a specific period of time (e.g., one month, one quarter, or one year).
2. Multiply that number by the total amount of time you anticipate that the customer will buy from you.
3. Add the lifetime value of any referrals the customer may provide.
4. Subtract your estimated cost to acquire and maintain the customer.

A simple example could start with a customer who generates $10,000 a month to your business ($10,000 × 12 = $120,000 per year). You might find that on average similar customers stay with you three years ($120,000 × 3 = $360,000 expected lifetime revenue). Most customers also give you one referral a year to another customer, also worth $10,000 per month ([$10,000 × 12 = $120,000] × 3 = $360,000 revenue from referrals). And this customer gives you a product idea that generates an additional $25,000. In this case, the total lifetime customer value is $745,000, with revenue coming in even after your business with this customer tapers off.

No doubt you will treat a customer you think is worth three-quarters of a million dollars of business more importantly than one who is worth only one $10,000 sale. When we calculate lifetime customer value, most of our customers are worth a whole lot more than we think. Lifetime customer value also keeps you focused on high payoff activities—like sales to your existing customers that are easier to close. In the long run, your profit will increase because you don't have to invest so much in bringing in new business.

FIVE CRUCIAL STEPS TO ASSESSING THE VALUE OF YOUR MARKETING EFFORT

So how can you improve—or, if you aren't doing anything at the moment, start—to assess your marketing ROI using the snapshot survey and other tools? Virtually all measurements can be completed by following these five steps:

1. Set Measurable Marketing Goals

Do you work in a business that measures success by the number of products, services, or ideas it sells? If so, tracking how, where, and how much your marketing is producing sales can provide critical insights. It will help you to set objectives, establish marketing budgets, isolate trends, and ensure short- and long-term growth.

What if tracking sales isn't the main goal of your marketing? Utility companies, for instance, may have a well-established customer base. A hospital or legal firm may be most interested in building awareness of the staff's expertise so that when people do need their services, they know where to turn first. A civic institution may want to know how it is perceived in the community as it considers plans for expansion, fundraising, or new memberships. For these organizations, it is useful to track attitudes, perceptions, and opinions, which generally *precede* behavior. Many businesses that rely on sales also benefit from measuring attitudes. From impulse buying to long lead time sales cycles, the attitudes and perceptions a prospect holds before making a decision influences the sale. So why not measure them?

A professional service firm wanted to measure the impact of offering less expensive health insurance. This was the second changeover the company had tried in a short time. The first shift, two years before, was a communications disaster that resulted in many employee complaints. This time the firm established three goals for its new transition:

Goal #1: *To present benefits information clearly and more thoroughly than before.* Managers first evaluated the materials used during the last changeover, along with the complaints they had received. They then developed an impressive communications program about the new benefits that included video briefings, a Web site, printed literature, and other materials. Next, they identified what results they wanted to achieve: higher employee satisfaction, fewer complaints. Finally, they looked for ways to quantify those desires in order to make them into goals.

Goal #2: *To reduce negative reactions to the benefits change.* Through a snapshot survey that followed the communications program, managers asked employees if they understood their new benefits, what they thought of them, and (for people employed during the last changeover) if the efforts to explain the new benefits were better this time than last. The survey showed employees were generally favorable about this change.

Goal #3: *To reduce the time that benefits staff devoted to the difficult and confusing changeover period.* The company measured this by looking at the telephone logs after each transition. They found that their benefits staff spent half as much time answering questions as during the first changeover.

Make no mistake. This effort worked only because of clear, measurable marketing goals. "Doing it better this time" wouldn't have been explicit enough to measure. Unless you have clearly defined marketing goals, there's no point in trying to measure your marketing ROI. You'll have an invisible, moving target to shoot for. First, make your goals clear, specific, and quantifiable. Then start thinking about the best tool or data to measure their impact.

2. Agree on What's Being Counted

Remember the National Aviary and its new bird theater? Toward the end of that job, my client called me frantically about a letter she had just received from a foundation who made a major investment to help build the new theater. Our snapshot survey clearly showed visitors who saw the show had a better visit than those who didn't see the show. So, I wondered, what could be the problem?

My client told me that the foundation wanted to know how the National Aviary's sales (admissions and gift shop) had improved since it had launched the shows, and particularly if the people who had seen the shows spent more money on average than those who hadn't. This is a great question, but it couldn't be answered with the snapshot survey the aviary had chosen. We could look at overall admissions and gift-shop sales data from before and after the bird theater opened, but we couldn't definitely tie any change in those numbers to the theater. To be more certain, we would have to have added a question to the survey about whether people had bought or planned to buy items, or to have run a separate survey of gift-shop customers.

In this situation, the ultimate client for the snapshot survey results was actually the foundation, not the National Aviary itself. And we had failed to agree with that ultimate client on what was to be counted and how. Measuring the visitors' experience produced important and useful data, but the foundation also wanted a more concrete analysis of the financial impact of its investment.

The best time to discuss exactly what you want to measure is, of course, while you're developing your marketing plan, not afterward. Before launching a marketing ROI assessment, ask yourself these four questions:

1. What data are you collecting, who's gathering it, and how do they get it?
2. How often do you collect data, and how will you know when to stop collecting it?
3. What will the data look like in the final report?
4. In what ways will the data help you improve your marketing, or how do you plan on using it?

The answers will help keep you focused on the right kinds of measurement.

How well do you know your customers? This might seem like a strange question, but do you know your customers' names, addresses, phone numbers, and e-mail addresses? Or are your customers more anonymous—people who wander into your store, or might (or might not) read a giveaway newspaper?

For many marketing ROI assessments, you need access to individuals who can tell you what impact your marketing had on them. This is especially true if you are trying more than one form of marketing to reach the same customers. Which technique was actually the most effective? The only way to find out is to ask your new prospects, and the only way to ask is to know who they are. Make sure you collect that data as part of your marketing ROI process. Then you can use a snapshot survey to gather more in-depth information from a select sample.

3. Use More Than One Measurement Tool

One of the best ideas for simplifying marketing ROI measurements is to think of them as one of two basic types: program measures and tactic measures. Program measures look at the overall impact of a program in terms of the big picture. Did it help increase sales, build market share, or accomplish some other important objective? Tactic measures tell you how effective a particular tool (news release, trade show, brochure, etc.) worked. Both types of measures can be helpful in evaluating your marketing, but expecting a tactic measure (number of media hits or impressions) to prove the value of an entire program (which is a combination of tactics and your "marketing mix") misses the point. There's no credible way you can, for example, say you built awareness for a new product by measuring only the number of media hits you got from the launch press release. You have to document awareness by asking your targets what they're aware of—and that's where the snapshot survey comes in.

Not all ROI findings are clear-cut, so "proof" from multiple sources is always best. Impressions (number of people who saw a news or trade article), baseline and follow-up opinion surveys, and sales that were generated from multiple marketing tools may not be persuasive measures by themselves. However, taken together, they point to a positive trend. One that's much more believable in terms of what's working and why.

Selecting the right tool. Each of the seven levels of marketing ROI require different measurement tools. For example, determining how many newspapers printed all or part of a press release might require the help of a professional clipping service. Measuring attitudes might require conducting a before-and-after attitude and perception survey. Measuring sales might require contacting all the customers who bought a product or service to ask how they learned about you and why they made their purchase decisions. There is no magic formula. Some ROI assessments are best measured using only one tool. Other assessments need several tools to get a better feel for what benefits can honestly be attributed to marketing.

FIGURE 10.5
Tools business-to-business companies use to measure their marketing ROI

Sales volume increase	61%
* Number of leads generated by tactic or program	60%
Tactic distribution (the number of press releases, pieces of direct mail, news releases, and other information sent out or delivered)	59%
* Number of new customers resulting from marketing	58%
* Awareness changes (percentage increase of customers'/prospects' awareness of product/service)	57%
Number of Web hits	54%
Impressions (number of articles multiplied by the potential readership of each publication)	53%
Total reach (circulation of articles and advertisements, plus distribution of literature)	53%
Content analysis (number of key messages picked up in the stories)	45%
* Advertising effectiveness (target audience delivery, awareness/recall, research completed by trade publications, etc.)	44%
Advertising equivalence (news story column inch or airtime multiplied by ad rates = "free advertising")	37%
* Comprehension (level of customer/prospect understanding of product/ service)	34%
* Baseline and follow-up opinion change surveys	33%
Ratio of marketing spending to sales volume	30%
Base: 430	

* Tools marked with an asterisk usually involve snapshot surveys or some other form of polling customers, prospects, or the public.

Several years ago, I completed an industry survey about how 480 leading business-to-business companies measure marketing ROI. (For a complete summary of these results, see Lloyd Corder et al., "PR Is to Experience What Marketing Is to Expectations," *Public Relations Quarterly,* Volume 44, Number 1, Spring, 1999.) It turned out that 10 percent of them do not measure marketing ROI at all. Of the 90 percent who do, they use a combination of measurement tools (see Figure 10.5).

4. Use Existing Measures before Creating New Ones

Before you build something from scratch, look around at what's already going on that you might be able to piggyback on. There are three obvious alternatives to collecting new data.

First, determine what's already being collected *inside* your company. Look at company records, call-ins, complaints, sales, accounting documents, old surveys, and anything else you can get your hands on. Someone may already be collecting data that might work as one of your measurement tools. It never hurts to ask. And you'll never know unless you do.

Second, wherever possible, modify existing data collection tools to do "double duty" as marketing ROI tools. You can do this by adding questions to existing customer surveys. Add survey questions to your Web site. Or have your receptionist start asking, "How did you find out about us?" after he or she greets callers.

Finally, look for external sources, such as industry surveys, rankings, and advertising publications surveys. I call this stuff "other people's data." One way a lot of colleges and universities evaluate themselves, although sometimes begrudgingly, is by rankings reported in the *U.S. News and World Report.* The State of Pennsylvania used site-selection magazine surveys published annually to help evaluate its economic-development marketing programs.

When you start looking around, you often can find that you don't have to reinvent the wheel to measure your marketing ROI.

5. Effectively Communicate and Present Your ROI Findings

As with most situations, the better the job you do communicating your marketing ROI results, the more your client, your boss, and even you will understand the program had an impact.

There's something magical in that old KISS formula: *Keep It Simple, Stupid!* Use simple sentences and statistics. Most people get lost quickly if you use statistics that are any more complicated than percentages or means.

Speaking of short, if you can limit your ROI presentation to one page or one slide, you're on the right track. Readers should be able to tell right away how well something is working. The next time you get a physical, ask to see a report of your blood work. Most of the results are one page and tell volumes about how healthy you are.

F l a s h   # 5 0

When summarizing and presenting your marketing ROI findings, try to keep your results brief (limited to one page, if possible). This will force you to summarize your findings and make them easier to present to others.

This should be your acid test: "Can a reasonably intelligent stranger grasp the essentials of your report in one reading?" If not, rewrite it.

THE BOTTOM LINE

What does it take to be better at marketing, achieve more of your objectives, win bigger budgets, and advance professionally? No matter what size your marketing budget, the simple answer is good marketing ROI. Marketing ROI no longer can just be a goal. It has to be a thoroughly planned and well-executed part of a comprehensive marketing effort.

With more planning, systematic measurement, defined standards, and actual research using the snapshot survey, you should feel less frustration and more confidence in your marketing decisions.

Just talking about marketing ROI doesn't cut it. Good marketers are quick to ask the question, "What have you done for me lately?"—whether they need to give the answer to their boss, their banker, or their own conscience. Great marketers use marketing ROI to *prove* their worth and *improve* their performance.

If you would like to learn more about *The Snapshot Survey*'s author, Dr. Lloyd Corder, and the services his firm provides, please visit *http://www.corcom-inc.com.* The site includes many valuable free articles, tip lists, and other resources.

You can also sign up to receive *C-Note$,* Dr. Corder's free monthly e-newsletter that contains valuable strategies and ideas for helping you more closely link marketing to sales, measure marketing ROI (return on investment), and become more personally persuasive and effective.

For more information, please contact Dr. Corder at:

Lloyd Corder, Ph.D.
CorCom, Inc.
Gateway Towers, Suite 240
320 Fort Duquesne Boulevard
Pittsburgh, Pennsylvania 15222
(412) 201-2636
(412) 201-2606 (fax)
corder@corcom-inc.com
http://www.corcom-inc.com

A

Ablak, Varol, 143–44
Accessibility, 71
Advertising, 163, 242
   see also Media coverage
   ad dollar value, 244–45
   awareness, 245–47
   content analysis, 245
   directory ad space, 238–39
   impressions, 244
   placements, 243–44
   publication surveys, 263
Advisors, 81
American Iron and Steel Institute, 168–70, 181, 182–83
Analyst reports, 64–65
Animal names, 152–53
Aquafresh Whitening®, 179
Aquarium concept, 190–92
Associated Press, 184
Atkins, Chet, 145
Attitude(s), 247–50
assessing changes in, 249
Attribute(s)
   evaluating, 72–74
   ratings, 70–72
   sample survey, 72
Audubon Institute, 191

B

Bacon's Directory, 178
Baldrige, Malcolm, 212
Baseline assessment, 249
Benefits, employee, 229–32
Bidding process, 63
"Blind" questioning technique, 66–67, 75

C

Board members, 81
Books
   as marketing tactic, 126
   news coverage and, 171
Boston Market Frozen Foods, 165
Brain drain (in Pittsburgh), 158–60
Brand acceptance, 249
Brand-reputation assessment, 7–8, 107–8
Brochures, 171
Budgets, 121
Buffett, Warren, 163
Business improvements, 211
Business plan, 112. *See* also Marketing plan
Business-to-business (B2B), 123–24, 262
   surveys, 172–73
Business-to-consumer (B2C), 123
Buyers vs. sellers, 188

Canned Food Alliance, 180
Career development survey, 214–17
Celebrity spokespersons, 175
Chat rooms, 64
Chefs Cooking with Style survey, 181, 182–83
Chemical manufacturer proposal, 193–94
Clipping service, 261
Closing ratio, 254–56
Coldtime Survey, 165–66
Communication, 211

awareness, 245–47
effect on attitude, 247–50
of employee benefits, 229–32
key messages, 245
technology gap, 109
Compensation packages, 226–28
Competition/competitors, 14, 61–86
   additional perspectives regarding, 78–82
   analyzing survey results, 85–86
   attribute evaluations, 72–74
   attribute ratings, 70–72
   case histories, 68–70, 75–78, 84–85
   competitive assessment survey (sample), 75–78
   discovering strengths/ weaknesses of, 65–70
   learning about, 64–65
   name/tagline/logo research, 149
   numbers and types of, 62–63
   personification questions, 74–78
   survey size/focus, 82–85
   web site analysis, 64
Conferences, 171
Confidentiality, 234
Conjoint analysis, 128
Consultative selling, 15
Consulting service, marketing, 124–26
Consumer personality demographic questions, 176–77

Consumer polls, 172
Consumer publications, 170–71
Contact evaluation studies, 250–54
Content analysis, 245
Controversy, 57
CorCom, Inc., 150
Corder, Dr. Lloyd, 265
Corporate image, 15
Credibility, 63
Current situation, reviewing, 118
Customer(s)
    see also Customer satisfaction/surveys; Target audiences
    attitude, 247–50
    education of, 144
    knowledge of, 260–61
    knowledge of competitors, 65
    lead generation and, 88–95. *See also* Lead generation
    "lost," 79
    perks, 108
    reasons for buying, 108
    relations, competition and, 62
Customer satisfaction/surveys, 7–8, 14, 63, 93–102, 247
    case histories, 93–95, 104–6
    as direct selling tool, 93
    importance/satisfaction ratings, 98–102
    lifetime customer value and, 102–6
    predominant themes, 106–9
    rating statements, 95–98
    survey, 67–70
Customer-service orientation, 71

D

Data analysis, 47–52
    editing surveys, 47
    hand-tallying results, 47–48
    importance and satisfaction scores, 98–101
    presenting, 56–57
    software and, 49–52
    summarizing results, 52–56
Database searches, 21
Decision making, 13, 14, 15
Differentiation, 185, 187
Directional feedback, 13
Direct marketing, 242
Directory ad space, 238–39
Distributor perspective, 79
Distributor satisfaction, 14
Drucker, Peter, 87

E

Efficiency, 71
Einstein, Albert, 31
Electronic marketing, 129–37
    e-mail newsletters, 134–37
    e-mail surveys, 24, 27–29, 232–33
    web site navigation, improving, 129–34
Emotional connections, 145
Employee(s), 9–10, 14
    see also Employee feedback
    benefits (communicating/ simplifying), 229–32
    compensation packages, 226–28
    competition from former, 63
    included in target audience, 209–10, 218
    increasing productivity/ satisfaction, 213–17
    job satisfaction, 211

    marketing specific ideas/ programs to, 224–26
Employee feedback
    career development survey, 214–17
    image/perception research, 81
    reasons to ask for, 210–12
    satisfaction/marketing awareness survey (sample), 219–24
    successful examples of, 212–32
    suggestions, 234
    surveys, 205, 219–24
    tips for gathering, 232–34
    using outside party to gather, 234
End users, 14
Enthusiasm, 45
Executive(s)
    interviews, 26
    job changes, 125
    perspectives of, 80
Experiments, 27

F

Face-to-face interviews, 21, 26–27
Fear 2000 survey, 166
Federal Communications Commission (FCC), 163
Feedback, 8–9
    community perspectives, 80
    coordinating brand names with, 82–83
    customer. *See* Customer(s); Customer satisfaction/ surveys
    directional, 13
    employee. *See* Employee feedback
    gathering, 45–47
    intercept surveys and, 25

Feedback *(continued)*
    for marketing plan,
        113–18
    opinion leaders, 81–82
    perspectives, 9, 79–81
    success stories, 212–32
Ficco, Jim, 3–4
Financial services, 9
Focus groups, 21, 22–23
    on employee benefit pack-
        ages, 229–32
    Pittsburgh Pirates logo
        and, 155–57
Follow-up assessment, 249
Ford, Henry, 111
Franklin, Benjamin, 185

G

Gambling/outlet mall prefer-
    ences, 196–97
General Dynamics, 225–26
Goals, measurable, 158–59
GoDaddy.com, 147
Graphic design, 46, 180
Gretsch Guitars, 145
Grin-and-Bear-It Survey, 166,
    179
Growth, 71

H

Hamburger Lovers Survey, 165
Heinz Boston Market Frozen
    Foods, 165
Hospital community percep-
    tion survey (sample), 93–95

I

Image, 15
    entrepreneurial, 83
    personification questions
        and, 74–78

in relation to competition.
    See Competition/com-
    petitors
Impact, boosting, 48
Impressions, 244
Industry publications, 170–71
Industry surveys, 263
Intercept surveys, 24, 25–26
Internal marketing. *See*
    Employee feedback
Internet searches, 64
    naming research, 146
Internet surveys, 27–29
Interviewing skills, 45–46

J–K

Job satisfaction, 211
Ketchum Advertising, 3
KISS formula, 263

L

Lead generation, 88–95
    case history, 93–95
    determining awareness,
        90–91
    product information,
        offering, 91–92
    soliciting referrals, 92–93
Lead tracking, 256
Letters, as name, 151–52
Leverhulme, Viscount, 235
Library research, 21
Lifetime customer value philos-
    ophy, 102, 104–6
Listerine, 174
Logos, 142–43
    communicating with, 148
    Pittsburgh Pirates, 155–57
    trade marking, 147
Loyalty, 14, 106–7, 108

M

Magazine coverage, 170–71
Mail List Pro 4.0, 135
Mail surveys, 24–25
Management
    communication and, 212
    interviews, 205
    perspective, 80–81
Margin of error, 17–20
    telephone surveys and, 23
Market leadership, 71
Marketing
    see also Marketing plan;
        Marketing research
    broad definition of, 209
    culture, strengthening,
        217–24
    decisions, 7
    effectiveness, 248
    evaluating tactics, 224
    experiments, 27
    four "Ps" of, 126
    goals, 258–59
    internal. *See* Employee
        feedback
    lifetime customer value,
        102–6
    "maintenance" marketing,
        111
    messages, 9, 15, 120
    objectives, 118–19
    pricing issues, 126–28
    return on investment
        (ROI). *See* Return on in-
        vestment (ROI)
    specific ideas/programs
        to employees, 224–26
    strategies, 119
    tactics, 120–26
Marketing plan, 111–39
    electronic marketing,
        129–37
    finalizing, 137–39
    gathering feedback for,
        113–18
    pricing issues, 126–28

Marketing plan *(continued)*
  specific categories for,
    118–21
  specific tools, selecting,
    121–26
  as subset of business
    plan, 112
Marketing research, 4
  basic types of, 20–22
  snapshot surveys com-
    pared to other types of,
    22–29
Mastovich, Dave, 209
Media coverage, 15, 163–84
  case study, 168–70
  media kits, 178–81
  pitching your story,
    183–84
  publishing findings,
    170–71
  publicity surveys, 171–78
  snapshot surveys and,
    164–70
  working with the trade
    media, 181–83
Media Director, 178
Media insights, 81–82
Media kits, 178–81
Media list, 178–79
Member surveys, 24
Microsoft, 150
Mine Safety Appliances (MSA),
  167
Mission statement, 71
Most Dangerous Place on
  Earth: Your Home, 167

N

Naming
  case histories, 143–44,
    153–54
  choosing a name, 146–53
  communication with, 148
  competitors and, 148–49
  generating names, 150–54
  Pittsburgh, 154–60

power of naming, 144–46
research, 15, 141–60
steps, 146–50
trademarks, 147
National Aviary, 250, 251–53,
  259–60
Natural names, 151
Needs assessment, 186, 203–7
  management training,
    206–7
  quantifying pain, 202–3
New product
  launch strategy, 8
  viability, 16
News coverage. *See* Media cov-
  erage
Newsletters, e-mail, 134–37
Newspapers, 170
News releases, 179
Nonrandom samples/non-
  probability, 16
North Way Christian Commu-
  nity Church, 101–2, 103
Notes, 45
Numbers, as name, 151–52

O

Observations, 21
"Odd price" theory, 128
O'Donnell, Rosie, 174
Ogilvy, David, 3
Onassis, Aristotle, 61
Online media, 171
Open-ended questions, 21
Opinion change, 249
Organizational Assessment
  and Opportunity Analysis
  (OAOA), 204–5
Outlet mall shopping/gam-
  bling preferences, 196–97
Output activities, 240–42
Outside interviews, 25

P

Pain motivation, 202–4
PDF files, 131
Performance, consistency of,
  107
Personal selling, 242
Personification questions,
  74–78
Perspectives
  buyer, 187–90
  employee, 210
  external, 79–80
  hospital community per-
    ception survey (sample),
    93–95
  internal, 80–81
  opinion leaders, 81–82
Phone answering systems, 107
Photos, in media kits, 180
Pittsburgh, Pennsylvania mar-
  keting, 154–60
Pittsburgh Pirates, 155–57
Place (product distribution),
  126
Placements, 243–45
PNC Bank, 157–58
Politeness, 45
Positioning, 118
Press releases
  ad dollar value, 244
  content analysis, 245
  impressions, 244
  placement, 243–44
Pricing, 107, 126–28
  conjoint analysis, 128
  "cost plus" formula, 127
  name value and, 144
  price competition, 70
  psychological aspects of
    setting, 128
Primary research, 21–22
PR Newswire, 179
Probability, 16–17
Product development, 10
Product distribution, 126
Product information, 91–92
Product maturity, 62

Product offerings, organizing, 145
Professional service, marketing, 124–26
Program measures, 261
Promotions, 7, 126, 242
Proper names, 151
Proposal(s), 33–37, 185–208
  background, 34
  buyer perspectives, 187–90
  current situation, 34–35
  need for marketing research, 35
  research recommendations, 35–36
  snapshot surveys and, 190–97
  timing, 37
  workflow, 36–37
Proprietary research, 125–26, 173–74
Prospects, 79
  education of, 144
  using names of, 145
Publications, 170–71
Publicity, 15
Publicity surveys, 164–70
  B2B surveys, 172–73
  celebrities and, 175
  consumer polls, 172
  humor and, 174
  proprietary research, 173–74
  questions for, 174–78
  scientific nature of, 171–74
Public relations, 163–64, 242. *See also* Media coverage

Q
Qualitative/quantitative research, 21–22. *See also* Market research

Questions
  "blind" question technique, 66–67, 75
  personification questions, 74–78
  taking time with, 45
  thought-provoking, 174–78
Quiz Show Survey, 166

R
Random samples, 16–17
  margin of error in, 19
Rankings, 263
Readership study, 246
Real estate agents, 200
Referrals, 92–93, 125
Regional Renaissance strategy, 155
Registered trademarks, 147
Reputation, 62, 70. *See also* Competition/competitors
Return on investment (ROI), 16, 104, 121, 235–64
  agreeing on what's being measured, 259–61
  asking "how did you find out about us?", 236–37
  assessing value of marketing effort, 258–64
  communicating and presenting, 263–64
  determining, 237–39
  existing measures, use of, 263
  knowledge of customers and, 260–61
  levels of ROI measurement, 240–58
  tools for measuring, 261–62
Reuters, 184
Ridge, Tom, 8
Riverlife Task Force, 158

Rudeness, 45
Ruth, Babe, 209

S
"Sales cookbook," 254–56
  adjusting prices, 256
  closing ratios, 254–56
  tracking and, 256
Sales presentations. *See* Proposal(s)
Sales process, 63
  determining cost of each sale, 238–39
  transforming, 199–202
Sales promotion, 242
Sales proposals. *See* Proposal(s)
Sales prospects, 253–54
Sampling
  randomness, 16–17, 19, 23
  representative, 17, 23
Scientific selling, 186, 198–207
  larger projects with, 198–207
  needs assessment, 203–7
  physicians and, 198–99
  quantifying pain, 202–3, 204–7
Scope mouthwash, 174
Scoping session, 201
Secondary research, 21
Sellers vs. buyers, 188
Selling a survey, 32–37
  key questions, 32
  promoting use of survey, 32
  proposal, 33–37
Seminars, 125
Service development, 10
Service offerings, organizing, 145
Service viability, 15
Simplified names, 153
Site maps, 130

Snapshot survey(s)
  see also Publicity survey
  applying findings from,
    137–39
  described, 11–12
  face-to-face interviews and,
    26–27
  focus groups and, 22–23
  genesis of, 3–7
  intercept surveys and,
    25–26
  mail surveys and, 24–25
  marketing experiments
    and, 27
  new media research and,
    27–29
  news coverage and,
    164–70
  prime situations for, 12
  questions answered by,
    13–16
  in sales presentations,
    190–91
  scientific selling with,
    198–207
  steps, 37–43
    asking right ques-
      tions, 37–43
    choosing participants,
      43–45
    gathering feedback,
      45–47
  successful decisions based
    on, 7–10
  telephone surveys and,
    23–24
  validity of, 16–20
Software analysis, of data,
  49–52
Special reports, 171
Star names, for products, 153
Supplier perspectives, 79–80

Surveys
  see also Snapshot survey(s)
  editing, 47
  scientific nature of,
    171–74
Syllable rearranging, 150–51

T

Tactics (marketing), 120–26
  measuring, 261
Taglines, 142–43, 146–50
  as business descriptor, 148
Target audiences, 24
  awareness on part of,
    246–47
  employees included as,
    209–10, 218
  intercept surveys, 25–26
  logos/typefaces and, 157
  mail surveys, 24–25
  in marketing plan, 119–20
TeamPA, 8
Team structure, 189
Technology, 71
Telephone answering systems,
  107
Telephone carriers, 200
Telephone surveys, 23–24
Testing surveys, 46
Three Rivers Park, 158
Top line report, 52–56
Total quality programs, 212,
  247
Tracking studies, 249–50
Trademarks, 147
Trade publications, 65, 125,
  170–71
Tradition, 71
Training and Development
  Journal, 171

Trend surveys, 125–26, 175
Trucking manufacturer pro-
  posal, 194–95
Trustworthiness, 71
Twain, Mark, 141

U

Upselling, 185
U.S. News and World Report,
  263
Usability testing (web site), 129
USA Today, 170
Utility providers, 200

V

Value, 71
van Westendorp, Peter H., 127
Victory Centre (MEC Pennsyl-
  vania Racing), 195–96
Visibility, 15
Vision, 71
Vocelli Pizza, 143

W–Z

Web site
  navigation, improving,
    129–34
  usability testing, 129
  web-based surveys, 27–29
White papers, 171
World Affairs Council (WAC),
  104–6
Writer's Market, 178
Ziglar, Zig, 213
Zoo exhibit concept, 190–92